CW00326272

STAR MAN

ABOUT THE AUTHOR

The son of world-renowned boxing trainer George Francis, who made world champions of British boxers John Conteh and Frank Bruno, Michael Daniel Francis was born and brought up in Camden Town. After thirty years on the road with various bands, he quit soon after his fiftieth birthday when one last event-filled tour with Kiss convinced him he'd had enough. He is now a consultant to the entertainment industry and lives with his family in North London.

Paul Elliott has worked as a music journalist for 18 years. His work has been published in *Q, Kerrang!, Sounds* and various other titles. He first met Michael Francis in 1989 while on the road with Bon Jovi.

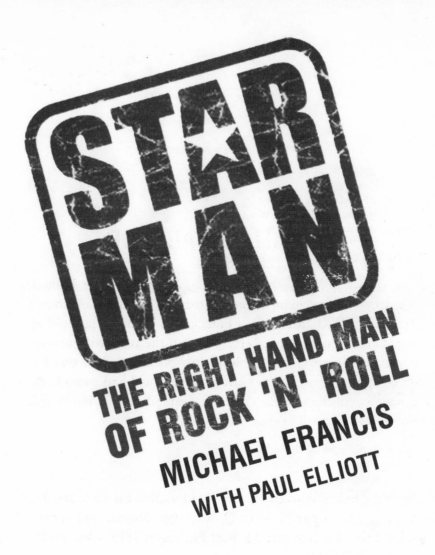

STAR MAN

THE RIGHT HAND MAN OF ROCK 'N' ROLL

MICHAEL FRANCIS
WITH PAUL ELLIOTT

SIMON &
SCHUSTER

London · New York · Sydney · Tokyo · Singapore · Toronto · Dublin

A VIACOM COMPANY

First published in Great Britain by
Simon & Schuster UK Ltd, 2003
A Viacom Company

1 3 5 7 9 10 8 6 4 2

Simon & Schuster UK Ltd
Africa House
64–78 Kingsway
London WC2B 6AH

www.simonsays.co.uk

Simon & Schuster Australia
Sydney

A CIP catalogue record for this book is available from the
British Library

ISBN 0–7432–3904–0 Hardback
ISBN 0–7432–3905–9 Trade paperback

Typeset by M Rules
Printed and bound in Great Britain by
Bath Press, Bath

'I always thought of *The Godfather* as the story of a great king with three sons. The oldest was given his sweet nature and childlike qualities; the second, his passion and aggressiveness; and the third, his cunning and coolness.'

Francis Ford Coppola

George Francis was a one-off. He was a man of huge passion and drive, a man who gave himself body, mind and soul to his family, and who kept his integrity in a rough world. George was a man you could trust with anything. This is the way I feel about him, as does everybody who was close to him.

George could talk a storm and loved to talk about himself, but it wasn't vanity: rather, he could just hardly believe a lot of what had happened in his life, and it was an amazing story. From humble beginnings on the streets of Camden Town, he became one of the very best boxing trainers in the world, and the first non-American to be voted Trainer of the Year in Sports Illustrated.

George Albert Francis died on 3 April 2002, but in many ways I still feel he is here with me, in me. George had a dream, what might at the time have seemed a crazy dream, but he made it come true by the sheer force of his personality and spirit. He had a blazing smile that said: 'Come on, get hold of the day, get on your front foot, and whatever the odds against you, with all your heart and soul, do the business.'

This book is dedicated to the memory of George Francis, my father, hero and best friend.

ACKNOWLEDGEMENTS

To my granddaughters Elle and Lia, my two little angels, thank you for giving me the future to look forward to.

And to my three beautiful children, Joanne, Daniel and Grant: it would take another book to tell you in words how much you mean to me. You are my life.

To my wife June, the love of my life, thank you from the bottom of my heart for all you have done over the years, not only for me and for our children but for the rest of the Francis family. You were a mum and a best friend to Simon, a daughter and a best friend to Mum, and for Dad, you were his soul mate. As Dad would say, truly, you are our guardian angel.

To Steve Pearce and all at Red Central, thank you for all your love and support during some very difficult times.

To Sally Partington and all at Simon & Schuster, thank you

for believing in our project, and for letting us take over your office for the last twelve months.

On behalf of the Francis family, thank you to all our close friends and family who are always the first to arrive and the last to leave. You know who you are.

Special thanks to John Conteh, Bunny Sterling, Frank Bruno, Doc McGhee, Gareth and Beth, Sting and Trudie, Charlie George, Michael Kirton, Graeme Fife, Howard Marks, St Dominic's Church, Cliff Ryan and all the artists that I have had the privilege to have spent some time with. And to the artists with whom I have worked I would like to say: don't take this personally, it's business.

Finally, I would like to express my gratitude to my co-writer Paul Elliott without whom this book would not exist. Paul and I have been friends ever since he came out to Kansas City in 1989 to interview Bon Jovi for *Sounds*. In February 2002 I had gone to Brighton to see Howard Marks reading from his book *The Howard Marks Book of Dope Stories* and who should I see a few rows in front but a familiar bald head above an even more familiar Arsenal shirt. Paul and I had dinner together after the show and he asked me about the diaries I kept of the tours on which I'd worked, and from that conversation *Star Man* was born. Listening to Howard was our inspiration, and Paul was the perfect partner, since he too has been there. As a rock journalist he has lived the life of sex and drugs and rock 'n' roll, even if only for days at a time. I could not have wished for a better companion on the road to publication.

CONTENTS

1

White toast

Jon Bon Jovi wants to punch my lights out. With both fists he strikes at my outstretched palms. Before every Bon Jovi gig, we act out the same boxing warm-up, a trick I learned from my father. Only this time it's different. This time there's a little extra in those blows. He might look like a girl with his glittering floor-length coat, tight leather pants and big hair, but his punches sting.

Here in Knoxville, Tennessee, in America's Old South, ten thousand fans are packed inside a sports arena and screaming for Bon Jovi. The noise is deafening as Jon faces me behind the heavy black curtain at the back of the stage.

I yell two words at him. 'White toast!'

Jon's face tightens and he slams even harder into my hands.

1

Right now, his band is the biggest in the world. Their break-through third album *Slippery When Wet* has sold eight million copies in America alone, topping the chart for fifteen weeks and producing two number one singles in 'You Give Love A Bad Name' and 'Livin' On A Prayer'. The current album *New Jersey* has also hit number one and sold more than two million inside four months.

Bon Jovi are superstars, but as I keep reminding Jon, they are nothing compared to Led Zeppelin. I worked with Zeppelin in the seventies when they were worshipped like gods and had a fearsome reputation fuelled by tales of violence, drug addiction, sexual excesses and a dark obsession with the occult.

Jon Bon Jovi is in awe of Led Zeppelin, like every rock-loving seventies kid, but while Bon Jovi can deliver a great rock 'n' roll show, their records are lightweight, lacking that raw edge of primal power and danger, and Jon is a pretty-boy pin-up. Bon Jovi are safe, mainstream. They're what Americans like to call *white toast*.

I look Jon in the eye. 'White toast.'

He'd love to knock me on my arse, but he's not big enough.

We have two minutes till show time. The other four band members are now standing with us in the half-light. Guitarist Richie Sambora wears a wide-brimmed fedora hat, a long white leather coat, black vest, black jeans and cowboy boots. He looks like the last gunslinger in town. Bassist Alec John Such has a sleeveless denim jacket over a silk shirt, rough shaven, his lean features heavily-lined, a smudge of eyeliner around his dark eyes and a cigarette at his lips. Keyboard player Dave Bryan is shirt-less under a leather waistcoat, with shaggy hair extensions down the length of his back. And drummer Tico Torres is all in white, his squat, stocky frame and dark complexion giving him the appearance of a Colombian middleweight boxer.

With two flashes of a pocket torch, I signal to tour manager Paul Korzilius that we are ready to roll. Thin Lizzy's 'The Boys Are Back In Town' is blasting over the PA system. Korzilius returns the signal: everybody is in position: my security team, and the sound and light technicians.

We go to black: The house lights dim and the roar from the crowd is incredible. The air is filled with the sweet smell of dope and a fog of dry ice creeps across the stage. The band's intro tape begins – the thundering drums of 'Lay Your Hands On Me'.

The adrenaline is pumping. Jon hugs me, smiles, then we push each other away. We're close, like brothers. He turns and runs out on stage. This is the moment when fear kicks in. You're open. It is my job to keep Jon safe, but once he is out there on the stage, anyone could get to him – an overzealous fan, or, worse, some drugged-up nutter. From here on in I am playing by instinct.

The arena has a high ceiling, with steep curves of terraced seating on all sides. As Jon runs the length of the stage, back and forth, drawing a frenzied response from the crowd, the people closest to the stage at the front and on each side can reach out and touch him. And no matter what I tell him, Jon will go into the audience at some point. For this reason, I have a team of four men grouped near the stage, all handpicked from the local event staff and ready to surround Jon and protect him if he leaps down into the stalls. I study the audience on all sides, looking for anything out of the ordinary: someone who is standing up but not enjoying themselves, not singing along to the songs. Members of my security staff are positioned around the stage looking to see what these people are up to. Two experienced guys do nothing else all night but patrol the front twenty rows. Over the years you develop a kind of sixth sense that helps you to spot the odd ones, the ones that could mean trouble. It isn't only when the band are on stage – from the moment the doors first open I walk the bars, the auditorium, everywhere; watching, listening, checking that everything's under control.

Tonight – every night – Jon is working his balls off. He always talks about the great rock 'n' roll front men, and tonight he is up there with the best. This is the fifty-third date on Bon Jovi's world tour and they are flying, but still ... I'm wearing a Led Zeppelin T-shirt, and when Jon looks to me at the side of the stage, I point to the Zeppelin logo on my chest, mouthing 'white toast'. Jon gives me the finger. Tico sees what is happening and sends his drumsticks flying within inches of my head.

The show is a good one, very good, and Jon is having fun as girls in the front rows lift up their tops to reveal their breasts. When Tico plays a drum solo, Jon saunters over to the side of the stage and chats to me while fixing himself a cocktail. A small table is set up with vodka, cranberry juice and ice. He calls it a Muff Dive. He sinks it in two thirsty gulps before dashing back to the centre-stage.

Richie is in equally high spirits. During the number one single 'Livin' On A Prayer', Richie plays a vocoder, singing into a mouthpiece attached via a tube to his guitar. But instead of making the 'wah-wah' sound of the record, he seizes the opportunity for a spot of subliminal advertising, stating over and over: 'Buy a T-shirt! Buy a T-shirt'. He looks across to Jon and they break into laughter. The two of them disappear behind Tico's drum kit and run down a flight of steps to little rooms under the stage where the band wait before returning to play an encore.

There are three rooms, each draped in black fabric and lit by dozens of white candles. One room is for Jon, one for Richie and the third for Tico, Alec and Dave. Even in a band as close as Bon Jovi, there is always some kind of hierarchy. In Jon's room there are towels, a change of T-shirt and an iced Muff Dive.

Alec stands at the entrance to Jon's room, beckoning me. He has a little problem I might be able to help him with – a groupie in the next room who has hustled her way backstage. We both know how she got here, by performing sexual favours for the Bon Jovi road crew. More importantly, Alec believes she may be the ugliest woman in Knoxville, if not the whole state. I find her talking excitedly to a clearly uninterested Dave Bryan. As Dave dabs the sweat from his face and chest with a towel, I lead the girl from the room, explaining that the band have to get back to the stage immediately.

'I want to see Alec!' she shouts over her shoulder as a burly security guard takes her by the arm and hurries her through a fire exit. I collect Dave and Tico from their room, then Jon and Alec, before checking on Richie. He is sitting on a folding metal chair, his feet on a table, and contentedly sipping a glass of brandy. The brandy is French, Louis XIII, and costs one thousands dollars per bottle. On the table sits a crystal decanter, a smoking joint in an ashtray, and a CD case on which five thick lines of cocaine are laid out. Normally we hide the cocaine from Jon, since he doesn't much like to see it around. He does not do cocaine. He never has. For a rock star he is careful, even abstemious, preferring to unwind with a good red wine.

'Don't fucking tell me,' laughs Richie, holding up his hands. 'I'm still white toast!'

'Not when we get to Vegas!' Jon says. 'Our boy is gonna kick ass!'

Our boy is Frank Bruno, the British heavyweight boxer, and in two days' time he will face 'Iron' Mike Tyson, the most feared fighter on the planet, for the heavyweight championship of the world. My father George is Bruno's trainer, and we have ring-side seats for the fight.

As he leads the band back to the stage for an encore Jon begins chanting. 'Bruno! Bruno! Bruno!'

When the band come off the stage, I wrap a large white towel around Jon's shoulders and we head to the dressing room. I pull two bottles of beer from an ice chest and hand one to Jon.

'Get showered quickly,' I tell him. 'We've got a plane to catch.'

Thirty minutes later, three limousines are delivering various members of Bon Jovi and support act Skid Row to an airstrip on the outskirts of Knoxville, where two Lear jets are ready to fly us to Las Vegas. Bon Jovi are using their own private plane to travel from state to state on this tour, but aviation laws do not permit large and noisy aircraft to land close to residential areas at night, so the smaller Lear jets have been hired at a cost of $20,000. For a band earning a million dollars a week, such an extravagance is easily affordable.

And besides, twenty grand is spare change compared to the money the band is losing by postponing the sold-out concert that was originally scheduled for the same night as the fight. Jon ordered the gig to be cancelled as soon as I told him the date. He has never seen a live boxing match before, let alone the heavyweight championship of the world. Moreover, this is a fight between the most feared boxer on Earth and a man whom Jon has come to know as a friend. Three months ago, Frank and my father came to one of Bon Jovi's four shows in London, and were guests of honour at the band's table during the after-show party at the nightclub Tramp. Since that night, Jon has talked about little else other than the fight.

The first of the Lear jets carries Jon and his brother Tony Bongiovi, plus Richie and Alec and Skid Row's guitar player Dave 'Snake' Sabo. At the rear of the narrow cabin, I sit beside Bon Jovi's manager Doc McGhee, a squat, rotund, round-faced Italian-American with more than a passing resemblance to movie star Danny DeVito. The four-hour flight passes quickly as we drink chilled champagne and speak excitedly about the fight. As the plane begins its descent, the lights of Las Vegas glittering in the blue-black desert night, we are drunkenly predicting a Bruno victory by a knockout in the first. Doc is using the tiny bathroom in the back of the cabin, so Richie relieves himself by refilling one of the empty champagne bottles.

My younger brother Simon, Dad's right hand man, is waiting

to greet us on the tarmac. A white stretch limousine delivers us to the Aladdin hotel on the dazzling, neon-lit Strip. Jon is exhausted and drunk but decides we should have one more drink before retiring. I do not need to ask for directions to the hotel bar: from the lobby, I can hear the boisterous singing of Bruno's supporters. Two hundred Englishmen are congregated in the bar, wearing football shirts or Bruno T-shirts, some draped in flags – the red, white and blue of the Union Flag, or the red Cross of St George. Bottles and glasses are raised aloft as a fat man in a beer-stained white T-shirt leads a loud rendition of the British national anthem. I recognise a few of the faces in the crowd, boxing fans I have known for years, plus a pair of notorious ticket touts.

Jon appears bemused but is grinning broadly. Simon offers us shots of bourbon and Jon proposes a toast 'to Big Frank'. I turn to see a guy in an England football shirt, standing a few feet from us, peering intently at Jon.

'Is that Jon Bon Jovi?' he asks.

'It is.'

'And he's on Bruno's side?'

'He certainly is.'

'Hey!' he shouts to his friends and moves unsteadily towards them, pointing back at Jon. I think about getting Jon out of here – there are a lot of big lads in the room and they are all very drunk and excitable. But as I move to Jon's side, a loud cheer sounds from the Bruno fans who have just been told that Jon Bon Jovi is here, and that he is a Bruno fan too. Within seconds, two hundred guys are shouting and applauding and waving at Jon. Jon laughs and waves back as they sing, to the tune of the Sixties hit 'Guantanamera', 'One Jon Bon Jovi! There's only one Jon Bon Jovi!'

Suddenly we are swamped by guys reaching out to shake Jon's hand, offering to buy drinks for us, and producing scraps of paper and beer mats for Jon to sign. So much for that one drink before we all go to bed. When we finally get out of the bar – tired, drunk and hoarse from singing – it is four in the morning.

In my room, the telephone's red message light is flashing. I tap the voicemail button to hear my father welcoming me to Vegas and telling me to meet him for breakfast at the Hilton hotel at eight. I have just four hours to sleep and sober up. I sigh heavily, kick off my shoes and stretch out on the soft bed.

I am gazing up at Frank Bruno, his arms aloft, the prone body of Mike Tyson at his feet, when the phone's shrill ringing wakes me with a start. 'You're late,' Dad chides me. 'Get over here now.'

2

Four corners of truth

I knock at the door of my father George's suite on the seventeenth floor of the Las Vegas Hilton. Each knock echoes in
my aching head. In my dry mouth I can taste last night's gin.
Dad pulls the door open and greets me with a wry smile. His
blue eyes sparkle and his weathered face is tanned from the
weeks spent training Frank Bruno in Arizona.

'Heavy night?' he asks.

I answer with a groan. We sit at a table overlooking downtown, a light heat haze over the grid of wide streets, the sky a
clear blue. The table is set for breakfast, a large basket of fresh
fruit at the centre. I take several long gulps from a glass of iced
water and pick a piece of toast from a small basket covered by
a napkin. The toast is cold. I pour a cup of coffee from a tall

9

silver flask, and wince as I swallow the first mouthful. It too is cold.

Dad laughs. 'I told you, you're late.'

'How's Frank?' I ask him.

Dad says nothing but nods slowly and smiles. Tomorrow is the biggest day of his and Bruno's lives. They have a shot at the world heavyweight title, the dream of every heavyweight fighter and every trainer. My father's career in professional boxing spans twenty-five years, in which time he has trained forty title-winning fighters, including the world light-heavyweight champion John Conteh. But the heavyweight championship of the world is the big one, and no British boxer has held this title since Bob Fitzsimmons at the turn of the 1900s, all of ninety years ago. For as long as I can recall – long before he ever discovered Frank Bruno – Dad has dreamed of this moment.

The one thing that stands in the way of his dream is reigning champion Mike Tyson, a bull of a man whose explosive punching power and brutal attacking style have had him dubbed 'the baddest man on the planet'. Since turning professional four years ago in 1985, Tyson is undefeated in thirty-five fights, of which only five have lasted beyond the sixth round and sixteen have been won either by knockout or by technical knockout in the first. From the first bell, Tyson overwhelms his opponents and batters them to the canvas. Where Muhammad Ali inspired awe, Tyson inspires fear. It takes a brave man to step into the ring to face him.

Dad has trained Big Frank to the peak of physical fitness. The training began, as always, with a punishing programme of long-distance runs on London's Hampstead Heath, a large and peaceful expanse of wooded parkland in the city's affluent north. These runs would conclude at Highgate Men's Pond, one of two small man-made lakes in a secluded corner of the Heath. Even in midwinter, when the Pond's deep waters would ice over, Frank would still be ordered to strip to his shorts and dive in. Dad was famous for putting his fighters through this torture. If

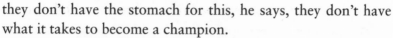

they don't have the stomach for this, he says, they don't have what it takes to become a champion.

For ten long months, Dad has been preparing Frank for this fight. Normally he would train a fighter for ten weeks before a contest, but these are not normal circumstances. The date of the fight has been postponed several times. On two occasions Tyson has sustained minor injuries; once when he broke his hand in a street brawl with fellow boxer Mitch Green, and once in a road accident.

In the past ten weeks, Dad and Frank have worked in isolation in the dry desert climate of Fountainhills, Arizona. A tough regime of ten-mile runs and dozens of rounds of sparring with other boxers have developed Frank's stamina and sharpened his speed and technique. Also, they have worked on tactics. Some fall within the rules of boxing as originated by the Marquess of Queensberry: others come straight from the streets of North London – what my father likes to call the university of life.

Bruno, he says, is ready. And now, at last, the fight is on.

Dad rises briskly from his chair. 'I've got work to do, son.'

I return to my hotel room to sleep off my hangover. In the early afternoon, I am woken for a second time by the ringing of the phone. The croaking voice on the line is that of Colonel Tom Parker, the elderly former manager of Elvis Presley. Back in 1976, I met the Colonel and Elvis here in Las Vegas while I was working for Led Zeppelin. In the ensuing years we have stayed in contact, bonded by our love of boxing.

The Colonel is in fact nothing of the sort. Born Andreas van Kuijk, he is a Dutch immigrant who has never served in the military, either in the US Army or in Europe. A former circus master with the reputation of a huckster and con man, Colonel Parker controlled Elvis Presley's career from 1956 until Presley's death in 1977. The Colonel is an enigmatic figure and great company, a witty man who always has a new tale to tell about the years he spent managing the greatest rock 'n' roll star of them all.

Jon Bon Jovi has taken to being called 'Elvis' on this tour and is desperate to meet the Colonel. The attraction is mutual: the Colonel is more than happy to meet the biggest rock star in the world. 'See you at ringside,' he says.

At six, the members of Bon Jovi and Skid Row dine at a Mexican restaurant, where Doc McGhee picks up the tab. There is one notable absentee from the table: Alec John Such, who has important business elsewhere in town. After several margaritas our hangovers are forgotten. At eight, Doc checks his watch and orders us to finish our drinks quickly. We rush back to the hotel and huddle around a table in the bar facing a giant video screen. The TV is tuned to a national sports channel, which has been previewing the big fight all day long.

At eight-thirty, a hush descends as a smooth-talking TV anchorman introduces the members of the panel who will be discussing the fight: a former boxer, plus two of America's foremost boxing writers, and last – clad in a white three-piece suit and slouching in his chair – Mr Alec John Such!

We whoop and cheer. All around the bar, people are smiling at us. We groan as the first three panellists forecast the result.

'Tyson in three.'

'Tyson in one.'

'Tyson in four.'

Now Alec: 'Bruno in five.' We cheer loudly and raise our glasses.

'Bruno hasn't got a chance,' one of the writers says, shooting a withering look at Alec.

'Oh yes he has,' Alec responds, reaching into his breast pocket to produce a chicken's foot. We laugh and cheer. The anchorman watches bemused as Alec dangles the foot before the camera. Rubbing his goatee with his free hand, Alec declares that he is the seventh son of a seventh son, and therefore has the gift of clairvoyance. 'If this chicken's foot touches Tyson,' he announces gravely, 'the prophecy will come true.'

'You're serious?' the anchorman splutters.

'Bruno in five,' Alec repeats with a knowing smile.

It is complete bullshit, of course, but Alec carries it off with style. I wonder if Colonel Parker is watching. The old trickster would love this.

A burly American fan seated at the bar is not amused. 'I thought you guys were from New Jersey,' he sneers at Jon. 'You should be supporting our guy.'

'No way, man,' Jon replies. 'Right now we're fucking British!'

He is still saying this at three in the morning when the barman pleads with us to leave so that he can close the bar. Jon is wearing a stupid grin and a Frank Bruno T-shirt given to him by one of the British fans. Truly, he is one of us.

25 FEBRUARY

The day of the fight. The day my father has waited for all his working life. He appears relaxed, confident and proud as he walks beside Frank Bruno in bright morning sunshine. At six feet and five inches, Frank towers over him, a light grey tracksuit clinging to the contours of his powerful physique. I follow a few paces behind, between Jon and my brother Simon. At the front and rear of the group are six security guards in black suits.

The walk is a brisk circuit of ten blocks, a little light exercise for Frank ahead of tonight's showdown with Tyson. Jon and I speak in hushed tones. We know not to disturb Dad and Frank. As we turn on to the Strip, passers-by shout to Frank and wish him luck. He does not hear them. He walks with a sense of purpose, his face impassive. A few fans ask for autographs and are politely declined by the security men.

The weigh-in is at noon. In a conference room at the Hilton, the press are gathered as the two fighters are weighed on scales before official adjudicators. We watch on TV in Jon's room and laugh as Tyson takes to the stage surrounded by an entourage of twenty, including his manager, the flamboyant Don King, and a gang of glaring black minders. Dad wears a Bon Jovi baseball

13

cap and regards Tyson and his people with a smile. He and Frank are not intimidated.

Bruno slips out of his tracksuit and steps on to the scales in just his briefs. There is not an ounce of fat on his 230-pound frame, just packed muscle. Still his face shows no sign of emotion.

'Do you think Frank can beat him?' Jon asks me.

'We'll know soon enough.'

We walk down to the hotel bar where the rest of our party is gathered. This being Las Vegas, the gambling capital of the world, we decide to place money on Bruno. His best chance will be in the first half of the fight: few fighters can stand up to Tyson's punches for more than four or five rounds, and only two men have ever taken him to the full distance of twelve.

I clear a table and make a note of each person's stake as rolls of hundred-dollar bills pile up. Between eleven of us, we raise a total stake of $12,000. We dash to the bookmaker's stall in the hotel's gambling hall and place the whole twelve grand on Bruno to win in six. The clerk cannot take our money fast enough. He offers us odds of 16-1.

Jon does the maths. 'That's a hundred and ninety-two thousand dollars!' he cackles.

'If he wins,' says Richie cautiously.

'Oh, he'll win,' Alec says, tapping an index finger against his temple. 'Trust me.'

One hundred and ninety-two thousand dollars. We were tense before. Now we are buzzing. Some of the guys remain in the gambling hall to play poker, others drift back to the bar. I return to my room to watch TV. Every news and sports channel carries the latest updates on the fight. Every pundit is backing Tyson. Archive footage shows him smashing opponents into submission. I switch to a movie channel and watch Sean Connery as James Bond in *Dr No*, flying the flag for Britain and beating up the bad guys. It feels good.

At six – four hours before the first bell will ring – we ride by limousine to the Hilton. We are all formally dressed, Jon in black suit and shirt, Alec in black tuxedo and bow tie. The lobby is crowded with Bruno fans, many of them a little worse for wear but singing happily. The Tyson fans are quietly confident. We are ushered into the VIP bar, where Sylvester Stallone holds court in one corner. An hour later, Colonel Parker glides into the bar, dressed in a black suit patterned with gleaming rhinestones, pale blue open-necked shirt and red silk cravat. The ensemble is finished off with a blue baseball cap bearing the name of country singer George Strait. The Colonel is flanked by two glamorous blonde showgirls in shimmering dresses. He is eighty years old but still knows how to make an entrance. I greet him with a smile and invite him to our table, where he sits between the giggling girls, entertaining us with his stories.

With a sly chuckle, the Colonel reveals the ease with which he made money during Elvis's residencies here in Vegas in the mid-seventies. Before the shows, programmes would be sold for three dollars in the foyer. Afterwards, the Colonel's staff would stand at the exits offering to buy back any unwanted programmes for a dollar-fifty. The Colonel had made half the cover price and he still had the merchandise: a true capitalist. For two hours, Jon asks numerous questions about Elvis, which the Colonel answers with the patience of a grandfather.

At nine-thirty, my brother Simon taps my shoulder. 'Dad said to bring Jon up to see Frank.' Simon leads us through the crowds and along a network of corridors to a door guarded by four of the hotel's security staff. They see Jon and wave us through. We walk up two flights of stairs to Bruno's dressing room. Simon knocks twice and Dad quietly beckons us inside. In the far corner of the room, Frank sits on a small sofa, his feet resting on a low table as he watches a TV game show. He offers a smile and gestures to the two empty chairs facing him. We sit and talk for a few minutes. It is difficult to find words to say to a man who is about to take on Mike Tyson. Frank is already dressed for the fight in white satin trunks and calf-length boots.

He wears a robe, brightly-coloured in the red, white and blue of the British flag, which lies open, a sheen of perspiration showing on his chest. I have known Frank for years, but I can only wonder what is going through his mind.

'Gentlemen!' my father calls from across the room. 'It's show time!'

We rise to hug Frank and wish him good luck. In Frank's embrace, Jon looks like a child. 'See you later, boys,' Dad says as we exchange tense smiles. In fifteen minutes I will see them climbing through the ropes. My stomach churns.

Outside the room, Jon turns to me in astonishment. 'I can't believe he's so cool, so relaxed!'

'Well,' I laugh, 'that makes one of us.'

The Hilton's 15,000-seater convention centre is filled to capacity for the big fight. Bon Jovi play to audiences of this size every night, but the buzz of anticipation in this arena is like nothing I have experienced before. With a rock show, the audience knows what to expect. Here, tonight, anything can happen. We are on a knife-edge: on one side, elation, on the other, despair.

Two security guards lead the Bon Jovi party to ringside. The house lights are still on, and pockets of Bruno fans cheer as they see Jon.

'One Jon Bon Jovi!' they chant. 'There's only one Jon Bon Jovi!'

Jon salutes them with two clenched fists raised above his head, then digs me in the ribs. He is pumped up, as if it is he who is about to climb up into that ring. As we take our seats in the second row back from the ring under bright overhead lights, Alec winks at me, a glint of mischief in his eyes, and scurries off towards an exit. To our right sits Colonel Parker: to our left, the greatest heavyweight champion of them all,

Muhammad Ali. The Colonel acknowledges Jon with a wave and the house lights dim. All eyes turn to the ring, where the master of ceremonies stands with a microphone.

'Welcome to the Hilton, Las Vegas, for the heavyweight championship of the world!'

The surge of adrenaline almost lifts me out of my seat. First to emerge is the challenger, Frank Bruno. Two spotlights are trained on the entrance and the roar from the British fans makes the hair stand up on my neck. 'Bruno! Bruno! Bruno!' British flags are waving all around the arena.

My dad steps into the glaring white light with Frank's red-gloved hands on his shoulders. The hood of Frank's robe covers his head, but his face is visible, his eyes focused dead ahead. They walk slowly to the ring, Frank bouncing on his toes and rolling his head from side to side to ease the tension from his broad shoulders. Dad pulls the top rope up for Frank to duck under and step on to the canvas. He holds one arm aloft and the Bruno fans cheer so loudly that I cannot hear what Jon is yelling in my ear. No matter: Jon's proud smile says it all.

For a few seconds, Frank stands alone in the ring, moving all the time to keep his muscles warm. He walks to one side of the ring and his brooding expression turns to a smile when he sees us standing and chanting his name. His smile disappears as the master of ceremonies announces the champion and spotlights illuminate the entrance where Tyson stands wearing black shorts and boots, no robe, and a look of pure menace.

'Look!' Jon shouts and points to the tier of seating to Tyson's left, where Alec is struggling to reach out past the line of security officials to touch Tyson with the chicken's foot. Tyson moves away towards the ring and Alec is left flinging his arms up in frustration. A great roar erupts around us as Tyson bounces up into the ring and fixes Bruno with a stare that has me thanking God that it is Frank and not me in that ring.

★

The referee calls the two fighters together at the centre of the ring and tells them that he wants a clean, honest fight with no low blows and no dirty tricks: and may the best man win. I remember Dad telling me as a child that the rules of boxing are the rules of life. And as the fighters move away to their respective corners to receive final instructions from their trainers, another of his maxims echoes in my mind. 'Four Corners of Truth' is a description he applies to the boxing ring. Once you are in there, he says, there is nowhere to hide.

Alec is now in his seat beside Jon. Agitated, he decides on one last desperate attempt to make contact between Mike Tyson and the chicken's foot. He jumps up to throw the foot at Tyson, who sits in his corner some thirty feet from us, but Alec's aim is poor and the foot whizzes through two sets of ropes and out into the audience. Within seconds, two giant security guards are lifting Alec out of his seat. It happens so quickly, I am unable to stop them dragging Alec away, but as I rise to follow, the first bell rings and I drop back into my seat. This is my father's greatest night: Alec will have to sort out his little problem on his own.

Tyson charges across the canvas and tries to catch Bruno cold with a lightning attack. Bruno counters the flurry of blows and puts some distance between himself and Tyson by using a double left jab. This is my father's plan: the double left jab to keep Tyson off balance, and the right cross, Frank's biggest punch, to knock him out.

Tyson drives Bruno on to the ropes ten feet from us and pummels away at Frank's midriff. The force of these punches is terrifying. With each impact, Frank grunts heavily, sprays of sweat coming off him in high arcs and covering the people in the first three rows. But Frank is surviving. He makes it to the end of the round, then rallies in the second by fending off Tyson with the left jab and smothering him with his big arms when he tries to get in close.

Bruno is faring better than any of the American pundits had

predicted, but in the third, Tyson delivers two crunching shots to the body which sink in so hard that Tyson appears to be struggling to pull his fists back out from Frank's ribcage. Incredibly, Frank finds the strength to push Tyson away and then lands a couple of good, solid punches of his own. The noise of the crowd is deafening, but I can still hear Dad's voice bellowing at Frank to keep pushing forward, to put Tyson on the back foot where he is less effective. It works – Frank stays on his feet for the third and fourth rounds – but in the fifth, Tyson's punches are finding their targets. The fight seems to be getting away from Frank when, astonishingly, as Tyson leads with his left, he lands a right hook to the side of Tyson's head that sends the champion rocking backwards.

For two seconds that seem like minutes, Tyson is dazed and vulnerable, his hands at his sides, his guard wide open. Jon and I are out of our seats, grabbing at each other in delirium and screaming at Frank to finish him off. This is the moment: one big punch and the heavyweight title is Bruno's. But Frank is even more shocked than we are to see Tyson reeling before him. He hesitates – and the moment is gone, the opportunity lost. As Frank advances, Tyson's head clears. He grips Frank at his sides and holds on for the bell. As the fighters walk to their corners, Tyson appears angry, Bruno disbelieving. Jon and I sink back into our seats, exhilaration draining from us.

'He had him!' Jon yells and shakes his head. The Bruno fans are still cheering their man, but there is resignation, and fear, in my heart. You do not get two chances against Mike Tyson. I think we can kiss goodbye to our $192,000. More than that, Frank's and my father's dream is over. I glance across the ring where Dad has his hand cupped at Frank's ear, barking orders, urging him to get back out there and try to win the fight again.

The bell rings for the sixth round and Tyson flies from his corner. Bruno is lost in the whirlwind as Tyson blitzes him with a rapid succession of rights and left uppercuts. Pushed to the

ropes just above our heads, Bruno shields his head with his forearms, but Tyson smashes through his defences with another
vicious uppercut to the chin that sends a jet of blood splattering
our shirts. The referee pulls Tyson away for a statutory standing
count, but the respite is brief. Bruno is stunned, a soft target.
Ten more punches and the referee is stepping between them. It's
over.

Dad embraces Frank and leads him to the corner. As he
consoles his beaten fighter, I sense that he is also consoling
himself. Both men have given it their best shot. There is dignity,
and honour, in this defeat.

Big Frank had performed like a hero, and had come so close
to fulfilling all our dreams, but the referee was right to stop the
fight when he did, sparing him from further punishment. He
could have been killed out there.

Jon turns to me with a sad smile. Neither of us can find words
to say.

The Bruno fans continue singing and waving their flags as the
auditorium empties under the amber haze of the house lights. As
we walk through to the VIP reception room Alec appears at my
side, offering reassurance that Frank did all he could. He tells
me he saw the whole fight: the security guards allowed him back
inside the arena when he explained that he was a member of the
biggest band in the world.

A small group of Bruno fans have talked their way into the VIP
room. They remain upbeat and proud that their man stood up to
Tyson and might even have won if he had followed up that
mighty right hook. Tyson's supporters are gracious in their praise
of Big Frank. Colonel Parker beckons us to his table and orders
several bottles of the best champagne, a notable gesture from a
man who is known never to give anything away for free.

We are enjoying a third glass of champagne when Dad arrives

at the table. The Colonel and the Bon Jovi guys shake his hand and tell him it was a great fight. He smiles and thanks them for their support. Frank is fine, he says, before drawing me aside. 'I've just spoken to Mum,' he says, his voice cracking from the exertion of shouting throughout the fight, and from the emotion of the occasion. 'I told her Frank was okay and that I'd make sure you're behaving yourself. Frank's too upset to come down.'

'You and Frank should be proud,' I tell him.

We exchange smiles and embrace each other. There are tears in his eyes, and mine.

'Those body shots were killing Frank,' he says after a few seconds' reflection. 'Tyson is the best I've ever seen. If he keeps himself right in his body and mind, he'll stay unbeaten for another ten years ...'

He pauses and sighs. 'But if Frank had landed one more right hander ...'

A few minutes later, Muhammad Ali joins us. Jon rises from the table to say hello and Ali tells him how my father taught him some tricks back in the seventies, when he met Dad at the Fifth Street gym in Miami, owned by his trainer Angelo Dundee. Jon is amazed but Ali insists that it is true. Dad smiles, a little embarrassed, and Ali drapes an arm across his shoulders. As Ali speaks, Jon hangs on every word.

When the long night of celebration and commiseration draws to a close, Dad looks at me, exhausted.

'I'll see you in London,' he tells me. 'Keep out of trouble.'

He turns to Jon. 'Look after the boy,' he says.

3

Gypsies, tramps and thieves

I was ten years old when I found out that my father was a bare-knuckle fighter.

'They had to carry your dad out of the ring last night,' my friend Lenny told me one winter morning as we trudged to school through icy rain. Lenny said his father had seen my dad fight the champion of the Gypsies. His eyes were wide with excitement. He said his dad had said it was the best fight he had ever seen.

I could not believe what I was hearing. Dad got up at 3.30 every weekday to get to work on the markets by 4 a.m., and he left the house long before the rest of the family got up. I never saw him until I got home from school in the afternoons, so Lenny's news was the first I knew about where he'd been last

23

night. I had heard the men in my family speak about bare-knuckle fighting with friends and neighbours. The sport was popular among working people, but was outlawed because it was so dangerous. The fights took place in warehouses or, if it was on the Gypsies' turf, in a field. Details of the location would be spread by word of mouth in the pubs.

The fights were brutal and would only end when one of the men was knocked out cold. Without gloves, the fighters would inflict terrible injuries on each other. They fought hard because in those contests, it was all or nothing: winner takes all. Each fighter would have the support of his own people, and they would place bets on their man. If a fighter won, his people also won: if he lost, his people lost.

The men who fought with bare knuckles did so because they loved to fight. But nobody in Camden Town loved to fight like the Gypsies did. These were tough people. They lived as a community within a community, and nobody messed with them.

The Gypsies had lived in Camden for generations. Where once they were tinkers, now they dealt in scrap metal and second-hand cars; or they were navvies, like many Camden Irish, standing in groups on the corners of Parkway and Camden Road in the early mornings waiting to be picked up for work. Though they were settled in Camden, most of them came from old Romany stock and were proud of their traditions. They weren't outsiders: on the contrary, they were as much a part of Camden Town as we were, and in the amateur boxing club my dad ran more than half the kids were Gypsies. There was no antagonism between them and the rest of the community; but there was a sense of identity, an almost tribal pride that could make itself felt as rivalry when the circumstances were right. It was like being part of a gang, in a way. Everyone knew who belonged to a Gypsy family and who did not.

My father was a hard man, and fighting was in his blood, as it was with a lot of the men on his side of the family. Many were either professional or illegal fighters. But I could not imagine

24

Dad taking on the champion of the Gyspies. He was much bigger than my father, at least forty pounds heavier, but from what Lenny was telling me, it sounded like Dad had put up one hell of a fight. Lenny had heard his father say that the fight could have gone either way until a knockdown in the tenth and final round. The Gypsy took the winner's purse, but both fighters took twenty-two pounds in nobbins – money that is thrown into the ring at the end of a bout if the crowd has seen enough blood.

After the fight, Dad had been taken to hospital. His urine was red: a certain sign of internal bleeding. My family were used to seeing him with a black eye. He said he got them sparring at the local boxing gym. Now we knew the truth. When Mum found out he'd been bare-knuckle fighting she made him promise he'd never do it again.

'If I see you like this once more, I'm off,' she warned. 'And I'll take the kids.'

Dad told her he would stop. And my dad never broke a promise.

In the years immediately after the Second World War, Camden Town was a tough, working class area of North London. It was here that I was born on 16 August 1950, at No.2 Dale Road, one of five terraced houses forming a small cul-de-sac. The houses were owned by British Rail, for whom my grandfather Will worked as a train driver. Our garden backed on to the railway tracks carrying the main line from London to Liverpool. For families like ours, who never travelled outside of London, Liverpool seemed like the end of the world. The garden filled with the noise of the trains and the smell of the diesel fuel. When the diesel smoke poured over the high red-brick wall, I could barely see the little pens where Dad kept chickens and rabbits.

Three families lived in our house. Mum's sister Doris and her husband Stan shared the top floor bedroom with their three children. On the ground floor there were three bedrooms; one for Mum's other sister Winnie and her husband Leslie, one for their six kids and another for Mum's parents Lily and Will. Mum and Dad had the larger of two rooms on the first floor. I shared a bed in the smaller room with my elder sister and brother, Mary and Billy. I was the youngest in the family – at least until my brother Simon was born fourteen years later. Altogether there were twenty of us in one little house.

The kitchen was the heart of our home, where people gathered to eat and to talk – not just the family but friends and neighbours who would drop by. Beside the kitchen, a tiny scullery was where the women did the washing in a stone sink and our Alsatian dog Peggy slept. From here, a door led to the backyard and the outside toilet. I hated that place. During the winters it was bitterly cold, and instead of toilet roll we had squares of newspaper tied to a length of string. To be safe, I would hide scraps of paper behind a pipe.

There was always someone in that toilet. That was okay for the grown-ups – they could just run over to the pub to use the toilet there, which was Granddad's favourite excuse for a drink – but for us kids it was a nightmare, always waiting, legs crossed, for the door to open. With so many people in the house, you had to be quick getting into that toilet.

If we needed to pee at night, we used a big pot under the bed. This was a problem for me when I was very young. I would panic and miss the pot when I was peeing. If Billy stepped in the puddle that I had left on the floor, I would get a whack on the back of the head.

And bath time was worse. A big tin bath hung on a wall in the yard next to the coal shed and a huge iron mangle that looked like a medieval torture device: it terrified me. All of us in the house took turns using the bath. I would dread Saturdays and Wednesdays, when it was my family's turn. We bathed outside in all weathers, and the eldest family members went first. Being the youngest, I was last in. Mum and Dad enjoyed a nice bath in clean, warm water, but by the time I got in, the water was cold and grey, and my brother always pissed in it. I would end up dirtier then before I got in.

Even fifteen years after the Second World War, most of the people in Camden were living in poverty. Few people owned motor cars: many local tradesmen still used horse-drawn carts, and trams were still in operation. If the people of Camden Town left their doors and windows unlocked, it was because few of them had anything worth stealing, and because it was a close community. In these streets, people helped each other. If a mother fell ill, another family would look after her kids. If a man were sent to prison, other families would make sure his family had food on the table. Elderly people were respected. We looked out for each other, and everybody in the neighbourhood knew each other by name.

The kids would play out on the streets until nine o'clock on summer evenings. I loved riding on a go-cart that my dad built from planks of wood stolen from the railway and wheels from an old pram. The streets were safe. Camden people were poor but we had love, loyalty, trust and friendship.

Because money was tight, Mum and her two sisters were always at the pawnbrokers, with its distinctive sign of three brass balls. Mum would pay a little extra to have her pawnshop parcels wrapped in brown paper, for privacy. Her wedding ring must have been in the shop more than it was on her finger.

Mum was so house-proud. The front doorstep was always spotless, and if you stepped on it with dirty shoes you were in serious trouble. My shoes often had holes in them, so I would cut two pieces from a cardboard box and slip them inside each shoe to keep from wearing holes in my socks. I would never dare to go home with dirty shoes. All of my clothes and shoes were hand-me-downs. I had to be careful not to mess my clothes, because I had only one set. Mum would wash them as soon as I took them off and dry them over a paraffin heater so I would have something to wear the following day.

Throughout these lean times, she always managed to put food on the table. My favourite treat was two big slices of white bread covered with butter and then topped with sugar. Another treat was broken biscuits, which I would collect from the corner shop. This was the place where the local women caught up on the gossip. Everything Mum bought would go on the slate, which she settled every Friday afternoon after Dad was paid for his work on the fruit stalls in Covent Garden and Inverness Market in Camden.

Working at the markets, Dad procured the little Christmas luxuries that he could not afford: fresh fruit and even a Christmas tree. One Christmas Eve, he returned from the pub carrying a big black bag. 'Happy Christmas!' he beamed, handing the bag to Mum. Inside was a fox-fur coat. Mum knew the coat must be stolen, but because Dad had no money to spare, she understood that he was simply doing whatever he could to put a smile on her face. Before I went to bed that night, I looked under the Christmas tree for presents: there were none. But in the morning there were twelve little parcels for all of us kids in the house. Tearing off the wrapping, we each found a fur hat with a little tail at the back, like the hat worn by the Wild West hero Davy Crockett. Dad could not believe his eyes when he realised what Mum had done with her fur coat, but when he saw the delight on all our faces, he smiled and gave Mum a big hug. It was the best Christmas present we ever had, and Dad knew how much it meant to all of us, Mum especially.

Dad worked incredibly hard and liked to unwind at the end of each day in the Mitre, a big public house on the corner of Dale Road that seemed like the happiest place in Camden. People could not wait to get in there as soon as they finished work, or whatever they had done during the day to make a little money. During the week the pub was filled with men drinking and playing cards, dominoes and darts while the women stayed at home. The place was always thick with smoke.

Half of the men worked for the railway, so there were a lot of parcels changing hands. The landlord claimed ten per cent of everything sold in the pub, and he took care of the police. A lot of wheeling and dealing was done in that pub. Everyone had something to sell: stockings, shoes, foodstuffs. The illegal book-makers also did a good trade.

At weekends, the women would accompany their husbands to the pub. If it was a warm evening, the parents might allow their kids to sit on the benches outside, where we would talk to a big fat man selling shrimps and jellied eels from a stall. Through the open door we could see the grown-ups gathered around a piano singing old wartime songs. Somebody in every family could play the piano. Sometimes the sing-song would carry on after closing time, and the whole crowd would go back to a nearby home. More often than not, it was our house.

My grandfather Will was always the life and soul of the party. When he wasn't singing at the piano, he would be telling his famous war stories, which seemed to have a different ending every time he told them. He seemed to spend his whole life in the Mitre, playing dominoes all night before staggering the few steps home. Will considered himself as a bit of a dandy, and was better dressed than a man who worked on the railways had any right to be. He always wore a suit with a white shirt and trilby hat, and when I was small I wanted to be a train driver like him.

My dad's father Albert was an illegal bookmaker and for many years he was the main man: the most famous man in Camden Town. Whatever petty crime had taken place, old Albert was involved somewhere along the line. Camden had its own criminal fraternity and, with its closeness to the heart of London's West End, many of the families had links with organised crime. The men of my family had a secret hiding place, under the shed at the top of the garden, where they kept money and a gun. So soon after the war, guns were easy to get hold of.

We had all kinds of people in and out of the house: some good, some bad. It was exciting. And because the house was at the end of a cul-de-sac, it was the perfect place for the men of my family to do a little business away from the eyes of the law. One man would keep lookout on the street corner and as a second line of defence, one of mum's sisters would sit on the doorstep with a couple of the kids. By the time any policemen managed to get into the house, the men would be over the back wall and escaping across the railway lines.

In this environment, I grew up streetwise, a real Camden kid. I realised from an early age that if I were to achieve anything in this life, I would have to do it on my own terms, by the force of my personality, and if necessary, by sheer physical strength.

As the son of the local hard man, I did okay. My elder brother Billy never got into fights and was never interested in boxing. But as the youngest kid in the family, I always felt I had something to prove. Luckily I was always big for my age and had a right hook that could knock out a horse. There was only one thing I was scared of, and that was my old man.

I hated every day that I spent at school. I was unable to read and write like all the other kids, and felt from the start that the odds were stacked against me. When I had to stand up and read aloud to the class, it killed me. I would break into a sweat as soon as I picked up the book, and my face would grow red and hot as the other kids laughed. That stuff would give me nightmares. None of my teachers understood my difficulties and my school reports just said that I was lazy.

I had one teacher, Mr Wilson, who pushed me too far. Not long after my eleventh birthday, I was at the back of the class, pretending to write down what he had written on the black-board, when I felt his hand strike me across the back of the head. The next few seconds passed in a blur. All I remember is standing over him as he lay stretched out on the floor. My class-mates told me I had laid him out with one punch.

At the disciplinary hearing, Mr Wilson sat nursing a black eye and looking nervous as my dad stared him down. He chose his words carefully to avoid upsetting the father of the kid who had knocked him out the previous day. I was suspended for two weeks before being put into a new class. As we walked home from school, Dad administered a long, hard lecture. 'You're throwing your life away, you stupid little sod!' He wanted me to have a better life than he had, but back then hardly anyone knew what the word dyslexia meant. My teachers certainly didn't and nor did Dad. He too thought I was lazy, even though he could barely read himself.

In 1962 we moved from the packed house in Dale Road to a council flat just around the corner. Our new home had three bedrooms and a bathroom. There was a room for Mary, a room for my parents and one for Billy and me. With all that space for the five of us it seemed like paradise.

Dad bought second-hand bicycles, one for each of us boys. We were the only ones on the estate who had bikes, so it was only a matter of time before some other kid tried to steal mine. I was round my mate Lenny's one warm summer day when I heard whispered voices through the open window. Out on the street a boy and a girl were standing beside my bike, glancing furtively around them. I knew them both. They were from a big Gypsy family who lived nearby in a rambling Victorian house. The men of the family made their living by buying, renovating and selling cars: their front garden was piled high with tyres, auto parts and other scrap metal. There were eight kids in this family, the girls as tough as the boys, and all of us on our estate were terrified of them. But I couldn't just stand there and watch them steal my bike.

I ran outside and confronted them. The boy lashed out at me, I grabbed him and the pair of us fell to the ground. As we rolled around in the street, I connected with a few good punches to his face. When Lenny dragged me off him, his nose and mouth were pouring blood. I straightened my shirt and rode home.

Mum saw the graze under my eye and knew I had been in a fight. When I told her what had happened, she went mad. I knew Dad would be angry too, so I crept out of the flat and back to Lenny's. Then I heard someone say that the Gypsy boy's father was on his way to my place to sort out my dad. This boy's father was a renowned drinker and fighter, a real wild man. I was petrified.

We ran as fast as we could back to my block, coming to a breathless stop at the foot of the staircase that led to our fifth-floor flat. Loud voices sounded from the balcony above our heads. We looked up to see the Gypsy boy's father hanging head downwards halfway over the railings. My dad had one hand on his belt and one on his collar, and for one frozen moment I thought that he was going to let him fall. Then he hauled him back to his feet and flattened him with a single punch. After that, none of the Gypsy fighters ever challenged him again.

4

Father and son

24 NOVEMBER 1962

A loud bang wakes me and I sit upright in my bed. My heart beats fast and my breath comes in short bursts. For a second I think I have woken from a nightmare. Then I hear my mother's voice, screaming my father's name. A heavy thud sounds against my bedroom wall and shakes the big wardrobe at the foot of my bed.

I jump out of the bed and fling open the door. Squinting at the bright light in the hallway, I see a tangle of bodies: there are five, maybe six men holding my dad on the floor. Dad's face is red and twisted as he struggles. A few feet away, two more men are pinning my mum against the wall.

I run towards her but one of the men grabs hold of me by the collar of my pyjamas and next thing I know I'm lying on the floor. I am desperate to help my mum and dad but my head is clamped between the knees of the man who is holding me down. I grab his leg and sink my teeth into his calf. He cries out and kicks me with his free foot, knocking me across the hallway. Mum screams again. Kicking wildly, she tries to break free of the men but they shout at her and tighten their grip on her arms.

Then I realise that she and the men are standing on a door that lies flat on the floor. It is painted red – our front door. Beyond them I can see the brick wall balcony outside the entrance to our flat, and above that, the black night sky.

A sharp click draws my attention back to where my father is lying prone under three bodies. Dad is now handcuffed to one of the men. Only then do I recognise the man's police uniform. Another of the men is also in uniform, the others in civilian clothes. Only then do I realise that my dad is being arrested.

As Dad rises slowly to his feet, my fear turns to anger. The police have come into our home and are taking my dad away. 'George Francis,' one of the men says, 'I am arresting you on suspicion ...' I do not hear the rest of the sentence. I just look at Dad, his head bowed. To me he had always seemed untouchable, a big man. Now he is being led away in handcuffs.

The other two men have let go of Mum. She is trembling as she tries to talk to Dad. One of the men – the one whose calf I bit – has rolled up his trouser leg and is rubbing a trickle of blood. I want to punch him, kick him, but I feel powerless. My brother Billy and sister Mary are standing in the hall watching in disbelief.

As the police lead him away, Dad looks back over his shoulder. His teeth are gritted and his eyes burn. He does not say a word but his expression is saying something to Mum, maybe to all of us: *it's going to be all right*. I think this is what he is saying. It is what I want to believe. I run through the open doorway onto the balcony and look down to see him being shoved into the back of a black police van. Mum calls me into the kitchen, together with Billy and Mary. Breathing hard to stifle her sobs, she says to us fiercely, 'Whatever it is, your dad's not done it.'

Our next door neighbour Dino has been woken by all the commotion and has come to make sure that we are all okay. 'Come on,' he says to Billy and me, 'let's fix that door.' I collect Dad's toolbox from a cupboard and hold the door upright with Billy while Dino screws the door back on to its hinges. Back in bed I lie awake for what feels like forever before Mum comes in and sits on the bed beside me. 'Don't worry,' she says softly. 'Dad will be home soon.'

Two days later, I run home from school to find him in the kitchen. 'They think I've done something bad,' he tells me. 'They've got me mixed up with someone else.' It is not until several years afterwards that I find out what his arrest is all about. There had always been rumours, at school and at the gym, that Dad had connections with various criminal gangs. Later on, the police even suspected him of being involved in the Great Train Robbery, since Buster Edwards was one of his closest friends. But they could never prove anything against him, and it nagged at them constantly. So this time they were determined to have him, even if they had to fit him up.

The following week when I come home I find Mum and Grandma seated at the table. Mum is crying and Grandma is holding her hand. They are startled to see me. Mum wipes her eyes and tells me to go to my room.

I sit on my bed, wondering where Dad is now. I know he is in trouble, and if the police have taken him away again it must be something serious. Only when his brother, my uncle Billy, calls at our flat the next morning do I realise how much trouble Dad is really in. I listen at the door while he and Mum are talking and I hear him say that Dad has been charged with three counts of armed robbery. 'They're putting him in Brixton,' Billy says.

All I know about Brixton, in South London, is that it is a place where people are sent to jail. A cold, sickening feeling comes over me. My dad is going to prison and I wonder if I will ever see him again.

★

6 December is better than any Christmas – my dad comes home. He is tired and pale, but his eyes have their usual sparkle as we greet him at the door. 'I have to go to court in January,' he tells us, 'but I'll be okay.'

For the next few weeks, when Dad leaves the house it is not to go to work at the markets but to meet a man named Bill Hemming, the barrister who will be defending him in court. We spend Christmas Day at my grandparents' house, but there are few presents. Dad explains that every penny he has is going to Mr Hemming. 'It's money well spent,' he says. 'Bill Hemming is the best in the business.' He tries to sound cheerful, but I have never known him be so quiet. Normally he is always talking and laughing and joking, but since the police first took him away, he has rarely smiled, and nor has Mum.

The trial begins on 3 January at the Old Bailey, where London's major criminal cases are heard. Each day, Dad leaves home with Mum at eight to be at the Old Bailey by nine-thirty. When they return, they are shattered. The first day, the trial is on the news at six o'clock: it feels strange and unreal to see Dad's face on TV and hear his name.

On the third day of the trial my uncle Billy gives evidence on Dad's behalf, and the next day so does Mum. Then Mr Hemming tells Dad he intends to call Mary, Billy and me. Billy is sixteen, Mary is fifteen and I am twelve, but Mr Hemming clearly believes we are old enough for our testimony to count.

That night I am almost too excited to sleep. I have seen court-room dramas on television and at the cinema, and I cannot wait to see what it is like in a real-life court, especially one as famous as the Old Bailey. Only when I think of Dad standing in the dock does my excitement turn to anxiety.

In the morning, we take a bus to Holborn Viaduct, then walk to the Old Bailey. It is a huge and imposing building and I feel nervous as we enter the grand entrance hall and I gaze up at the domed ceiling. At the door of the courtroom, we meet Mr Hemming, a tall man with dark hair slicked down with Brylcreem. He tells us not to worry, to answer honestly all the questions that he and the other barrister will ask us, and to speak as clearly as possible. Then he leads Dad through the tall, dark wooden doors. An hour passes slowly as we sit talking with Mum in a small room before a court official appears to collect Billy. Within fifteen minutes he returns with a shrug and a half-smile. Now it is up to me. The official walks me to the witness stand. I feel my heart pounding and my legs shaking as I look around the courtroom at the judge, the jury members, and the friends, family members and other onlookers in the public gallery. There is a hush in the room, the only sound our footsteps on the dark green carpet. I feel nervous yet elated: this is a real adventure.

An usher asks me to give my name and address then he hands me a stiff piece of card and a Bible and tells me to say the words that are on the card. Seconds pass as I stand there frozen, unable to read a line. The judge nods at the usher, who tells me to repeat it after him. As he talks me firmly through the oath a few words at a time I can sense the looks of sympathy from the jury. They are on my side.

As Mr Hemming approaches the stand I can't help thinking he looks rather comical wearing his white wig. He asks me where I was on the afternoon of 17 November 1962. I tell him I was at home.

'Was your father with you?'

'Yes, we watched *Bonanza*. We always watch it together on Saturday afternoons.'

'What time was this?'

'Five o'clock. We watch *Bonanza* after we've listened to the football results on the radio.'

'Thank you, Michael,' Mr Hemming says, returning to his seat beside Dad, whose tense expression gives way to a brief smile.

The prosecution barrister asks me if I am certain about the answers I have just given. 'Are you sure about the time that you watched *Bonanza* with your father?'

'Yes,' I reply. 'It's on at the same time every Saturday.'

'And you are sure that your father was with you on the afternoon of November seventeenth?'

'Yes, he never misses it.'

'That will be all,' he says.

Next day we wait anxiously for the verdict. From nine in the morning the hours tick by until at last we hear there has been a decision. Dad has been found not guilty on two counts of robbery with violence, but on the third, the jury is split and the judge has ordered a retrial.

★

It is a month before we return to the Old Bailey for the last day of the second trial. Dad has spent the previous night at Brixton prison. If he is found guilty, he will return to Brixton for fifteen years. If he is acquitted, he will come home to Camden with us.

We arrive at the Old Bailey in the early afternoon. Mum prefers to wait outside the courtroom. If Dad is found guilty, she does not want us to see him sentenced. The strain of the past two months has drained her: she looks exhausted and much thinner.

At a little after four o'clock, the doors to the courtroom swing open. I hear shouting from inside, voices I recognise, family and friends who have been watching the trial from the gallery. As people stream out through the doors, Mum clasps her hand tight around mine. Then Dad appears with his arm around Mr Hemming. All around them, people are patting him on the back and shaking Mr Hemming's hand. Dad disengages himself from the crowd and runs to us, embracing Mum and lifting her off her feet. When they part, he hugs Mary, then Billy, then me.

'It's over,' he says. 'It's all right.'

1963 had begun like a nightmare, but it ends like the sweetest dream. In the first week of September, less than a month after my thirteenth birthday, I fall in love for the first time. Walking home after playing football on Finsbury Park with my school friend Charlie George, I pass the Castle, a playground built for the residents of a new estate in the Camden Road. Two redbrick towers stand ten feet tall at the centre of a grassed area, surrounded by swings and a roundabout. Young children run in and out of the towers, watched by their parents. Among the older kids gathered around the swings, I notice a girl smiling at me. She wears black shorts and a red top and her dark hair is styled in a bob like the famous British designer Mary Quant. It is love at first sight, the way it happens in the movies.

I am too shy to go over and talk to her, but on the following afternoon, I return to the Castle and sit on the grass near the swings for an hour before she reappears. She sits on one of the swings, rocking gently, then waves to me. She tells me her name is June and we talk for an hour or more until the sun begins to dip in the sky. From then on we meet regularly. I am too young to think about having a serious girlfriend, but we visit each other at our parents' homes, and my mum takes to her immediately. On her first day at St Michael's School, I wait for June at the gates to walk her home.

Like every girl in my school, June is a fan of The Beatles, and has a crush on Paul McCartney. In the first week of December, I am walking with her from school when I tell her my exciting news: my sister Mary is taking me to see The Beatles' Christmas Show at the Astoria Theatre in Finsbury Park. June is aghast. 'I hate you!' she screams, punching me in the chest and running off to her home. A whole week passes before I see her again and she forgives me. I feel guilty that I am going to The Beatles' show and she is not, but I have never seen a pop concert before, and I am desperate to go. Besides, even if I did have another ticket, June would not be allowed to go with us because she is two years younger than I am, and her mother does not let her go out at night without an adult.

The concert is on Christmas Eve. Mary and I arrive at the Astoria in the early afternoon. Already, there are two hundred teenagers queuing at the door, huddled together in the cold. At five, we take our seats in the stalls. The show starts at six, but before The Beatles take to the stage, we must sit through performances from several other pop acts, including Rolf Harris, The Barron Knights, Cilla Black and Billy J Kramer & The Dakotas. The wait is agonising, especially for Mary, who joins in the chants of 'We want The Beatles!' each time there is a pause in the music.

When, at last, The Beatles appear before us, the noise from the audience is so loud, I feel it vibrate within me. Everyone jumps to their feet, and all around me, girls are screaming. Some are so excited they are crying.

The Beatles are wearing high-collared suits, their long 'mop-top' haircuts shaking as they sing. Mary's eyes are fixed on John Lennon, her favourite Beatle. He is my favourite also, although boys do not talk about things like that. I have seen The Beatles playing on TV, but as I watch them from a hundred feet away, it feels like a dream. They sing 'Love Me Do', 'Please Please Me', 'She Loves You' and their current number one single 'I Want To Hold Your Hand'. With each song, the screams grow louder, until it becomes impossible to hear the words. To my left, a pretty, dark-haired girl in a pink dress faints and is helped to her feet by her friends.

When The Beatles wave goodbye and run from the stage, it seems like only seconds since they first appeared. Mary is speechless, her face streaked with tears, as we put on our coats and scarves and walk to the bus stop. All along the Camden Road, Christmas lights sparkle in the windows of the houses. I can't wait to wake up tomorrow on Christmas morning, but there is another feeling inside me, another excitement that is deeper still. I don't know why, but after seeing The Beatles tonight, I sense that nothing will be the same again.

5

Uppers and downers

'Swinging London' the newspapers are calling it. It is the summer of 1966 and I am discovering a whole new life. There might be precious little glamour in the part of the city where I have lived for sixteen years, but in the heart of the capital, in the clubs and coffee bars of Soho, there is a buzz like nothing I have ever known.

Soho covers barely a square mile, but day and night, its narrow streets are crowded with people from every walk of life. On Carnaby Street, tiny boutiques offer the latest mod fashions: sharply tailored suits and pointed winkle-picker shoes for the guys, daring mini-skirts and brightly-coloured, knee-length leather boots for the girls. The surrounding streets form the hub of the city's entertainment business and its sex trade. In first floor windows above shops and restaurants, prostitutes' red lights shine from behind dirty net curtains.

Since leaving school at fifteen, I spend my days working with my father supplying fresh fruit and vegetables to the open-air markets of Covent Garden and Camden Town; but at night I, like thousands of young people, am drawn to Soho. After dark is when the place truly comes alive. The flashing neon signs of bars and clubs and sex shops bathe the streets in an exotic light. In tiny pubs filled with noise and cigarette smoke, boys flirt with girls as jukeboxes play the hot new pop records by The Beatles, The Rolling Stones, The Spencer Davis Group, Dusty Springfield and The Kinks. I feel like I belong here.

Although fresh out of school, I am big enough to pass for eighteen, the legal age for drinking alcohol. Mum and Dad have no idea that I am spending my nights in Soho. It is a simple deception. On the evenings that I visit June at her parents' flat in Camden Road, I tell Mum and Dad not to wait up for me. Dad has to get to bed early most nights in order to rise before 4 a.m. for work. When I leave June's, I catch a bus from Camden Town to Tottenham Court Road and the heart of the action. Provided I am home and in bed by two in the morning, nobody will be any the wiser. If my parents ever find out that I am going to pubs and clubs, they will be livid. And if they find out how I am financing this exciting new social life – by selling drugs – Dad will throw me out of the house. Everyone in the clubs is taking these drugs: little amphetamine pep pills – 'uppers' – that act as a stimulant to the central nervous system and give the user a buzz for a few hours. The most popular is Drinamyl, a compound of amphetamine and barbiturate, a sedative that takes the edge off the buzz and provides a smoother high. Because of their bluish colour and triangular shape, these pills are known as Purple Hearts.

I take my first Purple Heart at The Scene, one of London's most fashionable nightclubs. The doorman at the club is Terry, a boxer who trains at the Highgate gym where my dad works in the afternoons and evenings after his shifts at the markets. Terry knows that my friend Nicky and I are too young to be admitted to the club, but he lets us in and tells us he has something that will keep us dancing all night. He's not joking: the two Purple Hearts that we buy from him have us buzzing all night, and when I finally creep into bed at two-thirty, I stay awake for the next two hours until Dad comes into my room to get me up and ready for work. Nicky and I are hooked, but when we return to The Scene the following week, we do not have enough money to buy the pills. Terry has the solution to our problem: he tells us of his supplier, a Maltese guy named Mickey who works at another club, and suggests that we buy a bag of Purple Hearts from him and then sell them in the clubs and pubs at a profit. All we need is enough cash to buy the first bag: after that the pills will pay for themselves. I borrow the money from my sister Mary, telling her it's to buy a present for June.

Ever since, I have visited Maltese Mickey at his house in Kentish Town every Friday afternoon. I buy ten pills, one each for Nicky and me, and eight to sell at two hundred per cent profit. Our scam is working nicely until one Thursday night after Christmas, when I come face to face with a real drug dealer. Nicky and I are at The Scene, talking to two pretty girls, when a stocky, dark-haired guy steps between us, jabbing a finger at my face. I recognise him instantly. He is from a well-known South London family, hard men whose business is drugs and prostitution.

'I've heard you've been selling gear in here,' he says with a half smile.

'Not me, mate,' I reply.

'Shut up,' he snaps, the smile replaced by a snarl. 'I know what you're up to, and if I see you in here again you'll fucking regret it.' Eyes bulging, he asks repeatedly if I understand his warning. I nod and resist the urge to knock him cold with a right hander.

He walks away with a swagger to rejoin his gang near the bar. The two girls have disappeared. As Nicky and I finish our drinks, the gang members stare at us through a throng of dancing people.

'Where shall we go tomorrow night?' Nicky asks.

I smile. 'We'll come here.'

★

Friday morning at Covent Garden is bitterly cold. As Dad and I unload sacks of potatoes and boxes of oranges from his cart, he pauses, his breath rising into the cold air in great clouds of white.

'You alright?' he frowns.

'Fine,' I reply, realising that this is the first word I have said for the best part of an hour. All this morning I have been thinking about the guy who threatened me last night at The Scene. Time and again I have run through the same scenario in my mind: he threatens me a second time and I hit him with everything I've got; he falls to the floor and his gang back off. I must go back to the club tonight. I told Nicky that I would, so I can't back down.

I meet Nicky at nine at the bus stop on Camden Road. I am wearing a black mohair suit, a Christmas present from my parents. I want to look like I mean business, so that these guys understand that they are not dealing with a kid. First we head for the Ship, a pub on Wardour Street. We drink a couple of whiskies to settle our nerves, and pop a Purple Heart. At ten-thirty we arrive at The Scene. Terry waves us through the door and we walk downstairs. The music is loud, the warm air thick with smoke. My legs feel heavy as I walk to the bar, my adrenaline running high. A beer soothes my dry throat and calms my shaking hands. There is no sign of the South London gang. I look to the dancefloor and my gaze fixes on a girl dancing wildly, shaking her blonde hair to the beat, a white mini-dress revealing long, slender legs. I recognise the song, 'Uptight' by Stevie Wonder, and also the guy dancing with her – Nicky. I smile to myself. He really is a fast mover.

The Purple Heart is kicking in. I feel sharp, confident. I order another beer and walk out to the dancefloor just as The Rolling

Stones' 'Nineteenth Nervous Breakdown' begins. I see Nicky and the blonde girl at the far end of the room. Dancing before me is a girl in a black roll-neck sweater, mouthing the words of the song. I close my eyes, the rush of amphetamine warming my blood. I sway on my feet for a few seconds. Then I feel a blow to the back of my head and hear the crash of breaking glass. My head swims and I fall to the floor, my face impacting against hard wood. Pain comes with a jolt. I lift a hand to my head and feel warm blood running through my hair. A boot thuds into my ribs and I roll over on to my back, dazed and blinking. I see the shape of a man looming over me, a flash of something catching the lights above – a broken bottle that smashes into my face, once, twice, slicing into my mouth.

Suddenly I am lifted up and dragged across the floor and up the stairs, freezing air filling my lungs and bringing me to my senses. I am pushed against the brick wall of an alleyway. My whole body sags but two men hold me up as a familiar face comes into focus before me, the leader of the South London gang.

'You don't fucking listen, do you?'

He pulls out a shotgun from inside his coat and pushes the barrel up under the side of my jaw. This is it, I think, I am going to die. He leans in close and whispers in my ear.

'If we ever see you around here again, you're dead.'

He lowers the gun from my face and his two pals let go of my arms. I slump helplessly to the floor. Overwhelmed by pain, fear and nausea, I sink into half-consciousness, staring dumbly at the flashing pink neon sign of the strip club across the road, until I hear Nicky's voice beside me. Between us we staunch the blood from the jagged gash in my mouth before Nicky hauls me into the back of a taxi, where I black out.

When I come round, in Charing Cross Hospital, Nicky is speaking to a nurse. He turns to me with a grin. 'They did a job on you, mate.' He tells me I have fifty-six stitches in my face and head, and twelve under my tongue. I feel lucky to be alive –

except that now I am frightened to go home. I can imagine all too vividly what Mum and Dad will say.

★

When my brother Billy wakes up the next day and the first thing he sees is my face in the next door bed, he lets out a startled scream. In the bathroom I inspect the damage in the mirror. My face looks twice its normal size and my head is covered by so many bandages that I look like Boris Karloff in *The Mummy*. I have two black eyes and a broken nose and ugly black stitches running along my top lip. It is as if I have been in a road accident.

Several times, Dad asks me if I know who attacked me, but I stick to the story that Nicky and I have agreed: I was whacked outside the Tally Ho pub in Kentish Town; I was jumped from behind; I never saw my assailant. If Dad ever finds out who did this to me, he will not go the police. He will sort it out personally. I know he will get to the truth sooner or later, because the South London gang are part of a family who also work on the markets, and people talk. I only hope that Dad does not discover the reason why these guys battered me.

It is a full month later when Nicky informs me that the South London gang have taken a beating. The word is that Dad and three of his boxers surprised the gang in their local pub on The Cut, near Waterloo Station, just south of the River Thames. The fight was so brutal that one of the gang lost an ear. Dad has not said a word to me about it. Nicky and I agree to stay clear of The Scene and keep out of trouble.

In the first week of February I return to work with Dad at Covent Garden. We arrive at the market-square in the blue-grey half-light of early morning. As Dad parks the car, a second-hand Morris Minor that has seen better days, I see a group of beautiful young women entering a club in one of the side streets. The sign above the door reads 'Middle Earth'. I decide that I must investigate this place as soon as possible.

Three days later, I am walking through the door. The club has three floors linked by a single narrow staircase. I stare in disbelief at the beautiful young hippie girls dancing all around me. The warm, heavy scent of dope smoke fills the air. If this is flower power, count me in.

As I head to the bar on the top floor, a guy with long hair and an army-surplus greatcoat tugs at my sleeve. He is selling tabs of LSD. I have not taken acid before, but if I am ever going to try it, it might as well be here and now. For the price of a day's wages, he hands me a small square of paper with smudges of colour on each side. He tells me to place the paper on my tongue for a few minutes, then chew and swallow.

Exotic music, like nothing I have ever heard, lures me to the dancefloor. The room is hot, the atmosphere heady. The multi-coloured lights above my head are dazzling, mesmerising. The lights seem to hover in the air like spaceships. The beautiful hippie girls change shape before my eyes, their faces expanding and contracting. I know I must be hallucinating, but what I see appears real.

I am losing all sense of reality. A couple dancing next to me mutate into alien form, like Martians in a Saturday morning picture show. After dancing for what feels like an hour, maybe two, I walk through the crowd to the stairs and feel as if I am floating down to the basement room, where Indian music throbs within me. I see a huge bed covered in naked bodies. I reach out to touch the bed to see if it is real, and feel water moving beneath my hand. Great waves rise up ten feet to the ceiling. Then a hand takes mine and I turn to see a girl with a pretty oval face pulling me down on to the bed among the waves. As I lie back, closing my eyes, I feel her unbuttoning my jeans and taking my cock in her mouth. When I open my eyes again I am startled to see people on the ceiling. I begin to panic before I realise that there is a mirror above the bed. The shock brings me back down to earth: I see myself in the reflection, lying between other bodies; then I see the girl who is blowing me. She is enormous, all of four hundred pounds, with thick rolls of fat at her sides, and now she is manoeuvring her bulky thighs towards my face. I slip underneath her and scramble off the bed, tripping over with my jeans wrapped around my ankles. I pull them up and dash upstairs. Searching frantically for the exit, I stumble across the dance floor, bumping from one person to the next. Each of them has the face of the girl on the bed. The music is overpowering, a dizzying, hypnotic pulse. I feel the waves from the bed washing up over my head, then something pulls me from the crowd, a hand on my arm, and I emerge blinking into bright daylight. A girl – she looks just like June – is standing with me in the street, asking me if I am okay. My head begins to clear.

'I've got to get home,' I say. The girl smiles and disappears back inside the club. I shiver against the cold and begin walking towards the tube station. Everything appears normal: the street, the sky, and the people walking past. I feel groggy, yet relieved. The clock above the tube station reads 9.25. I must have been inside that club for twelve hours, although it feels like a few minutes. I make a mental note to myself: stick to Purple Hearts.

Since the fight at The Scene, Nicky and I have found a new club nearer home, the Downbeat in Green Lanes, North London. The club operates in a large room over a pub and hosts gigs by up-and-coming artists like Georgie Fame. I am still buying pills from Maltese Mickey, but selling only to my friends.

It is a Friday night in late February. Nicky and I and a group of ten other friends are in high spirits. It is the end of the working week and we have been drinking for a few hours before heading to the Downbeat. We are all buzzing: Mickey was not kidding when he promised me that this batch of Purple Hearts is the best he has ever had.

A mod band is playing. They are nothing special, but there

are lots of girls in the club, so we are all happy. Nicky is chatting to two pretty, giggling sisters when a tall, blond guy, immaculately dressed in a blue suit, marches across the room and prods Nicky's chest, warning him to back off from the girls. I move quickly to Nicky's side and immediately we are confronted by several of the blond guy's gang. I recognise one: his name is Roy, an ex-boxer and a real bully.

I know what is coming but I fail to see the first punch: it slams into the side of my head and sends me reeling backwards into Nicky, my beer glass smashing on the floor. A mass brawl ensues. Girls scream and the band stops playing as fists and boots fly.

I drag a guy off Nicky, but as I throw him to the floor, Roy catches me off balance, knocking me through a doorway and tumbling down a long flight of stairs.

I lie there, dazed, as dozens of people flee the club in panic, clattering down the stairs and jumping over me as I struggle to get up. Then I see Roy coming towards me. I wince, anticipating a boot in the face, but he brushes past me and runs off down the street. For a second I feel lucky. A bastard like Roy will always kick a man if he is down. Then I realise why he has vanished: someone up there must be badly hurt, or even dead.

I grab the doorframe to pull myself up, and breathe a sigh of relief as Nicky appears, his face bloodied and frightened. 'Come on,' he yells, 'let's go!'

We don't stop running until we reach the gates of Finsbury Park. Bent double with the pain in my sides, I fight for breath. 'What happened?' I ask, wheezing.

'One of their boys got stabbed,' Nicky says. 'I don't know who did it, but it looked bad.'

We walk back to Nicky's house and I sleep on a sofa downstairs. In the morning we are drinking tea in the kitchen when Lenny and Jimmy, two of the friends who were with us last night, call at the back door.

'One of them's dead,' says Lenny.

51

'Fucking hell,' groans Nicky. We are in serious trouble. At least a hundred people witnessed the fight. It will not be long before the police come calling.

I walk home with fear in my heart. At the entrance to our estate, a police car is parked. I turn back and find a red telephone box on the street corner. Dad answers my call and my heart sinks. 'The police are here,' he says gravely. 'You'd better come home, son.'

6

The man who fell to earth

In the first week of March 1967, I am interviewed at Stoke Newington police station in North London, in a small room sparsely furnished with a wooden table and four grey plastic chairs. Because I am aged sixteen and legally a minor, I am accompanied by my dad. The police repeat their questions over and over, testing my version of events. Over and over I tell them what happened: that I was at the club with friends, we were assaulted, I was thrown down the stairs and I left the club without witnessing the stabbing. Altogether my interview lasts eight hours. Policemen come and go, taking turns to hammer me with questions, trying to make me slip up or change my story. The detectives take regular breaks, but for me there is no respite. I am exhausted, hungry, and very, very frightened.

All I want to do is to get this over with and go home. When

at last the officers rise and it's clear that it is finished, I am flooded with relief. So when one policeman begins to read aloud from a sheet of paper, 'Michael Daniel Francis, you are being charged with affray ...' I still do not understand the implications of what he says. It is only when the one with the charge sheet continues, 'You will be remanded in custody until your case goes to trial ...' that it hits me. I am not going home. Far from it. They are going to lock me up.

A policewoman tells my dad that he will have to leave without me. Dad tells me not to worry, since I have done nothing wrong. He tells me to keep my head up, to watch my back and trust no one. They are sending me to a young offenders' institute in Ashford, Kent, some fifty miles south-east of London; but he promises to visit every day.

After Dad is gone, I am led downstairs to a cell. I stare at the cream-coloured walls for what feels like hours and wonder how Dad will explain to Mum that I am not coming home. I wonder how I will cope. I'm not concerned about the other inmates. I know that I can look after myself if I have to. But I have never been inside a cell before and already I have discovered I can't stand it. Being banged up like this for weeks, months, or longer is a prospect I am terrified to face.

A burly policeman unlocks the door and takes me to a holding room where three of my friends are gathered: Lenny, Jimmy and Pat. Before they can say a word, I sense from their glum expressions that they too are being sent to Ashford. There is no sign of Nicky. He was lucky: no one ever fingered him for being at the club.

For fifteen minutes we wait in silence, trying hard to stifle our apprehension. Then we are led outside to where a large black van stands ready. The back of the van is divided into solid metal cubicles, several on each side. They are cells in miniature, each with its own small window, a grille in the door and just enough room to sit down. Most are already occupied with men collected from other London police stations. As soon as we are loaded into four of the empty cubicles, the doors slam shut behind us and the van moves off with a lurch.

Through the tiny window I see familiar North London streets. I recognise Camden Road and feel a sharp pang of regret. At the end of the rows of cells, two police officers sit, chatting idly to each other as we drive. One is looking forward to going to football at the weekend. It makes me think of all the things that I will not be doing; Soho, the Mitre, evenings with June, Mum's roast Sunday lunch.

The first stop on our journey is Pentonville Prison, where four of the men are taken out of the van. Another three are delivered to Wormwood Scrubs. We pass the Houses of Parliament, over Westminster Bridge, and east to the outskirts of the city before entering green countryside. I have travelled outside of London only on the rare occasions when Dad has taken the family to seaside resorts like Brighton and Margate for day trips in the summer. Now, as rain thrums against the window, I feel a long way from home.

It is almost dark when the van swings down a steep incline and under a railway viaduct to the forbidding entrance of Ashford Institute for Young Offenders. The building resembles a fortress, with high grey walls and dark blue gates of solid iron set between two tall pillars. Through the window, I can see the gates closing behind us. 'Welcome home, lads,' one of the policemen mocks.

Released from the van we are led across a courtyard illuminated by spotlights. Barbed wire is strung in four lines at the top of the walls. Once inside, our personal possessions are taken from us. The duty officer signs us in, then signals for the policemen to depart. We are taken to a nearby room where we are told to strip. Nervously we remove our clothes and stand shivering, while a prison warder snaps on a pair of white rubber gloves. In turn we are each instructed to bend forward while a cold finger is inserted inside our rectums. This process – preventing inmates from bringing drugs inside the facility – is as humiliating as it is discomforting. When it is done we are handed bundles of prison-issue clothing. We dress in silence as the guards look on.

From there, we are led, one by one, to our cells. Mine is high up on the second floor. It is ten feet square and furnished with a steel washbasin, a two-tier bunk bed and another, single bed on which two black teenagers sit playing cards. They look up and nod as the door clangs shut behind me. At least they seem friendly enough. I find out their names are Robert and Keith. Both of them are seventeen, and have convictions for burglary. They ask how I got here and when I describe the fight at the Downbeat, Robert emits a wry laugh, as if he has heard my story a thousand times before.

'It will be lights out soon,' he says. 'You take the top bunk.'

'I need a piss,' I reply. Robert points to the floor near the washbasin, where there is a circular hole a foot wide. He grins. 'I hope your aim is good.'

At nine sharp, the single naked bulb clicks off as I lie in my bunk, staring at the ceiling. Through a small barred window, I can see the blue-black night sky. I think of home, of my family and friends, people who love and care for me. I promise myself that when I get out of here I will stay away from clubs in the future, back off from fighting, work hard, and make sure I never end up in a place like this again.

I hear a train rattling over the viaduct, then a second some time later, and so on through the night. The minutes pass like hours, the hours like days, until at last dawn breaks. The morning wake-up bell comes as a relief.

I soon discover that every day the routine is the same. The wake-up bell rings at six. At 6.15 the cell doors open and we slop out. Each inmate carries his bucket to the latrines, and for several minutes each landing is pervaded by the smell. Three times a week we are permitted to have a shower. We make our beds: the screws come round and check that they meet the regulation standard, and if your bed fails the inspection you lose your privileges for the day. Breakfast is at 8.30 and is over by 9 a.m. Then it is back to the cell. Exercise is in two lots: one group in the morning and one in the afternoon. It is just like you see in old black and white prison movies: under the gaze of the warders we walk a continuous circle round and round the yard. We are not allowed to stop. We are not supposed to talk, although if you are quiet you can get away with talking under your breath. Lunch is from half past twelve to half past one. We eat in shifts. The meals are disgusting; as bad as the worst school dinner I ever had. Yet even though it is horrible – tasteless, greasy and overcooked – food is still the highlight of our day. Visiting time is also in two sessions: mid-morning or mid-afternoon. There are no visits at weekends; but from Monday to Friday, because I am on remand, I am allowed a visit every day. For those who have been convicted, visits are reduced to two a month. At the end of each day we have half an hour in which we can go to the library or the chapel. Supper consists of a cup of tea and a biscuit in the cell. The light goes out at nine. Seven days a week, day in, day out, this becomes my life.

It doesn't take me long to learn the rules. You have to learn fast or else. Most of the screws are okay but there is the odd one who relishes power and likes to beat up any kid who is stroppy or foolish enough to step out of line. On the second day I find out which of the inmates to watch out for. It is at the end of exercise, just as we are dispersing back to our cells. I am standing with Keith and Lenny and Jimmy and Pat when something makes Lenny laugh. 'What's so fucking funny?' snaps the lad who is next in line. He too is with his mates, and all of them look mean. Before he can answer, Lenny is knocked to the ground. Beside me, Keith mutters quietly. 'Don't start anything with those lads,' he warns. 'They'll murder you.'

It is only a turn of phrase, but I get the point. Later, when we are back inside the cell, Keith and Robert advise me on the best way to survive. There are two gangs in particular who like to think they run the place: one is Jamaican, the other white. It is not a good career move to challenge either one. What happened to Lenny was a rite of initiation, a message to let us know who is boss. We should not retaliate, but keep ourselves to ourselves. If we stay quiet, we will not be troubled again. This is not how it would happen in Camden Town, but I am in Ashford now. This is not my turf. I realise that I have to keep my head down if I want to get out of here in one piece.

On the fifth day, in the canteen, a familiar voice calls my name. Derek is a young Irish boxer who has trained in Highgate with my dad between spells in correctional facilities. Dad speaks highly of him, and reckons that he could make a solid professional if only he would stop whacking people outside of the ring. I am not surprised to learn that Derek is awaiting trial on charges of aggravated assault. We talk briefly before he moves off to take his place in the queue. As Derek walks away, I notice that the guy who thumped Lenny is watching us. He nods his head slowly, a gesture of respect. Derek, it seems, is a good friend to have in here.

Dad's visits help me through the long months inside. He brings June with him whenever her mother and her school work permits. In the visiting room, tables are set out in lines with one chair on the near side, for the inmate, and two opposite for his friends and family. Visitors must remain seated; we are not allowed to touch. The first day sets the pattern: Dad brings me news from home, with special words of encouragement from Mum. He says that she cannot come because she has two-year-old Simon to care for, but I know the truth is that after all that has happened, it is just too painful for her to see me here. Dad looks tired – he has driven straight down from the markets in his battered Morris Minor – but he does his best to keep my spirits up.

The guard calls time. Dad takes a deep breath and looks up

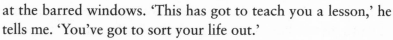

at the barred windows. 'This has got to teach you a lesson,' he tells me. 'You've got to sort your life out.'

'I'll see you tomorrow,' he says.

Being locked up is either something you can live with, like my cellmates Robert and Keith, or you hate it, as I do. Every day I tell myself I will be out soon. I never lose this belief. Boredom is the hardest thing. Towards the end of the summer, I am given a job in the kitchens with Derek. The work is arduous – peeling potatoes and washing plates until my hands are as shrivelled as an old man's – but it means I spend less time locked up in my cell, for which I am grateful.

The one good thing that comes from my time in Ashford – apart from the fact that it puts me off pursuing a life of crime – is that I teach myself to read. Letters are a lifeline, although I have to get used to the fact that those that come in are opened and read before they reach me, and any I send in return must be left unsealed. Keith writes my letters for me, and reads me the letters I get, until finally he suggests he should help me to learn to read them for myself. With his encouragement, gradually I overcome my word blindness, and grow to love reading. Every few days after that Dad brings me books from Mum, and the hours in my cell pass more quickly as my reading skills improve.

It is eight months before I return to London, to the Old Bailey, for my trial. As we are driven up from Ashford in a prison van, Lenny, Jimmy, Pat and I sit silently in our individual cubicles, fervently hoping that we will be released. When we enter the courtroom, I look up to the public gallery and see Dad sitting with June and my old friend Charlie George, and my heart lifts.

For me the trial is astonishingly brief. The police only have one witness who placed me at the club on the night of the stabbing, and now she is uncertain. She is no longer willing to swear in court that I am the person she saw. My barrister appeals instantly to the judge, claiming that I have no case to answer. The judge agrees: the case against me is dismissed. For Lenny, Jimmy and Pat, however, it does not end so well. Each of them is convicted of affray.

In the hallway outside the courtroom, I am reunited with Dad and June and Charlie. There are tears and hugs, just as there were on this very spot for my dad four years ago. As we walk out into the street, June clings tightly to me as if she is afraid to let go of me ever again. I turn to look back at the Old Bailey's grand façade, and vow never to return.

7

The first cut is the deepest

It is a frosty morning in January of 1968 when I realise exactly how much my parents sacrificed to secure my release. I had heard that when Dad himself was on trial in 1963, friends and family scraped together the money for his legal fees, and a hat was passed around at the Mitre across the road. In all the times that he visited me in Ashford, Dad never told me how he was raising the money to hire the barrister who would defend me in court. He told me not to worry about it, that I had enough to think about.

On the day I return to work at Covent Garden, my uncle Billy finds me sipping a cup of tea at the stall in the corner of the square while Dad is collecting orders from the market office. Billy has a face like thunder. He speaks in a low whisper, but the force of his words is like a slap in the face.

'I'm telling you this so that you sort your life out,' he says.

'Your mum and dad used their life savings to get you out of that place. A barrister like that doesn't come cheap. They were going to use that money as a deposit on a new house, but now they're stuck in that council flat for years.'

I feel sick to the stomach. I swallow hard, unable to look him in the eye.

'You've brought trouble on yourself. You can't go around fighting every night. You've got to straighten out. You owe it to your family ...' Billy's face softens slightly. He smiles and ruffles my hair, relenting. 'Just don't let your dad know I've told you this,' he says. 'It's good to have you back.'

Billy slips away before Dad returns, whistling. He is eager to finish the day's work so that he can get to the gym and resume training a promising new boxer, Bunny Sterling. In the eight months I spent inside on remand, Dad has made a momentous decision. He has given up the amateur club he ran for so many years in Camden and begun to train professionals, in a new gym in the back room of the Wellington, a Highgate public house. Bunny is his first big hope. Born in Kingston, Jamaica, Bunny, at twenty, is one of the best young middleweights in the country. Dad thinks he has what it takes to be a champion, and spends all his spare time honing Bunny's ring-craft in the busy Highgate gym. In fact, as I later discover, it was Bunny himself who persuaded Dad that he should take this step. Having won every amateur prize that was open to him, Bunny refused to turn professional unless Dad agreed to train him. He said he would not do it with anyone else.

When we finish work at three o'clock in the afternoon, Dad drops me off at home, pausing only for a cup of tea and a sandwich before driving up to Highgate. When he has gone, I linger alone in the kitchen, pondering what my uncle Billy said. I feel guilty that I have cost my mum and dad the chance of moving to a better home, but the more I think about it, the more I realise how much I must mean to them, and how indebted I am. Dad has always been generous in helping others: last year, he raised money for a local hospital by pulling his market barrow, fully loaded, from Covent Garden to Brighton and back, a round trip of one hundred miles. And for me, he would do anything. I understand this now more than ever.

★

I take on extra work, putting asphalt covering on roofs with our neighbour Dino, so that I can give a little more to Mum and Dad each week. It is not a fortune, but I know it will help as they begin saving again. Also, I work as Dad's assistant at the gym. He offers to pay me, but I tell him I am happy to work for free. I travel with him from Covent Garden to Highgate, three or four days a week. I scrub the canvases and concrete floors of dirt and blood, and act as second corner man during sparring: ensuring that the boxers' hands are properly bandaged inside the gloves before they are tied, and providing them with water to drink between rounds. I consider it an apprenticeship. Lacking any academic qualifications, I have no career plan.

Now that I am spending many hours each week at the gym, Dad encourages me to box. Perhaps he thinks that I could benefit from the disciplines of boxing, or that it will provide an outlet for the aggression that might otherwise lead me into more trouble out on the street. Within a matter of weeks I am competing at amateur level, at middleweight, for Hampstead Boxing Club, but despite Dad's best efforts to prepare me, I win only three of twelve fights. I have a powerful right hook that can put a much bigger man on the canvas, but I struggle against quicker opponents. And while I can take a punch to the body or even to the side of the head, if I get hit on the nose, my eyes water, my head spins, and I am finished.

In two of the bouts, I am disqualified for foul play: nothing nasty, just a few little tricks that Dad has taught me, like nudging an opponent with the shoulder to unbalance him before delivering a big punch. Every fighter bends the rules a little here and there, Dad says. I am simply not sly enough to get away with it.

My twelfth and final fight is at the London Polytechnic, in a grand hall with ornate, gold-painted balconies and a glittering chandelier hung from the high ceiling. The boxing ring stands at the centre of the room. At the far end of the hall, facing the entrance, is a wooden stage set with a long table and a dozen chairs.

The hall fills with five hundred people before the first of ten fights, each scheduled for three rounds. As I stand with Dad in a corner of the room waiting for the guest of honour to arrive, a few familiar faces from Covent Garden approach us to wish me luck. Among them are members of two of the most notorious families in London, both with reputed links to underworld crime; but to those who know them through working on the markets, they are trusted friends. Several of them shake my hand and tell me they are looking forward to my fight. I cannot wait to get it over and done with. Dad and I both know that I am not good enough to win amateur prizes, let alone make the grade as a professional fighter. I want to win this fight for Dad and for my friends from Camden who are here to support me, then quit when I feel like I am ahead.

The master of ceremonies, a thin man in dress suit and bow tie, steps into the ring and calls a hush in the room. He makes a brief welcoming address before gesturing towards the entrance. 'Ladies and gentlemen, will you please welcome tonight's guest of honour – from the world of pop music, Mister Cat Stevens!'

All eyes turn to see an exotic figure with a mane of long dark hair and a white fur coat that reaches to the floor. He has a straggly beard but his features are delicate, almost feminine. He is flanked by two stunning blonde girls; one wearing a shiny red plastic raincoat, the other wrapped head to toe in a long Afghan coat. There is a glow, an aura, about them. People stare in disbelief, as if these strangers have landed from another planet. I, too, am mesmerised. I have seen The Beatles on stage, but never have I felt so close to a famous and glamorous pop star. I do not know much about Cat Stevens, other than that my sister Mary liked his first hit single 'Matthew And Son', and that he wrote PP Arnold's hit 'The First Cut Is The Deepest'. But as I watch him take his seat up on the stage, a beautiful girl on either side, I long to see the world through his eyes: a world far beyond the confines of Camden Town and Covent Garden, a world of magical places and limitless possibilities . . .

'Come on,' Dad says, grabbing my arm and bringing me suddenly back down to earth. He leads me from the hall to the dressing rooms downstairs, where I change into boxing shorts and boots and work through a few warm-up exercises. Dad wraps my hands and ties my gloves and I sit tensely for five minutes before I am summoned to the ring.

My friends and supporters shout their encouragement as I size up my opponent, a lean, rangy army cadet with cold blue eyes and tattoos on his forearms. He looks confident. I turn to Dad in my corner, he slips a gum-shield into my mouth, and the first bell rings.

For two rounds, I barely lay a glove on the guy. He is quick on his feet and has a longer reach. I try to cut off the space in the ring, to close him down and catch him with some combination punches, but he eludes me and stings my face with sharp jabs. Once or twice he lands solid uppercuts to my chin, but I stay on my feet and keep plugging away, working for an opening. The audience appreciates my effort and determination. I come out for the third and final round with renewed energy, landing a few good shots to the body and one to the side of the head, but it is too little, too late. The last bell sounds and the referee brings us together at the centre of the ring, lifting my opponent's arm to signal his victory. Loud applause echoes around the hall as Dad wraps a towel around my shoulders and we walk back to the dressing room.

At ten o'clock, when the last fight is finished, Cat Stevens rises to present trophies to the winners. The master of ceremonies stands with him on the stage, announcing the winners' names. When all have collected their little tin cups and shaken Cat Stevens' hand, one cup remains on the table. I am shocked when my name is called. The prize is awarded for the best fight of the night. My legs are shaking as I step up to the stage.

'Great fight,' Cat Stevens says to me with a smile. I mumble a thank you and try not to stare at the girl nearest to me as I walk away.

Late that night, when I place the little cup on the table beside my bed, I feel a sense of relief knowing that I will never fight in the ring again. Boxing will always be part of my life – it is in my blood, after all. But as I close my eyes to sleep, it is not the fight I remember, it is the electrifying feeling in that room when Cat Stevens walked in. That buzz is better than any drug I have experienced, and for days, weeks, months, it is all I can think of.

By the turn of the seventies I am attending two or three rock concerts each week: The Rolling Stones, Led Zeppelin, and Steampacket, featuring a brilliant young singer called Rod Stewart. Then, in May 1970, my life is turned upside down. Since I was released from Ashford, June and I have grown closer than ever. We have even talked about marriage. We are sitting together in her bedroom on a warm early summer evening when she tells me she is pregnant. I am both elated and terrified. I am not yet twenty years old, and June has just turned seventeen. A child will be a big responsibility for us both. I take June's hand and ask her to marry me. She smiles and says yes.

We are married at the Town Hall in Finsbury Park on 3 July, a bright summer morning. Joining us at the reception party in a nearby restaurant are family and friends, including Charlie George, who is now a celebrity, having established himself as a regular in the Arsenal football team. In the evening a friend drives us to the seaside resort of Brighton on the south coast, where we stay for five days at a bed and breakfast hotel, on a budget of thirty-four pounds. When we return to London as man and wife, I move out of our council flat to share a room with June at her parents' home in Camden Road.

Back on the market, Dad has exciting news. His young boxer Bunny Sterling is to fight for the British middleweight title. This, truly, is the big time. If Bunny were to win, he would be the first immigrant ever to claim a British title belt. And for Dad, such a victory could help propel him towards his ultimate goal: to be a full-time professional boxing trainer. He could quit the markets for good.

On 8 September 1970, at London's Royal Albert Hall, Dad's dream comes true. Bunny defeats the champion Mark Rowe with a clinical display, cutting Rowe so badly that the contest is stopped in only the fourth round. In the weeks after the fight, Dad receives hate mail branding him a 'nigger lover' and 'white witch doctor'. He laughs when he tells me about these letters. 'Idiots,' he says. 'They should recognise Bunny for what he is – a fine boxer and good man.'

At the year's end, Dad has yet more cause for celebration. On New Year's Eve, he becomes a grandfather for the first time. At seven in the morning, June gives birth to a daughter, Joanne. I rush from Covent Garden to the hospital in Gower Street and arrive to see June cradling our child, her face flushed with joy. Joanne is the image of my mother Joan. Holding her in my arms, I feel happiness like nothing I have ever known.

When June falls asleep, I walk back to Camden in a blissful daze. Mum and Dad take me to the Mitre, where our friends insist on buying drinks for the father and grandparents. Mum and Dad's eyes sparkle, their faces radiating pride. Their boy is now a man.

It is only three years since I was released from Ashford but it now feels a lifetime away. I know how much it pleases my parents to see me become a father, to give them a grandchild, and to begin a new generation of the family. After all that my mum and dad have done for me, this is the best gift I could give them in return.

8

Gods and monsters

On 17 March 1972, St Patrick's Day, June gives birth to our second child, Daniel, a brother for little Joanne. In the same month, there is also a new arrival at my parents' home. John Conteh is a gifted young boxer, still just nineteen years old, who relocates from his native Liverpool to turn professional and train with my father. John is of mixed race and is drawn to work with Dad after hearing about his success with Bunny Sterling and other black fighters.

To help his new protégé adjust to life in an unfamiliar city, Dad invites John to stay with our family in Camden Town. For two months, he shares a room with my eight-year-old brother Simon. Dad chuckles as he tells me how, shown where he would be sleeping, John was delighted to see the red and white wallpaper, thinking that Dad had decorated in the colours of Liverpool Football Club to make him feel at home. Dad explained that red and white are also the colours of the local team, Arsenal, and that Simon was a devoted Arsenal fan.

When I first meet John Conteh at the gym in Highgate, he laughs as I remind him who scored the winning goal for Arsenal against Liverpool in the previous season's FA Cup Final: it was my old friend Charlie George. I had watched the game at Wembley Stadium with Charlie's father Bob, and we cried together at the end. Charlie's long hair and cocky attitude make him a cult hero with the Arsenal ·fans. Like myself, he is a Camden bad boy made good.

Conteh, too, has a bit of the devil in him. Tall and good-looking, with the kind of ready wit that the people of Merseyside are famed for, John is a charmer. He is also, by Dad's reckoning, a born champion. He has a solid punch, a big heart, and a desire to win that separates the great from the good. On 1 October 1974, Dad's prophecy comes true when Conteh defeats Jorge Ahumada of Argentina at London's Wembley Arena to win the world light heavyweight title. The fight lasts the full fifteen rounds, with both fighters drawing on every last vestige of stamina and courage. When the final bell rings and the referee holds Conteh's arm aloft, I watch from ringside as John and my father embrace. There are tears in my eyes. Dad has a world champion. Not since the birth of Joanne have I seen such joy in his face.

It is a few days after the fight when John says he has a friend coming to visit the gym. He won't say which friend: he just smiles and tells us we are in for a pleasant surprise. At around five o'clock in the afternoon, Paul McCartney walks through the door. He is dressed simply in faded blue jeans and a white T-shirt under a heavy overcoat. Immediately he is laughing and joking with John, and saying hellos to the other boxers. There is a buzz in the room, just as there was when Cat Stevens entered the hall at the London Polytechnic on the night of my last fight. Yet this is different. Where Cat Stevens was putting on a show with his white fur coat and a girl on each arm, Paul turns up alone, without any fanfare, and is relaxed and chatty. Paul McCartney is one of the most famous men on the planet. He has no need to draw attention to himself: it just happens, wherever he goes.

John Conteh and Paul have become good friends in the year since John was invited to a country house near London's Heathrow airport to pose for the cover of Paul's album, *Band On The Run*. The cover photograph has a gang in prison uniforms trapped against a wall in the glare of a searchlight, as if caught in the act of breaking out of jail. The members of this gang are Paul, his wife Linda and fellow Wings band-mate Denny Laine, plus John and five other celebrities – TV chat-show host Michael Parkinson, actors James Coburn and Christopher Lee, singer Kenny Lynch and gourmet-turned-politician Clement Freud. The album has recently topped the charts on both sides of the Atlantic, which pleases John no end.

John introduces Paul to my father. 'This is the man who made me into a world champion,' he says. Paul smiles and asks Dad if it is really true that he makes his boxers jump into Highgate pond in the middle of winter. 'It toughens them up,' Dad says, and they laugh. As I shake Paul's hand, John mentions that he and I are going to a cinema in London's West End on 30 October to watch a live screening of Muhammad Ali's world title fight against George Foreman. Paul asks if he can come with us. I am speechless.

'Of course you can,' says John.

On the night of the fight, I go with John to pick up Paul from his home in St John's Wood. On the way to the screening we talk about the fight, which is being staged in Kinshasa, Zaire; hence its billing as The Rumble In The Jungle. At thirty-three, Muhammad Ali is considered by many to be past his best and too old to be attempting to regain his world heavyweight title. Moreover, the champion,

George Foreman, is the hardest puncher in the business. Much as we would love to see Ali triumph, each of us predicts a Foreman victory.

We leave the restaurant in the early hours of the morning. We could walk to the cinema in Leicester Square in just a few minutes, but for Paul's safety we are delivered by car to a side entrance, where a friend of John's is waiting to take us to our seats. The cinema is filled to capacity, the atmosphere highly charged.

The fight is the most astonishing I have seen. Ali dominates in the first round yet spends much of the next four against the ropes as Foreman drives punches into his midriff. We watch in disbelief as Ali sways on the ropes, either unable, or unwilling, to escape the battery of heavy body shots. Surely, John says, nobody can take so many punches as Ali is taking, especially from a guy like Foreman. But in the eighth round, with Foreman exhausted, Ali comes off the ropes to deliver a flurry of punches that have Foreman tumbling to the canvas. We jump to our feet, punching the air in celebration, Paul's eyes wide in amazement. People around us are out of their seats and cheering wildly. Foreman rises in a daze and is counted out on his feet. In the centre of the ring, Ali is mobbed. He has done it. Ali has proved us all wrong, proved the whole world wrong. He is world champion again.

Exhilarated, we walk out into the cool air at sunrise. The chauffeur is waiting to drive us to Paul's north London home. As we speed through the deserted streets, Paul turns to me with a smile. 'I could use a guy like you.'

For a second or two I think that I am imagining things, that the excitement of the fight has gone to my head – but Paul is serious. He tells me he does not need a full-time bodyguard, but he would like me to be around when he is staying in London. 'It's a deal,' I say, and we shake hands. When we arrive outside the large walled house, Paul and John get out of the car, and the chauffeur takes me on to Camden Town. Gliding through the silent city alone in the back of a Daimler, it doesn't feel real. I can't believe this is happening to me.

June stirs from her sleep as I slip into the bed beside her. 'You'll never guess who my new boss is,' I whisper in her ear. She yawns and tells me to go to sleep. When I tell her it is Paul McCartney, on whom she had such a crush as a teenager, she digs an elbow in my ribs. 'Shut up,' she groans, 'you're drunk.'

My first job with Paul McCartney is as a security guard when Wings play at the Astoria in Finsbury Park – the very place where I had seen him perform with The Beatles on Christmas Eve 1963. At the end of the show, an eight-seater mini-van is backed up to the stage door so that Paul and Linda can make a quick exit – a 'runner'. I wait beside the van as the driver keeps the engine ticking over. When Paul and Linda appear, led by the tour manager, I help them into the van then jump into the back seat. As soon as the van moves off, two nervous teenagers, a boy and a girl, appear from behind me. 'Paul, can we have your autograph?'

How these kids managed to sneak inside the van I have no idea. As Paul turns to face them, I panic. I could get fired for this. When Paul laughs and begins chatting to the kids, I breathe a little easier. Paul and Linda sign the fans' album covers and Paul hands them the towel he has used to wipe the sweat from his face, a special souvenir. We stop outside a tube station so that the teenagers can get home safely.

'Sorry about that, Paul,' I say as the van door shuts and the couple wave goodbye.

'No problem,' he chuckles. 'They were nice kids.'

My next assignment with Paul is to accompany him to a party in Soho. Led Zeppelin are celebrating the release of their new album *Physical Graffiti*. Since I first saw Zeppelin playing in a London club in the late sixties, they have become the biggest rock band in the world, and the party is suitably lavish.

Hundreds of people fill a private club, drinking champagne as the album plays at deafening volume. I lead Paul through a crowded hallway and into the main room just as a tall man with long blond hair smashes a smaller man to the floor with a punch that Muhammad Ali would have been proud of. People look on in shock as the blond man calmly gestures to two waiters to remove the prone body from the room.

'Paul!' a voice calls out. A giant of a man stands before us, his enormous bulk seeming to fill the room. At over six feet and heavily built, with a bush of a beard and thinning hair pulled back in a ponytail, he dwarfs the people around him. He squashes Paul in a bear-like hug and invites him to join a table at the far corner of the room, where Led Zeppelin's singer, Robert Plant, sits amid a group of people on a crescent-shaped sofa. Paul signals to me to stay close. I stand nearby absorbing the music as a gentle blues gives way to Zeppelin's signature crunching hard rock. A redhead wearing a beautifully decorated black Japanese kimono offers a joint. I politely decline. 'Not while I'm on duty.'

I chat to her for some time until I'm distracted by a sudden movement to my right. A man in blue denims has a chair raised above his head as he approaches the table where Paul is seated. I move swiftly to block his path and order him to put the chair down. He throws out a hand to push me aside and does not see my fist coming. It connects with his jaw and sends him and the chair crashing to the ground. He is out cold.

I feel a hand on my shoulder and turn sharply, my fist clenching. A blond man smiles – the man I saw knocking the other guy out the moment we arrived. 'Thanks for that,' he says, motioning to the denim-clad figure lying flat out on the carpet. 'Sit down and have a drink.' Two more staff are summoned to drag the unconscious man from the room. Neither one seems in the least bit fazed by this duty: clearly such scenes happen in here every day.

The blond man introduces himself as John Bindon, Led

Zeppelin's head of security. I sit beside him at the far end of the crescent-shaped sofa, across the table from Paul and the bearded giant. Handing a glass of champagne to me, he asks me who I am and why I am here. I explain that I work for Paul, and ask him who the guy is to whom Paul is talking. The big man is Peter Grant, the manager of Led Zeppelin. I know the name, and I have heard stories about his uncompromising and intimidating style of management. Seeing him up close in the flesh, I understand why he inspires such fear. Bindon tells me that the man I punched is an enemy of Grant's.

'What about the guy you belted tonight?' I ask.

'Just some drunken prick,' he sniffs. 'It happens all the time.'

After a few minutes, Paul rises to leave the table. 'It's okay,' he says to me. 'You stay here.' As Paul departs, Peter Grant beckons to me. I shake John Bindon's hand and walk around the table to sit in the place vacated by Paul.

'I saw what you did earlier,' Grant says in a thick, husky, nasal whisper that makes him sound like Marlon Brando in *The Godfather*, only with a cockney accent. 'I might have a job for you.' He produces a business card from the pocket of his red silk shirt and tells me to call his office the following morning.

It is noon on a bright spring day when a black Daimler glides to a halt outside the terraced house where I live with June and the children, just a few streets from where I grew up in Dale Road. I open the door to a small, ginger-haired man who introduces himself as Norman. He is to drive me to Peter Grant's country retreat, Horselunges, near Eastbourne on the Sussex coast. As I slide on to the back seat, my elderly neighbour Frank leans on the little iron gate outside his house and asks if I am going to a funeral. You do not see many Daimlers in the streets of Camden Town.

The journey takes us though beautiful countryside, up and over the hills of the Sussex Downs, past farms and quiet villages. Marking the entrance to Grant's estate are two tall brick pillars mounted with stone eagles. A long driveway sweeps up through an avenue of mighty oaks to a stately manor house parts of which date back to the fourteenth century. Encircling the house is a moat, which we cross via a creaking wooden drawbridge. I feel like I am travelling back in time to the Middle Ages.

Norman leads me inside the house to a vast reception room lined with bookshelves and warmed by a log fire. I sit in a green leather armchair, in awe of the place and nervously anticipating my audience with Peter. I try to make small talk with Norman while one hour passes, then two. Every so often the panelled ceiling creaks with the heavy tread of someone upstairs pacing slowly to and fro. When Norman raises his eyes towards the sound and says laconically, 'He's up. He's about.' I realise it must be Peter. At last I can stand it no longer. 'So when are we going to see him?' I ask. But Norman is clearly as frightened as everyone else is of his employer, and displays a marked reluctance to leave the comfort of his chair. Finally he takes pity on me; but when he comes back it is clear that my wait isn't over. 'Peter won't be able to see you today,' announces Norman, frowning slightly, 'but he would like you to stay the night.'

I pass the afternoon walking around the house and grounds with Norman as my guide. He tells me there is a secret subterranean passage leading from the cellars of the house to the village church one mile away. I smile as I envisage Peter walking through the tunnel by the light of a lamp, then emerging from the pulpit to terrify a Sunday morning congregation. Norman advises me not to venture upstairs unless I am summoned by Peter. It is Peter's domain, he says, and his alone. At nightfall, I eat supper with Norman in the kitchen. The chef is busy preparing a third meal, which he places on a silver tray beside a bottle of wine. 'I'll take this up and be off,' he says.

It makes me uneasy that Peter has been here all this time while

I have been at the house, and yet he has not seen me. He's entitled to his foibles, sure, but this is way beyond normal. Retiring to one of the small guest bedrooms, I wonder what I might be getting myself into. There is a powerful aura about Led Zeppelin and Peter Grant. The band is phenomenally successful, yet maintains a dark secrecy. I have heard tales of wild excesses during Led Zeppelin's American tours, when drummer John Bonham is said to have driven a motorcycle through hotel corridors in a drunken frenzy. It is also reported that the group's guitarist and leader Jimmy Page lives on the shores of Loch Ness in a house once owned by the late Aleister Crowley, the infamous occultist, philosopher and writer variously described as a Satanist, a drug addict and 'The Wickedest Man In The World'. Peter's archaic retreat seems no less strange, with its moat and drawbridge and secret tunnel, and the master alone upstairs, withdrawn from the outside world. For all his astronomical wealth and fame, Paul McCartney is a warm and approachable man. The same cannot be said of Led Zeppelin and their colossus of a manager. I think again of the party in Soho, the casual violence of John Bindon, and how my own show of force has drawn me into Led Zeppelin's menacing orbit.

In the morning I could walk away from all this. Perhaps I should, for the sake of my wife and children, for my parents, and for myself. Violence and drugs, the very things that saw me banged up in Ashford, are the grimy underside of the world I'm about to enter. Yet this is also a world of excitement, of power and riches and glamour, and its gravitational pull is strong. When a smiling Peter Grant meets me for breakfast the next day, I decide I have had enough of shifting sacks of potatoes on the markets.

May 1975 marks my initiation as a member of Peter Grant's staff. I work as part of John Bindon's security team for Led

Zeppelin's four shows at Earl's Court in London, for which a total of 51,000 tickets had been sold in less than two hours. These are the best gigs I have ever seen: better than The Beatles, The Rolling Stones, The Who or The Jimi Hendrix Experience. Their performance is magical. Jimmy Page is a slender, almost girlish figure, yet the sounds he conjures from his guitar resound like thunder around the huge arena. Robert Plant is the definitive hard rock singer, strutting with his shirt open to the waist and shaking a mass of blond curls. John Bonham – bearded and barrel-chested – thumps his drums so hard I can feel the reverberations in my whole body. And at the right of the stage, as if existing in his own little universe, John Paul Jones plays bass and keyboards with a sullen countenance.

Here at Earl's Court and during the ensuing months, I serve my apprenticeship in the business of rock 'n' roll. I learn quickly to respect the authority of those trusted members of Led Zeppelin's inner circle. Tour manager Richard Cole is like John Bonham's twin, only slimmer. His long dark hair and beard frame a boyish face with a rough complexion. Cole is tough, with a brusque manner and a cruel wit. Such a personality is a prerequisite for the job. By contrast, stage manager Clive Coulson, a blond and fresh-faced New Zealander, exudes calm. He and Cole have John Bindon to do any dirty work. Bindon is Peter Grant's enforcer. At over six feet tall, thickset with unkempt long blond hair, Bindon cuts an imposing figure. I have been around some tough guys in my twenty-five years – boxers, gang members and prisoners – but if I were to choose one man on whom my life depended in a fight, it would be John Bindon. I have heard from other members of the Zeppelin entourage that in a one-on-one situation, Bindon is unbeatable. If this guy is not smiling, I keep my distance. It is also known that Bindon is hung like a horse: his favoured party trick involves hanging ten half-pint beer mugs from his erect member.

Bindon had begun his career as a promising young actor. In 1967 Ken Loach had cast him alongside Carol White and

Terence Stamp in *Poor Cow*, and he also had roles in the seminal seventies classics *Performance* and *Get Carter*. He was known to be a friend of Princess Margaret's, whom he met on the Caribbean island of Mustique. In an era renowned for its hard-drinking, hard-living actors, Bindon elevated the epithet 'hellraiser' to a whole new level, and as the film parts began to dry up it was no surprise that he gravitated towards the rock business, a world where he could encounter like-minded souls.

The band themselves are quiet by comparison, especially John Paul Jones, who spends much of his time in his hotel room. Jimmy Page is thoughtful and intense, highly intelligent, and oddly prone to throwing up because of pre-show nerves. Robert Plant is sociable and very funny, and so too is John Bonham, unless he is drunk. 'Bonzo' – as he is known to friends and fans alike – can be the sweetest guy in the world and is a loving husband and father. But when he and Richard Cole hit the bottle, which is more often than not, they turn unpredictable, and no one, save for Peter and the other band members, is safe.

It is Peter I feel closest to. His reputation as a tyrant and a bully is justified: his huge size intimidates everyone he encounters, and when he loses his patience, he spits and splutters with rage, terrifying and humiliating any who dare to challenge him. More than once, with hindsight, he asks me to take risks, or puts me in situations I should never have been in. Mostly this involves transporting various items on his behalf, and one time I find myself standing on the tarmac of a European aiport in the middle of a security alert, surrounded by soldiers, with several ounces of hash stashed down my boots. Fortunately I was the one person they decided not to search. Yet in the months I spend working with him both on the road and at the manor house, I grow to like the man behind the myth. Publicly demonised, privately he is warm, generous, and open. Jimmy Page, especially, he loves like a son.

Also he is the best teacher I have known. From him I learn

who does what, and why each of their jobs is important. On any tour, the life may be wild but everyone knows exactly what he is doing. The pieces have to fit together like cogs in a machine.

The tour manager is responsible for the welfare of the band when they're on the road, and also the logistics of getting from place to place. He takes care of transport; hotels and flights, the crew buses and the trucks that carry the band's equipment: instruments, sound and lights. Even in the seventies a band with a stage set like ELP or Genesis would fill three or four long-wheelbase artics: thirty years later with stadium bands it isn't unknown to have twelve. Getting that lot overnight from, say, Sheffield to Glasgow is a doddle. But getting from somewhere like Stockholm to Athens in forty-eight hours is no joke. The tour manager holds all the passports. He has contacts at every border and in every airline and if he is good he is worth his weight in gold. The converse is if you slip up once, you're history. In a job like that you can't afford mistakes.

The tour manager is the band's liaison for press and promotion, radio and TV. He is responsible for getting the band to the venue on time, and also, on the night, for making sure they get paid. With most bands it is the tour manager himself who does all the settling up with the promoter after the show. But the biggest bands – those who can sell out arenas – have accountants who travel with them. Finance on that big a scale is too complicated for anyone other than a specialist to handle.

Where the show itself is concerned the stage manager is the most important person on the tour. He controls every aspect of the show apart from the band. Later, as shows become bigger and more complex, this function will split into two, with the production manager taking the major role while the stage manager concentrates on what actually happens on stage. But back then, in the seventies, the stage manager is in charge. He is always the first person in and the last to leave. He is responsible for hiring and firing the crew, from the roadies, technicians and engineers that travel with the band to the local loaders we use at

every gig. He works hand in hand with the crew on the night
and also makes sure that everything runs to time. At each venue
there is a curfew, normally 11 p.m., by which time the band is
contracted to leave the stage. If they overrun they can pay a
hefty fine – nowadays up to $1,000 per minute – and it is the
stage manager's responsibility to see that they don't.

The sound and lighting engineers are the artists of the tour.
It's a world away from the sixties, when a single bank of
speakers and a spotlight was enough. Prog rock, with its experimental sounds, and bands like Pink Floyd with their fluid,
coloured psychedelic backdrops have changed all that. Now
every note is monitored and modified by the mixer, and the
lights are keyed in to an electronic sequence that changes with
every chord. These guys have skills that can make or break a
show, and the best of them can command a fee to match.

Then there's the crew themselves. When the show ends the
band's work is done for the night, but for them it is far from
over. They have to dismantle the stage, the lights and sound,
and load it all on to the trucks for the next venue. All the equipment is packed away in flight cases, each of them named and
numbered: Upper Stage Left Number Two; Light Cases 40 to
60; Jimmy's Guitars – Les Paul; Ovation 12-string; Double
Neck plus Violin Bow. Everything is always loaded in the same
order so that when it is unloaded at the next gig it can go
directly to where it needs to be. Precision is vital. Every piece of
equipment has its place, and everyone knows where it is. If one
single item goes missing the next day's show could be in jeop-
ardy, and the roadie who misplaces something better watch
out.

The riggers have it toughest of all. At 11.30 p.m. they are
climbing up into the roof to bring down the rigging which holds
the lights and sound: in an arena, that could be as high as 150
feet. And as they are the first ones to start setting up in the
morning, that means they can be at the venue for eighteen
hours. If the crew get one or two nights in a hotel bed in a week

they are lucky. If not it is load-in, do the gig, load-out, sleep on the bus, drive maybe 500 miles; get up, load-in, do the gig, load-out and so on five days a week for weeks, sometimes months on end. In the US it is not that bad. The roads are easier, there are motels everywhere, and everyone speaks the same language. In Europe and South America it is a different story. It takes a special kind of temperament to be a roadie. Most of them are mavericks of one kind or another. In America in the seventies many are Vietnam vets, restless men with troubled pasts who are running from themselves.

Each musician also has his or her own personal roadie who takes care of the instruments for the band. Somewhere around the nineties these become known rather formally as guitar or drum technicians. But these guys need to know quite a bit about the instruments they look after, and many are talented players who just never made it in a band. The personal technician to the lead guitarist may have twelve guitars to take care of, and by 5 p.m. they must all be tuned and ready to play. If a guitar string breaks on stage he must have one prepared in a split second and be on stage to replace it as soon as his man has taken the old one off. If he screws it up he is in big trouble, in front of maybe 25,000 punters.

It is also his job to see that his man has whatever he needs on stage to keep him happy, whether it is water, drink or drugs. And he has another role. If a girl in the audience takes the guitarist's fancy, it is up to him to relay the invitation and to make sure that the girl is in his man's dressing room under the stage before the end of the show. In all my years and in all the shows in countries around the world I have seldom known the offer to be turned down. The girl could be there with her mum and dad, her boyfriend, her new husband. It never mattered, and ninety per cent of the time it would end in some form of sex. In most of the bands I worked with that was the most important thing, and the reason that most of them took up the guitar in the first place.

★

But the pivotal figure for any band is their manager. Ultimately he hires the tour manager, the production manager, and pretty much everybody else. He plans the band's career trajectory and – in theory at least – looks after their interests. He negotiates with the record company executives and with the band's agent, who books the live shows. Above all he has to be a dealmaker, and a good or bad manager is what makes the difference between a band that gets rich and one that ends up broke.

Where lucrative deals are concerned, Peter Grant is a master. Like myself, Peter endured great hardship during his South London childhood, and while he now lives like a lord and has the money to indulge his passion for fine art, he has not forgotten where he comes from. In fact, it is those very street smarts he developed as a youth that he has used to make Led Zeppelin the richest rock stars of their generation. In doing so, he has revolutionised the music business.

In the UK, Led Zeppelin have never released a single. This, Peter believes, enhances the band's credibility among rock fans who despise pop music and would be appalled to see Led Zeppelin appear on a mainstream TV show like *Top Of The Pops*. There is a certain irony here, given that the theme music for *Top Of The Pops* is a reworking of Zeppelin's 'Whole Lotta Love', by bluesman Alexis Korner's CCS. More importantly, the absence of singles focuses attention on the group's albums, which generate much greater revenue.

In North America, Peter has rewritten the rules of touring. Such is Led Zeppelin's popularity in the United States, where their album sales have eclipsed those of both The Beatles and The Rolling Stones, that the group's live performances break all attendance records. In 1973, they played to 56,000 people at the Tampa Stadium in Florida, beating an eight-year record held by The Beatles for their legendary show at New York's Shea Stadium. From such power, Peter Grant exacts the maximum leverage. Concert promoters accustomed to a fifty-fifty split of box-office receipts are issued with a stark ultimatum: either Led Zeppelin take ninety per cent of the gate money, or the promoter loses the show. As Peter explains, ten per cent of Led Zeppelin is better than fifty per cent of any other band.

Peter has weaknesses, among them a heavy cocaine habit – which is why he spends so many days and nights alone upstairs at Horselunges, the meals taken up to him returning barely touched. On one occasion, Mitch Fox, the managing director of the Led Zeppelin-owned record label Swan Song, flies in from New York to consult Peter about a new band he is thinking of signing to the label. Norman collects Fox from the airport and brings him to the manor for a scheduled appointment at two o'clock, but by six, there is still no sign of Peter. Norman suggests that Mitch stay the night. Two whole days pass. For hours on end, I play snooker with Mitch in a drawing room. He hears Peter's footsteps above, but says nothing. Eventually, Peter sends a message via Norman: it has all been a misunderstanding, and Mitch should return to New York. He does so none the wiser, but a much improved snooker player.

Early in 1976, I am summoned to Las Vegas to attend Peter while he negotiates a deal to bring Elvis Presley to Britain for a concert tour. It is my first journey across the Atlantic, and a huge culture shock. I travel alone and find a limousine driver waiting for me at the airport, holding a placard bearing my name. He leads me out to the parking lot in bright sunshine, a dry breeze warming my pale skin. The black stretch limousine is the biggest car I have ever seen. As the limo speeds along a ten-lane freeway towards the city, I ease back into squishing black leather upholstery and gaze out at the vastness of America: the flat brown desert plains, the soft reds and blues of the surrounding mountains, silver skyscrapers shining over downtown Las Vegas.

I have seen the city's famous Strip in movies, but to the naked eye it appears more surreal than ever. Even in daylight, the neon signs dazzle. The limousine pulls up at the hotel beside a cream-coloured soft-top Cadillac, the kind of car I dream of owning. I walk under a canopy of shimmering gold lights into a lobby dominated by a green-lit water fountain. A pretty blonde receptionist presents an envelope with a message from Peter. I place my suitcase in my room on the seventh floor and head up to Peter's suite on the fifteenth. The main room is huge, decorated in rich hues of brown and orange, and offering spectacular views of the city from windows that reach from floor to ceiling. Peter is in a solemn mood. Elvis's manager, Colonel Tom Parker, has declined his proposal. Elvis has never played a concert in Europe and is unlikely ever to do so. As an illegal immigrant, the Colonel does not even hold a US passport, and since he never travels outside the United States, nor does Elvis. The deal is dead, but Peter remains on friendly terms with the Colonel, and has accepted his offer to meet for cocktails at his hotel suite this evening. 'Dress smartly,' Peter tells me.

We arrive at seven and Colonel Tom Parker greets Peter like an old friend. He is dressed in a blue suit with a white open-necked shirt and blue silk cravat. His eyes sparkle, but his thin hair and sagging figure betray his sixty-five years. We sit in enormous high-backed chairs as a waiter mixes drinks at a bar in the far corner of the room and Peter and the Colonel trade stories about their business deals. When Peter mentions that my father is a boxing man and the trainer of a world champion, the Colonel's face lights up. His knowledge of John Conteh and other fighters is impressive.

After an hour, the Colonel rises from his seat and invites us to meet Elvis. We follow him to the elevator and up to the penthouse suite. A tall man with a measured Southern accent opens the door to a dimly lit room chilled by air-conditioning. At the centre of the room, surrounded by a gang of six men, stands Elvis Presley. His considerable bulk is clad in a blue velour running suit and there are dark rings around his eyes, but his welcome is courteous, and his presence magnetic. During the past eighteen months I have worked with Paul McCartney and Led Zeppelin, giants of popular music, but to shake the hand of the original King of Rock 'n' Roll is an experience I shall never forget. It is an experience made all the more special by the warmth of his smile, and his easy manner of conversation.

I am still buzzing when I return to London with Peter two days later. He has a new job for me: he wants me to act as personal minder to another of his clients, a singer with a reputation every bit as fearsome as his own. 'If you can handle this guy,' he says, 'you can handle anything.'

9

Desolation angels

Bad Company is Peter Grant's second love after Led Zeppelin. The group formed in 1973 following the break-up of Free, one of the great British blues-rock bands. Free's singer Paul Rodgers and drummer Simon Kirke joined with guitarist Mick Ralphs, formerly of glam rockers Mott The Hoople, and bassist Raymond 'Boz' Burrell, ex of progressive rock act King Crimson, and a supergroup was born. Bad Company's debut album topped the American chart in 1974, and their success has continued with more million-selling records and sold-out tours.

In 1979 the band is releasing a new album, *Desolation Angels*, and touring Britain and America. My job is to protect Paul Rodgers and keep him out of trouble. Given his taste for drinking and fighting, it will not be easy. Paul Rodgers is a seventh dan in karate and a real tough customer. A few years

back, Peter had asked if my father would allow Paul to spar
with John Conteh. Dad had laughed at the suggestion: Conteh
was a pro, a world champion, and he would knock Paul clean
out of the ring. Paul was insistent, however, so Dad arranged for
him to visit the Highgate gym and try a couple of rounds with a
junior lightweight champion from Uganda named Cornelius
Boza Edwards. To Dad's surprise, Paul held his own in the ring.
Also there that day was the respected boxing expert and TV
commentator Reg Gutteridge, who had come to watch the sparring. When he saw Paul, he asked Dad, 'Who's the new guy?
He's a bit tasty.' When Dad told him Paul was a rock star,
Gutteridge thought he was joking.

Looking after Paul will be a challenge, but that is not why I
have reservations about touring with Bad Company. June is
pregnant again, and while the baby is not due until October, I
am reluctant to leave her for months on end. Mum tells me not
to worry: she and Dad live just a few streets away from our
house, and will visit June three or four times a week. I accept the
job knowing that June will not be on her own; and besides, I
will be earning the kind of money that most of the people who
live in our street could only dream of.

The tour begins on a rainy night in Edinburgh. Clive Coulson,
Led Zeppelin's stage manager, is now acting as tour manager for
Bad Company. I like having him around, and I quickly strike up a
rapport with the guys in the band. Paul is solidly built, handsome,
with dark, wiry, shoulder-length hair and the air of a man who
has seen and done it all in his twenty-nine years. Mick is slender,
with soft, almost feminine features and a ready smile. Simon has
lank blond hair and an easy-going manner. And Boz, with his
dark hair, beard and calm disposition, has me thinking of the
pictures of Jesus I saw in books at school.

The show is stunning: no fancy theatrics, just a great rock band with a singer whose soulful rasp makes him the best in the business. After the gig, we drink in the hotel bar. Paul cradles a glass of Bushmills whiskey and eyes the other band members with disdain as they sneak off to the toilets to snort cocaine. Paul's loathing of hard drugs is not surprising: three years ago, his friend and former Free guitarist Paul Kossoff died mid-flight from Los Angeles to New York of heart failure at the age of twenty-five, the result of years of heroin addiction. Some of the tension eases from Paul's face when he speaks of the time he spent sparring at Dad's gym, but the omens for this tour are not good.

After the next date in Glasgow, the local promoter invites the band to a club, where a VIP room is filled with booze and girls. At three in the morning, I walk downstairs to check that our limousines are waiting outside the door. I stand at the foot of the steps as the band walks down towards me, accompanied by five or six of the girls. Suddenly a guy comes barrelling down the stairs and grabs at the arm of the brunette clinging to Simon Kirke. As I step between them, he takes a wild swing which misses by a good six inches. I push him against the wall and twist his arm up behind his back, at the same time yelling to Simon: 'Get in the car!'

'That's my fucking wife!' the guy screams, squirming in my grip.

Four of his friends come thundering down the stairs. One of them smashes a bottle over my head: it breaks, gashing my scalp and soaking me in red wine. I tighten my hold on the first guy as a mass brawl breaks out around me. Even the girls join in, scratching and kicking, before several security guards manage to drag them all out into the street.

I can taste the wine mixing with my blood and running into my mouth. Not a bad little drop, I think to myself as I adjust my hold on the guy and manoeuvre him to the door. I leave the poor bastard slumped drunkenly on the steps. Soon he will have to make his way home and wait up for his wife to come back smelling of booze and sex.

I see the band safely into the cars and make my way to the nearest casualty department. The cut on my head is sewn up with twelve stitches: a fine introduction to life on the road with Bad Company.

★

When the tour reaches Birmingham, I receive a call from Peter. He is coming to the show with Robert Plant and John Bonham, both of whom were born in the Black Country and now own estates nearby. Bonzo is hosting a party at his farmhouse after the show. Before they arrive, I run out to the nearest off-licence to pick up a crate of Peter's favourite wine, the Liebfraumilch Blue Nun.

They arrive at the venue, an old Odeon cinema, at eight, one hour before Bad Company are due on stage. Peter is dressed for this special occasion in a black shirt and trousers with a red cravat and matching shoes, an outsized turquoise ring dangling from one ear. Robert and Bonzo wear everyday jeans and T-shirts. They sit in the dressing room, drinking and chatting, until Clive Coulson calls the band to the stage.

With Peter, Robert and Bonzo watching from the wings, Bad Company raise their game by a couple of notches. Every show on the tour has been a triumph, but tonight they give everything they've got. When Bonzo takes up a seat beside Simon Kirke on the drums and Robert joins Paul Rodgers centre stage, the audience goes wild. Together they run through two classic rock 'n' roll songs from the 1950s, before Robert and Bonzo acknowledge the crowd and depart.

The dressing room fills with members of the Swan Song staff, groupies and sundry hangers-on. After an hour, a convoy of five limousines plus the Bad Company tour bus heads for Bonzo's farmstead along narrow country lanes. From the bus, we trudge through soggy grass to a converted barn, in which a Harley Davidson motorcycle hangs from the rafters above a full-size drum-kit. Champagne and cocktails are served from a well-stocked corner bar, and a fug of dope smoke rises to the ceiling. Like Paul, Bonzo can be a terror when he has a few drinks inside him. I think of the last time I saw him, at the Rainbow Room in Los Angeles, with a pint in one hand and the other clamped round the throat of some pest who had been annoying him. He was holding the guy about two feet off the floor. But tonight, with his wife and son Jason at his side, he is relaxed and happy, and a pleasure to be around. He plays a test pressing of the forthcoming Led Zeppelin album and Jason plays along on drums, to the guests' delight. When at last we stumble out of the barn at six in the morning, the sun is up above the trees. Dead on my feet, I wonder if I can survive another two months on the road.

Peter appears at my side, a bottle of Blue Nun clutched in one huge hand. He draws me close to him. 'The guys really like you,' he tells me. 'Just make sure Paul gets back from America in one piece.'

The first date of the American tour is in Dallas, Texas, and we pick up almost exactly where we left off, with a fight. The promoter, keen to treat the band to some authentic Texan hospitality, takes us to a bar with an exclusively redneck clientele, clad entirely in denims and cowboy hats. Dozens of these guys look up from their drinks and pause over their pool games to stare at the long-haired strangers entering the room: it feels like we are walking into a bad Western movie.

Within a few minutes, Paul is challenging one of the locals to an arm-wrestling contest. His opponent wears a denim shirt, cut off at the sleeves to reveal Popeye-sized biceps, and a Stetson as broad as a motorcycle wheel. If you can't fight, my dad says, wear a big hat – but I would prefer not to test this theory in here. Paul and the cowboy are locked in a struggle for minutes on end. Neither is prepared to concede. Eventually I lean in close to Paul and hiss in his ear: 'Let him win, and we can get out of here alive.'

'Fuck off,' Paul snorts. When he does lose a few minutes later, my relief soon turns to dread. His pride wounded and countless shots of tequila in his belly, Paul is on a short fuse. I see him squaring up to a pair of truckers but I move in fast to defuse the situation, dragging Paul towards the exit and out into a waiting limo. On the ride back to the hotel, Simon, Boz and Mick barely speak a word. They have seen incidents like this more times than they care to remember.

In El Paso, where Texas borders Mexico, a rowdy, drunken crowd throws firecrackers at the stage to show its appreciation of the band. After the gig, we head for a strip club where the band is treated to intimate performances in a private room decorated like an opium den with tapestries and floor cushions. When Paul rises to go to the bathroom, I follow. My instruction from Peter Grant is never to let him out of my sight. As Paul stands in one of the stalls, the door left open, two skinny young Latino men come bustling in and call out to him, offering up a bag of strong-smelling dope and pleading to be allowed to join the band's private party. Paul warns them not to bother him when he has his dick in his hands. Too fucked-up to comprehend, they protest loudly as I steer them out of the bathroom. I stand barring the door and they move away, muttering darkly. It is time to get the band out of here.

I lead Paul back to the private room, where several of the strippers are preparing to leave with us for the hotel. Then, alone, I walk out of the fire exit at the rear of the building to tell the two limos to pull round to the front. As I turn back towards the lights of the club the two Latinos are waiting for me. One of them is stooped and reaching inside his boot as if feeling for a knife. I know they are not here to sell me that bag of weed. I punch the lad nearest to me – a fast, hard right hander that has him keeling over and cracking his skull on the concrete – and turn to see the other, still crouched, looking up at me and pulling a tiny silver derringer pistol from his boot. Before he can raise the gun I swing a foot into his face, sending him sprawling backwards and the gun skittering across the ground. I slam the fire-door shut behind me and rush the band out of the club through the front entrance with three strippers in tow. We leap into the limos and speed back to the safety of the hotel. In the bar I order a large gin and tonic and tell Paul about the crazy Latinos and the gun. He grins, shakes his head and drains his glass of whiskey.

Within the hour, the hotel manager appears at my shoulder and requests that I follow him to the lobby. Waiting there for me are three police officers and the two Latino youths. One of the cops, also Latino, tells me I must accompany them to the police station. Without further explanation, I am marched outside and bundled inside a car, my protests of innocence met with stony silence.

At the police station, I am led to a cell enclosed by three brick walls and one of green-painted steel bars. The Latino officer and the two kids follow me inside while the two other officers lock the door and stare blankly through the bars.

'You assaulted these kids,' the officer snaps at me.

'He threatened me with a gun,' I begin, but the officer slams a fist into my belly and I sink to my knees, doubled over in pain. He brings his knee up sharply into my face, crunching my nose and cutting my top lip. Grabbing my hair, he tilts my face upwards and indicates the kid who had the gun. 'This is my son!' he rages. I know what is coming. Fists and boots rain down on me from the policeman and the kids. I curl up into a ball on the floor and wait for the beating to stop. It does so only when the three of them are breathless and laughing.

I am left alone in the cell for an hour before I am taken back upstairs and charged with assault. Clive Coulson arrives, shouting and banging the desk when he sees my bruised and bloodied face. He calls Peter Grant's attorney in New York, who advises me to enter a guilty plea on a lesser charge, which will secure my immediate release pending a fine. I am relieved when the attorney says that Peter will take care of the fine: $1,500 is more than I earn in two months.

★

From Texas, we fly to New York, where Bad Company are to perform at the prestigious Madison Square Garden. As befits a superstar rock band, we fly in a private plane, a customised 24-seater Vickers Viscount with the Bad Company logo on its side. The pilots are Vietnam vets, survivors of numerous missions over hostile jungle territory. Their uniform: blue jeans and Bad Company tour jackets. The stewardess is a slender strawberry-blonde named Linda, who serves cocktails in huge mugs with 'Bad Co.' on one side and our names on the other. Dosed up on painkillers to soothe my bruised ribs, I fall asleep within minutes of take-off, oblivious to the noises emanating from the tiny curtained-off space at the rear of the cabin, where Boz is being entertained by a well-known groupie, Connie, from Little Rock, Arkansas.

New York is one of the two main hubs of America's music industry, Los Angeles being the other. On the eve of such a high-profile gig, Paul is content to drink in the hotel bar before retiring at midnight. I am grateful, as I have a busy day ahead. Dad has brought one of his boxers across the Atlantic for one of the most bizarre fights ever staged, and tomorrow he and I will be reunited.

I rise early to meet Dad at his hotel off Central Park. Both he and his boxer Bunny Johnson, a black heavyweight, appear tense, and with good reason: the fight is to take place inside Rahway State Penitentiary, one of America's toughest prisons, where Bunny's opponent James Scott is an inmate. Before his arrest, Scott was the number one contender for the world heavy-weight title, and this fight is the second he has fought while serving his time behind bars. Peter Grant, in New York for the Bad Company gig, has allowed me to take the day off on two conditions: I report back to Madison Square Garden by seven o'clock, and I do not take Paul Rodgers to the fight. Much as Paul would love to come with us, Peter does not want his star going anywhere near a prison filled with murderers and drug dealers, and besides, Paul needs to rest before tonight's show.

During the past couple of weeks, Dad has conducted several of Bunny's training and sparring sessions inside London's Pentonville prison before an audience of inmates. This, he says, will prepare Bunny for the intimidating atmosphere ahead. But an hour out from New York, as we drive up to the jail, we are shocked into silence. Its sheer size is overwhelming, and before we reach its walls we pass through five checkpoints manned by armed guards. Memories of Ashford come back to me, my palms moistening with sweat.

A makeshift dressing room has been set up in the chief warden's office, where the warden warns us to expect a hot reception from the prisoners watching the fight. They will all be backing Scott, a cult hero within these walls. Once Bunny has changed and warmed up, we are escorted by six warders through to the gymnasium, where several hundred inmates are seated on bleachers surrounding the ring. At Ashford I hated the warders, but here I am reassured by the presence of fifty or sixty of them, patrolling the room with batons drawn. Without their protection, the prisoners would tear us apart. They jeer and spit as we step up to the ring, their catcalls turning to cheers when Scott ducks through the ropes and stares hard into Bunny's eyes. In the corner, Dad splashes Bunny with water from a bucket and issues the final instructions: keep moving and using your jab, and don't let this develop into a street fight.

From the first bell, Scott is all over Bunny, his heavy body-shots landing with such force that I can hear the impact over the clamour of hundreds of prisoners baying for blood. Scott is hell-bent on beating up an Englishman to prove to all the hard men inside this place that he is still the boss, and unless Bunny can knock this guy out quickly, he could get badly hurt. Bunny is fighting with all his heart, but after four rounds, Dad is ready to throw in the towel. Scott spares him the trouble: in the fifth, the referee stops the fight. The prisoners are up on their feet and yelling as I help a shell-shocked Bunny from the ring and we hasten for the exit, our heads bowed. Only when we are on the freeway and heading back to New York do I feel the muscles loosen in my shoulders. I breathe a sigh of relief, happy at least that we have got Bunny out of that place alive.

★

Backstage at Madison Square Garden, Peter Grant holds court with the heavy grace of a Mafia don. In a private room furnished with plush sofas and lit by candles, he welcomes Dad and Bunny as his guests. We are joined by Paul Rodgers, asking Dad and Bunny about the fight. As a gesture of thanks for the time that Dad let him spar in the Highgate gym, Paul tells me to give Dad and Bunny seats at the side of the stage for the show. From here, in the wings, they will have a view of the band that none of the audience sees, not even those in the front few rows. They will be on the stage itself, mere feet away from the action. To be that close to musicians at work is a rare intimacy and a real privilege.

The house lights dim to whoops of delight from the sell-out crowd. Hidden from view behind the stage curtain, the band is gathered beside a black grand piano, which is then wheeled out on stage by two members of the road crew, invisible in the darkness. Paul walks out to the piano alone, and as he plays the first chords of 'Bad Company', the band's eponymous signature song, a single spotlight beams down on him. The noise from the audience almost drowns him out as Paul sings the opening line, 'Company, always on the run ...'

Simon is seated behind the drum kit; Boz and Mick are walking out on to the stage. Then suddenly Paul is looking back over his shoulder towards the crew with fury in his eyes. On the flat lid of the piano, under Paul's nose, a fat joint is smoking in an ashtray beside a glass of wine and three thick lines of cocaine showing bright against the polished black wood. Every night – before Paul leaves the dressing room – the other band members

share a spliff and snort a few lines of coke off the piano, unbe-
known to the drug-hating Paul. Now their little joke is
backfiring, and we are panicking. Paul is likely to punch
someone out as soon as the set is over. One of the roadies scoots
across the stage and crouches half under the piano. His hands
appear on the piano lid as if performing a magic trick, groping
around blindly before locating, and then delicately removing,
the ashtray and the wine glass. One hand sweeps away the
cocaine in a little puff of white dust.

Fortunately the show is the best of the tour, the band inspired
and the atmosphere electric; and Paul comes off the stage
smiling as he wipes the sweat from his face. The crew can
breathe easily again, relaxed in the knowledge that none of
them will get thumped.

There is a celebratory air when the band dines after the show
at Patsy's, a fine Italian restaurant, where Paul and Dad swap
stories into the small hours. Before we head to a club for a gig
by the legendary guitarist Les Paul, I say my goodbyes to Dad
and Bunny, who are flying home to London on the following
afternoon. I feel a pang of envy when we part. I would love to
go back with them, to see June and the children; but the job
comes first, and my place is with the band.

We head west in high summer for the last few shows, beginning
in Las Vegas, where, as a starstruck new kid, I had first met
Elvis Presley back in 1976. It is almost two years now since
Elvis died on the bathroom floor of Gracelands, his Memphis
mansion, a religious book at his side and a cocktail of
sedatives – codeine, morphine, Quaalude and Valium – in his
bloodstream: an ignominious end for the King of Rock 'n' Roll.

On the night before the show, we are stepping onto the side-
walk outside the MGM Grand Hotel when the sudden sound of
gunfire shatters the late night air. Instinctively, we scramble for

cover beside the nearest limo. Peering over the hood I can see where a black sedan has screeched to a halt in the traffic; three police cars, red lights flashing and sirens wailing, in pursuit. Four men pile out of the sedan, firing shots from handguns and semi-automatics as they scatter. Instantly one is cut down as the police return fire. From the cars jammed in the street, people flee in terror, cowering amid the thunder of gunfire and the crack of shattering glass. As they stream towards the hotel entrance, I grab Paul and Boz and rush them inside the lobby, closely followed by Simon and Mick and the girls. All around us there is confusion and shouting, sobbing and fear.

I push through the crowds, dragging Paul behind me, and make for an exit at the rear of the building. Within a few minutes, I have persuaded the driver of one of the MGM Grand's courtesy buses to take us back to our hotel five blocks away, where we steady our nerves with a handful of drinks before heading up to our rooms. I sit up in bed, watching the local news channel reporting on tonight's shooting. The gang that the police were chasing are drug dealers, one of whom was shot dead. Two policemen are also dead, and another is critically injured. The remaining three gang members are in police custody. Three kilos of cocaine have been recovered from the sedan. I reflect that in a city founded on gambling, there will always be those who are reckless enough to gamble with their lives. They do so every day and night on the roulette wheels and the card tables, and tonight, it has played out on the street before our eyes.

My own brief career as a drug dealer ended the day I was sent to Ashford, but in the past few months, drugs have wormed their way into my life once more. Around a major rock band like Bad Company, drugs are freely available: cocaine, dope, pills; something to take you up, and something to bring you back down again. There is a perpetual motion to a tour, a daily cycle of plane and bus rides, gigs, hotels, clubs and bars. The hours are long and one day blurs into the next. Cocaine revives a tired body and mind and keeps you alert. Often it is the only way to keep going. It is a social drug, not a solitary one, and in every city, at every concert hall and club, there is always someone eager to sell you some more. By the time we reach Los Angeles, I am snorting two or three grams of coke per day and popping sleeping pills or tranquillizers to knock myself out whenever I find a few hours in which to rest. Some of these pills have hallucinogenic side effects: within twenty-four hours of our arrival in LA, Clive Coulson finds me inching along a hotel corridor and clinging to the wall by my fingertips, believing in my delusional state that I am walking a narrow path above a precipice.

Over four days in Hollywood, the band sees little daylight, preferring the dark ambience of the Rainbow Bar & Grill on Sunset Boulevard. In this, Hollywood's most famous rock club, English rock stars are feted as royalty. Like Led Zeppelin before them, Bad Company are indulged with women, booze and drugs in the upstairs VIP room. Everyone in the room is either a rock star or a drug dealer or a close associate of either; or else a music industry power broker, or one of an elite band of groupies. Here, anything goes. Great mounds of cocaine are snorted while groupies kneel beneath tables to administer blow jobs: only when shooting up heroin do the participants seek the privacy of the bathroom.

At dawn, the party moves on to the hotel, where girls queue outside the band members' rooms, waiting their turn. The noise draws numerous complaints from other hotel guests, but this has been a feature of the tour. At Seattle's Edgewater Inn – made famous when Led Zeppelin's roadies 'pleasured' a groupie with a red snapper fished from the sea via a hotel window – Bad Company's after-show antics disturbed the sleep of a ten-pin bowling team whose rooms were on the other side of the corridor from the band's. Several times that night various agitated members of the bowling team protested, to no avail. When the team checked out the next morning they left their bags lined up outside their rooms. Unable to resist, I ran to the bath in Bad Company's suite, which was full of fish the guys had caught while larking about last night, and scooping up armfuls – amongst them a live mud shark and one slippery pink octopus – I placed them surreptitiously in the unattended bags. We stood at the hotel entrance and watched them drive away, all unaware that each of the bags stowed carefully on the roofs of their vehicles was carrying a fish. How puzzled they looked as we stood there grinning to wave them on their way . . .

Before we leave Los Angeles for the flight home to London, Peter thanks me for a job well done. I have taken a few bruises, kept Paul on the straight and narrow, and prevented the band from getting their heads blown off in Las Vegas. Peter tells me to take some well-earned rest before the next big job he has lined up for me: Led Zeppelin's homecoming shows which will headline two nights at Knebworth , spread over consecutive weekends.

On board the flight to Heathrow, I close my eyes but cannot sleep. Although I feel mentally and physically drained, I need a pill to put me to sleep, and I have none. I gulp down three gin and tonics and several miniature bottles of wine, but still my mind refuses to let me rest.

Memories of the tour run through my head like some demented slideshow. Some of them make me smile. I remember a night in Detroit when one of the roadies got so drunk that he passed out and fell into a stack of speaker cabinets, bringing two of them crashing down on stage. The band, to their credit, ignored him and played on.

I remember the morning in Kansas City when I found Boz asleep in his bed beside the hotel swimming pool. Boz later explained that he could not sleep because of the noise from the room next door to his, where Paul was partying with friends:

his solution was to drag his bed outside to sleep in peace beneath the stars. He was wearing sunglasses when I woke him.

I remember great shows, good times; but also bad.

The crowd that the band attracted could be wild, and on more than one occasion things almost got out of control. Their preferred method of showing their approval was to throw cherry bombs at the stage. These would explode with a deafening bang; one time one landed so close to Simon Kirke that it blew him clean off his drum stool. Another landed right next to where Dad and Bunny were sitting the night that Paul invited them on to the stage. They jumped out of their seats and ran for the shelter of the dressing room. Bunny said afterwards it had frightened him more than Rahway State Prison had done. It was impossible to stop them all, short of searching every single punter. But night after night was enough to turn anyone into a nervous wreck.

Under the surface, there were always tensions, and there were days when the guys would barely speak a word to one another. On more than one occasion Paul has threatened to come to blows with the other band members, even his old friend Simon. The problem was they had gone down so well in America that days before they were due to go home the tour had been extended by three months. Even a band at the top of their form needs downtime, and they didn't get it. Worse, they had it snatched from them just as they were starting to relax, the end in sight. Those final twelve weeks were the killer. All of us felt the strain. For the band, with hindsight, it was a bad mistake. They had been on the road too long. That was the price they paid for success, and the beginning of the end for Bad Company. Less than two years later, the band had split apart.

10

Swan song

It is early July 1979, a few weeks short of my twenty-ninth birthday, when my dad calls me into the office at the back of the Highgate gym. He pours two mugs of tea and sits across the table from me, stony-faced.

'What's all this I hear about you taking drugs?' he asks me bluntly.

In the two weeks since I returned to London following the Bad Company tour, I have continued taking cocaine and sleeping pills. One of the guys working at Peter Grant's Kings Road office provides me with the drugs. I am also drinking heavily, mostly gin and tonic, and it shows in my face, in my sallow skin, and in my erratic moods.

Dad says that June is worried about me, and I feel sick. June is pregnant and I should be taking care of her. He tells me he understands how hard I have been working, and how easy it is to get hooked on coke and pills in such an environment. But he has seen John Conteh lose his spirit, his sharpness and his world title to booze. And he reminds me of what I stand to lose if I do not get clean: my wife, my kids, everything that is truly important to me.

When I leave the gym, it is early evening. Dad offers me a lift home but I decide to walk. The warm air clears my head. I find June in the living room watching television with Joanne and Daniel sitting either side of her on the sofa. She tells me that they have already eaten dinner, and that mine is in the oven. Before I go to the kitchen, I walk upstairs to our bedroom and quietly open the wardrobe. From the pocket of my leather jacket, I remove three wraps of cocaine and a bottle of pills, then step through to the bathroom to flush the entire stash down the toilet.

By the time I have taken my dinner plate from the oven and settled into an armchair, Daniel is asleep, his head resting in June's lap. He has been ill for two days with a cough and a high temperature and June has booked a doctor's appointment for the following day. I eat half of the dinner – my appetite weak from all the drugs I have been taking – then carry Daniel up to the bedroom he shares with Joanne. As he sleeps, his breathing is laboured, wheezing. I sit beside the bed for a few minutes, mulling over the things Dad said to me earlier, wondering how I would feel if my own son was too strung out on drugs to take proper care of his family.

These thoughts are still turning over in my mind as I lie in bed that night, restless with guilt and drug withdrawal. Finally, fatigue overwhelms me and I drift into sleep. I am woken by a loud choking sound from the children's room. I sit upright in bed and hear Daniel fighting for breath. Panic rises inside me as I run to lift him from his bed. His face is pale and sweating and his chest heaving with exertion. June is quickly at my side. Her eyes are filled with fear. We live next door to a hospital – the Whittington in Highgate – so I pull on some clothes while June wraps Daniel in a blanket, then I run the fifty yards to the Emergency Department with him cradled in my arms.

Daniel has pleurisy, and for several hours that night it is touch and go. The next day I phone Peter to tell him I have to miss the meeting he's called to talk through plans for Led Zeppelin's Knebworth shows. 'Your family comes first,' he assures me. 'If you need anything, you only have to call.' The following afternoon, when June and I get home after visiting Daniel, Peter's black Daimler is parked outside our door. Norman presents June with a bouquet of beautiful white flowers and a basket of fruit for Daniel, then hands an envelope to me, in which I find two hundred pounds in cash and a note from Peter wishing Daniel a speedy recovery. It is a thoughtful and generous gesture, and one I will always remember. Daniel improves with each day, and within two weeks he is back at home with us. Returning to work, I feel closer to Peter than ever before.

Fifty miles north of London, Knebworth House is a stately home set in two hundred acres. Here in the beautiful Hertfordshire countryside, under summer skies, Led Zeppelin are to play two shows, the first on 4 August and the second a week later. It is four years since the band last performed in Britain, and 140,000 tickets have been sold for each of the two nights.

On 2 August, the Zeppelin entourage is installed in a grand country hotel ten miles from Knebworth House. Every room in the hotel, one hundred or more, is reserved for the next ten days. My room is one of six linked by internal doors, which when opened create a single long suite. Various members of the entourage pass from room to room throughout the day and night, often with a girl or two. Rock music blares from different rooms as people gather to talk, drink and take drugs. I decline the many offers of cocaine, but accept a couple of joints to help me to sleep.

At around nine each night, the hotel's bar fills with assorted road crew and staff from the Swan Song office. Into the small hours, tales of debauchery are swapped, and with each passing hour, the stories grow more outrageous. Outside, a team of security guards, all ex-army officers, is on duty, ensuring that the band and crew are not intruded upon, either by fans, media or would-be hangers-on from the music business.

On the day of the first show on 4 August, the four members of Led Zeppelin appear tense as they wait before heading out to the stage. It seems incredible that the most successful band of the decade should be nervous in the run up to a performance, but the Knebworth shows are the biggest of their career, and it has been a long time since they faced their British fans. Peter delays their entrance until the sun is setting behind the stage. Ever the perfectionist, he is determined that Led Zeppelin's homecoming should be the ultimate rock 'n' roll spectacle.

I stand at the top of a long wooden ramp leading up to the stage, a flashlight in my hand, ready to guide the band on their last few steps before they walk out under the stage lights. I glance out at the audience, a sea of faces in the blue twilight, stretching as far as the eye can see. Hundreds of cigarette lighters are raised; tiny flickers like stars in a sky. The cooling air is thick with excitement and anticipation.

I turn to see Peter leading the band up the ramp, followed by four security guards. Suddenly, a young man, a fan who has somehow breached the backstage security, scrambles up the side of the ramp and lunges at Robert Plant. Immediately he is grabbed by one of the guards and thrown from the ramp, falling six feet to the ground. The band walks on as if nothing has happened. When they reach the stage, still hidden from the audience by a towering line of amplifiers, Peter huddles them together, their arms linked, as if in prayer. Then they walk out into the bright lights to a heroes' welcome.

The show is a triumph. Standing at the back of the stage, close to the drum riser, I feel every kick of Bonzo's bass drum.

The band look different from the last time I saw them perform – their hair shorter, their clothes more conservative – but their power remains undiminished. Jimmy appears pale, thin, emaciated, but his playing is spellbinding. As the sky darkens from blue to black, dozens of campfires are lit around the perimeter of the field, blazing orange.

After three hours, the band takes its final bow. I wait at the foot of the ramp as Jimmy and Bonzo are led to a waiting limo, Robert and John Paul to a second. I jump into a third car with Peter and Richard Cole and we follow in convoy, escorted by two police cars. Before those campfires have burned out, we are safely back at the hotel. Jimmy and John Paul retire to their rooms while Robert and Bonzo receive guests in the crowded bar. Bonzo is still drinking with Richard Cole when I walk unsteadily from the bar to my bed at dawn.

The next afternoon I find Peter in his suite with two policemen, studying a selection of aerial photographs of the concert site shot from a police helicopter. Peter asks the two officers to estimate the audience numbers. They agree on a figure somewhere between 250,000 and 280,000 – more than double the official figure as confirmed by the promoter. Even if the police are correct, there is no way to prove exactly how many people were at the show, but Peter is fuming at the thought that thousands of fans have been admitted without tickets. These fans will have paid cash on entry – and Peter has not seen any of the money. When the promoter arrives at the hotel a few hours later, Peter invites him into his suite while I wait in an adjacent room. After two hours, the promoter emerges looking twenty years older.

The second show proves anticlimactic. Perhaps it is the rain that dampens the audience, or technical glitches that interrupt the band's flow, but there is not the same celebratory atmosphere as

107

there had been the week before. Back at the hotel bar, however, the road crew is in high spirits, the job done. And having resisted temptation for so many days, my resolve crumbles. I find myself sitting in the hallway outside my room at six in the morning with four of my fellow crew members, cocaine tingling in my brain, my nose clogged. When a room service waiter arrives with our break-fast on a trolley, none of us can muster the energy to stand up, so we ask the waiter to set out the food on the hall carpet. The waiter clicks his tongue in disgust as he wheels the trolley away, no doubt counting the hours until we leave. I try to eat but the coke has killed my appetite. I struggle to my feet by sliding my back up against the wall and walk down to the bar, where people are slumped in chairs as if they had been gassed. One guy is asleep on the bar counter. Half-empty bottles of champagne, spirits and wine litter the floor.

Peter enters the room with a worried expression. He tells me in his croaking voice that there's a guitar case full of money in his room and that we must get it out of there as quickly as we can. This is pure cocaine paranoia, but I do not wish to argue with Peter. Gently, I assure him that the money is safe, that we have ex-army guards all over the hotel, and that nobody could get past them. Peter is still coked out of his mind and is not to be comforted: he is convinced that a gang of robbers is trying to break into his suite as we speak. We walk up to the suite and Peter makes an urgent call requesting a helicopter to collect the guitar case. He summons four of the security guards to the room. Thirty minutes later the buzzing of the rotor blades is rattling the glass in the windows as the helicopter lands just behind the car park at the rear of the hotel. Flanked by the guards, Peter marches out across the tarmac, shielding his eyes against the sun with his left hand while clutching the guitar case tightly to him with the right. He stoops a little when he nears the whirring blades, and offers up the case to the Swan Song employee sitting beside the pilot. As Peter stands back to watch the helicopter rise and turn away in a slow arc, the backdraft ruffling his hair, a weight seems to lift from his shoulders.

After Knebworth, I am relieved to return to normal life in Camden. Although I have gone back on my resolution by taking cocaine on that last night in the hotel, I have broken the habit. With each day, my mental and physical health improves. Led Zeppelin's new album *In Through The Out Door* is released in September and tops the charts in the UK and the US. It is business as usual for Peter and the band. Peter calls to ask if I am available to work on Zeppelin's forthcoming European tour, but with our third child due in a month, I tell him I would prefer to stay at home. He accepts my decision on condition that I will join the band's American tour in the autumn of 1980. On 25 October, a few hours after the birth of my second son, I call Peter to tell him that I have named the boy Grant in his honour. For the first time since I have known Peter, he is at a loss for words. When, finally, he expresses his pride, he sounds happier than at any point in the past four years.

The new decade begins with a call regarding a favourite client in trouble. Paul McCartney has been arrested at Japan's Narita airport and charged with possession of 219 grams of marijuana. He is jailed for ten days, then released to fly home. Paul's chauffeur collects me en route to the airport, where the head of security allows us to clear customs via a channel normally reserved for visiting foreign dignitaries. With press photographers massed on the main arrivals floor, we slip away unnoticed from an unmarked exit. As we drive to his country home in Rye, near the Sussex coast, Paul is so exhausted he can barely speak. Once inside the house, I notice a group of fans and photographers gathered on the public footpath that passes within fifty feet of the kitchen window. They can stand there all day and all night for that matter but that's the closest they're going to get.

In the morning, a night's sleep behind him, Paul can begin to relax. At midday he rolls a joint and we walk from the back door through the gardens and out to the woodlands at the far reaches of his property. After a few long pulls on the joint, we are both laughing about the whole drama.

Paul's wife Linda arrives in the early evening with their children, who are of similar age to mine: Mary, aged ten, is a year older than Joanne; Stella, at eight, is a year older than Daniel; and their young son James is two. As Paul hugs and kisses his kids I wish I were back at home, but I have already agreed to Paul's request for me to stay with him for a couple of weeks until the storm has blown over. I sleep in a small guest bedroom and speak with June every day on the phone. The McCartneys rarely venture out of doors except to walk in the garden. Only at the end of the second week do they resume a normal life, when the whole family dines at the local pub and I keep watch for opportunistic journalists or photographers. They are wonderful people and I feel sad saying goodbye. Linda is a sweetheart, the perfect companion for Paul, and their children are bright, happy and wholly unaffected by their father's wealth and fame.

During the spring and summer I work with an old school friend who is now a landscape gardener. It is hard work, but it pays the bills and allows me plenty of time with June and the kids ahead of Led Zeppelin's American tour, which is scheduled for October. It is early on the morning of 26 September when the phone call comes – but it isn't the one that I have been expecting. The voice on the line is Peter's, but I can hardly make out what he is saying. Thinking that he is calling from another country, I ask him to speak louder. There is a lengthy pause.

'Bonzo's dead,' he tells me, his voice faltering. 'We found him yesterday at Jimmy's place.'

I try to speak but no words come.

'I'll call you again soon,' Peter says, and hangs up.

The news spreads rapidly on the radio and TV. I listen over and over as the story is repeated throughout the day and night:

John Bonham, thirty-two-year-old star of the rock group Led Zeppelin, has been found dead at the home of the group's guitarist Jimmy Page. The cause of death is believed to be asphyxiation due to excessive consumption of alcohol. A verdict of accidental death is expected. So far there has been no comment from the group or its management regarding Bonham's death or the future of the group ... In my heart, I know that it is over.

On 15 October, five days after Bonzo's funeral at a small parish church in Worcestershire, I journey to Peter's home. He appears somehow smaller, a shadow of the man who has dominated the music industry for the best part of a decade. The death of his friend has sucked the life out of him. We talk for two hours, mostly about the good times, before Peter says he needs to rest. He summons Norman to drive me home and proffers a weary handshake. As I follow Norman to the door, I turn to watch Peter walking heavily upstairs, and instead of a giant I see a broken man.

A little more than seven weeks later, on 9 December, June calls urgently to me from the kitchen. Holding Grant in her arms, she is listening intently to the radio. 'It's John Lennon,' she says, her face drained of colour. 'He's been shot.'

As the voice on the radio confirms that Lennon has been murdered – gunned down outside his apartment in New York City – I think immediately of Paul and how his heart must be breaking. The Beatles' split was as bitter as any divorce but, together, John and Paul wrote songs that changed the world and touched millions of lives. I think of Christmas Eve 1963, when they stood on the stage of the Finsbury Park Astoria, a night I remember as if it had happened just days ago. I think of June's tears when I told her I had a ticket for the concert and she did not. I look at June now and there are tears in her eyes once more.

I walk across the room and draw her to me. She lays her head against my shoulder and sobs. Between us, Grant shifts a little in June's arms. I wonder whether Peter has heard about Lennon's death, if it has caused him to grieve anew for Bonzo, or if, sadder still, he is locked away upstairs in the great house, alone and oblivious to the world.

I hear John Lennon's 'Imagine' playing over the radio, and it feels like a requiem; not just for its writer, but for an era.

11

The plastic age

The new decade has brought yet more changes with it. At the end of 1980 the three surviving members of Led Zeppelin announce their decision to dissolve the band following the death of John Bonham. Just as the Rolling Stones' disastrous 1969 concert at Altamont had signalled the death of the sixties, after a young black man, Meredith Hunter, was stabbed to death by bikers as the Stones played, so the demise of Led Zeppelin marked the end of rock's golden age. The writing had been on the wall as far back as 1976, when the sudden explosion of punk, with its two-minute thrash perfected by bands like The Sex Pistols, The Clash and The Ramones, turned dozens of seventies rock bands into dinosaurs overnight. A handful of giants had the musical stature to ride the upheavals that swept the business on both sides of the Atlantic, and Led Zeppelin, with their roots sunk deep in the bedrock of authentic raw blues power, were the last of them.

Now British music has a different sound: the new romantic style of Adam & The Ants, Duran Duran and Spandau Ballet, and the electro-pop of The Human League, Soft Cell and Depeche Mode. One of the UK's brightest stars is Gary Numan, who by the age of twenty-three already has two number one singles with 'Cars' and 'Are Friends Electric?' And in 1980 I receive a call from Tony Webb, Gary Numan's father and manager, asking me to join his boy's forthcoming tour.

Working with Gary and his family is, in its own unique way, every bit as strange as the rarefied world of Peter Grant and Led Zeppelin. The Webbs are working class people from Hammersmith in west London. Before managing Gary, Tony worked as a bus driver at Heathrow airport. His wife Beryl takes care of Gary's on-tour wardrobe, which consists mainly of black PVC jump suits. Gary's image is that of an android from a science fiction movie, but off stage, he has a warm personality, if a little withdrawn. The fact is he is happiest when piloting his single-engine Cessna aeroplane, high up in the clouds. But Gary and his family are such genuine, good-hearted people, I fear for them in a business as cruel as this. Gary's tour manager is an old friend of his and a former schoolteacher. Richard Cole he is not.

We tour for four weeks in Europe and the shows are bizarre to say the least. Gary glides around the stage in a little motorised spaceship on hidden wheels. His band are uniformed robots in identikit black jump suits with hair of various fluorescent colours. Out in the audience there are hundreds of Numan clones, dressed even more outrageously than the star himself. And at the side of the stage, watching proudly, are dear old Tony and Beryl.

Paul Gardiner, the bass player, is full of mischief. I see a lot of my younger self in Paul. He is a London lad, cheeky, with a boyish grin and a taste for booze and drugs. Each night, while

Beryl is making beans on toast for Gary after the show, Paul is sneaking off to buy a bag of speed, dope or pills. I advise him to slow down a little, to keep from burning out, but Paul is young and headstrong, and is forced to leave the group before we head to the US.

Although Gary is enjoying a top ten hit in America with 'Cars' in the summer of 1980, he remains a cult artist whose cropped and bleached hair, lipstick and eyeliner draw a homophobic reaction in the bars and clubs he visits. The fact that Gary is straight is of no consequence to a bunch of drunkards looking to pick a fight. After two close scrapes during a single night in Detroit, I ban Gary from going out at night unless we are in a cosmopolitan city like New York or Los Angeles.

Texas is not known for its liberal attitudes, and it is here that the tour finishes. We are nearing the end of an overnight road journey, six hundred miles in all, when we pull in at an interstate truck stop. It is early morning: too early, I hope, for the locals to be out of bed. I order the band to stay put while I take a look around, then step out of the bus into brilliant sunshine. Shielding my eyes against the glare, I see dozens of people are staring at me from the windows of the restaurant. Their expressions are puzzled. Our tour bus, loaned from a country and western singer, has dramatic and brightly-coloured scenes from the American Civil War painted the length of each side, but if these people are expecting to see Dolly Parton or Kenny Rogers emerging from the bus, they are in for a surprise.

I walk past a row of giant trucks: each has chrome-work polished to such a shine that I can believe the old adage that truckers treat their rigs better than they treat their wives. Inside the restaurant, twenty road-hardened guys sit on tall stools at a long bar eating breakfast. The other tables and booths are filled with more truckers and a couple of families. In one corner, beside racks of candy, beef jerky, music cassettes and road maps, a jukebox with pulsing red and blue lights plays an old Glenn Campbell classic, 'By The Time I Get To Phoenix'. As one of the guys at the bar pauses with his coffee cup at his lips and looks me up and down, I wish I too was on the way to Phoenix, anywhere but here, but the smell of frying bacon makes me swallow with hunger.

A waitress in a pink checked dress – in her forties and a little rough around the edges – asks me if I would like a seat at the bar. I tell her I have ten people with me. Her smile drops as she looks past me to see them coming through the door: still half asleep, their faces smudged with last night's make-up, their hair in messy tangles of pink and green and blue. The waitress leads us to a couple of empty tables at the far end of the room. As we pore over the menus, a fat man in a baseball cap calls to me from the nearest booth.

'You boys in some religious sect?'

'No, we're from England, a rock 'n' roll band.'

He nods and goes back to his steak and eggs. Then Gary appears at the door, white as a corpse, with Tony and Beryl at his side. Everyone in the room turns to stare. Three truckers sneer at Gary and shift in their seats. I have experienced this kind of Texan hospitality before when I was with Bad Company. There are a lot of guys in this place who would like nothing better than to make trouble for people like us. I feel my heart beat faster, my hands tightening into fists. If this is going to end up like Custer's Last Stand, I won't even have a guy like Paul Rodgers fighting alongside me.

I must act quickly.

I check my watch and tell the band that we haven't time to sit and eat. If they go back to the bus, I say, I will bring their food out to them, and they can eat as we continue on our way. Oblivious to the hostility around them, they exit, chatting happily. When I follow them on to the bus a minute later, minus their breakfasts, and tell the driver to set off for Dallas, they sulk like five year-olds. None of them has any idea that I might just have spared them from the worst beating of their lives.

This naivety is typical of Gary and his rather quaint little family business. With his bus-driver father cutting the deals and his mother ironing his spacesuits before the gigs, Gary Numan is never going to take over the world. But after what happened to Peter Grant and Led Zeppelin, perhaps he and his family are better off as they are.

★

When I return to London in the summer, Dad has another world champion. Cornelius Boza Edwards, the youngster who sparred with Paul Rodgers two years ago, has won the world lightweight title against the gritty Mexican Rafael 'Bazooka' Limon, in a gruelling, dirty fight that went the full distance in searing California heat. But there is sadness in Dad's eyes when I meet him at the gym. Davey Long, an ex-boxer and close friend of the family, has died at the age thirty-four, following a long illness. Davey had endured unimaginable pain for many long months, refusing morphine so that he could think and speak clearly during the last precious hours he shared with his wife and children.

All of my family attend the funeral. The wake is at the Irish Centre, a social hall in Camden Town, where I stay long after June has taken the children home. The mourners eat pie and mash before gathering around a piano to sing traditional songs. With a belly full of gin, I join in a chorus of Vera Lynn's wartime standard 'We'll Meet Again', my arms around members of Davey's family and tears streaming down my face.

When I get home, the phone is ringing. Deke Arlon is a friend of Dad's who manages Dennis Waterman – the star of two of Britain's best-loved TV series, *The Sweeney* and *Minder* – and the pop star Sheena Easton. Deke wants me to join him in Los Angeles to watch over Sheena who, in the space of a few months, has become one of the biggest stars in America. It is an incredible transition for a twenty-two-year-old from Glasgow who first came to prominence via a cheesy British TV talent show called *The Big Time*.

In May, Sheena's first American single 'Morning Train (9 To 5)' hit number one and sold a million copies. Now, just two months later, she is celebrating a worldwide hit with 'For Your Eyes Only', the theme to the James Bond film, in which she is seen singing the song during the opening title sequence, the first singer to appear on screen in a Bond movie. This, truly, is the big time, and Deke needs me to protect his delicate young star. I feel a little fuzzy with drink and drained by the emotion of the day, but I could use the money.

'Okay,' I say wearily, 'I'll do it.'

'Great,' Deke chimes. 'I'll have a car pick you up at seven.'

'What?' I splutter. 'Tomorrow morning?'

'Yes. I need you out here right away.'

I place the receiver in its cradle and walk through to the kitchen to make coffee. I need to sober up before I wake June and tell her that I am flying out to LA in the morning. I know that it is tough on her and the kids when I leave home for weeks, even months at a time. But for a poor boy from Camden Town without a formal qualification to his name, it is not a bad career.

It certainly doesn't seem too bad as, twenty-four hours later, I sit with Deke in the polo lounge of the Beverly Hills Hotel, sipping cocktails and trying not to stare at the two old fellows seated at a table thirty feet away. They are Bob Hope and George Burns. We talk for an hour or two, mostly about boxing, before Sheena arrives, looking stunning in a long black dress. As I stand to greet her, I am shocked at how tiny she is. Even in heels, she is no taller than five feet, but she looks every inch the superstar, with flawless skin and beautiful dark eyes. Only her accent gives any indication that this is just a young girl from Glasgow who was singing in pubs only three years ago. Her manner is assured without being arrogant, and she has a quick wit and a dirty laugh. We hit it off instantly.

One of my first tasks is to guard her on a trip to Chile, where she is to appear at a festival staged in a football stadium near

Mum and Dad on their wedding day, Euston Town Hall, London, May 1945. Mum was seventeen and Dad sixteen years old.

LAND'S END
1908
WOLF ROCK LIGHTHOUSE 8
JOHN-O-GROATS 874
SCILLY ISLES 28
LONGSHIPS LIGHTHOUSE 1½
KENTISH TOWN 296

Outside our house in Dale Road, Camden Town, 1953. Clockwise from front: me, my cousin Christine, my brother Billy and sister Mary.

At Lands End with my mum in 1962. This was the first time I'd been outside of London.

Three generations of the Francis family. Left to right: me, my father George, and my sons Grant and Daniel. This was the last picture taken of my father, in January 2003.

John Conteh, the new world champion, celebrating with my wife June at the Star pub in St Johns Wood, London, 1974.

My wild days in the swinging sixties with velvet flares and a Lord John top: hiding out from the heat in Ibiza with a couple of friends.

Early days: on tour with Led Zeppelin in the USA.

Contract negotiations with Bill Tansley, Sheena Easton's co-manager, at George Martin's famous studios on the island of Montserrat.

Looking out for Bon Jovi as they do the tourist thing outside Madison Square Gardens before their first headline show at the legendary New York venue in August 1987.

Fun in the sun: Richie and Jon in Jamaica for the MTV Awards in 1987.

Jon Bon Jovi (left) and Richie Sambora incognito on the Slippery When Wet tour in Australia. The disguise was the only way I could get them past the 5000 fans camped outside our hotel.

With Bubbles, Michael Jackson's pet chimpanzee. Tokyo, September 1987.

Bon Jovi's touring staff, 1987. This is how many people it takes to stage a rock show every night. Doc is at the drum kit with me above.

Celebrating with Jon and his wife
Dorothea at their wedding party,
New York City, 6 August 1989.

Bowling with Jon and his wife Dorothea in
Kansas City. Jon won everything, including
the shirt off my back.

My 39th birthday at the famous George pub in London's East End. Jon is laughing at me trying on the butler's outfit he bought me from Harrods.

Having a laugh with Richie Sambora at Cheng-Du, a Chinese restaurant in Camden Town which was a Bon Jovi favourite.

Bundled up against the cold in Red Square, Moscow. From left: Richie Sambora, manager Doc McGhee and Jon Bon Jovi.

Cover story: part of a sequence which was taken for the cover of Sounds in April 1989. It was 8.00 a.m. when this was taken: I am wearing Jon's glasses after an all-night party, and Jon is wishing he hadn't lent them to me . . .

the capital, Santiago. Many South American cities have high crime rates, and visitors are warned against kidnapping. There is not enough time for me to travel ahead of Sheena to work on security in advance, but when I call the Chilean promoter, he assures me that we will be met off the plane by a special police team, plus a representative from Sheena's American record company.

On the flight from LA, I am Sheena's sole companion: her band is travelling separately a few hours later. As we disembark from the plane, two men approach. Tall, unsmiling, wearing sunglasses and leather jackets, they flash their police badges from their wallets and request that I hand over our passports. I am reluctant to do so, but they insist. We pass quickly through customs to the arrivals gate, where the woman from the record company is waiting for us, but as she calls to me, the policemen wave her away and lead us briskly through an exit to two police cars. When I ask why we were not permitted to speak to her, and why there is no limousine for us to travel in, they offer no reply. I open the rear door of the first car for Sheena to sit in the back, then walk around to the front passenger door.

'No,' says one of the policemen. 'You go in the second car.'

'No way,' I tell him. 'I travel with her, always.'

The policeman pulls his jacket open to reveal a gun in a shoulder holster, but I am not about to leave Sheena in a car with two guys I met just thirty minutes ago. I jump into the passenger seat and nod to the driver, but as he smiles and says hello, the policeman opens the driver's door and pulls him out of the car. After a brief conversation, the policeman then sits at the wheel and makes a show of withdrawing the gun from its holster and placing it on the seat between his legs. I turn to Sheena and tell her that everything is okay. She smiles weakly. I am not sure that she is convinced.

The policeman drives fast from the airport and along a steep, winding road, skirting mountains, the second car close on our tail. The tyres screech as we round a sharp bend and then accelerate into the straight. Nervously feeling for my seatbelt, I ask the policeman to slow down a little. He grunts and points behind us. In the wing mirror, I see a third car closing fast on the second. The policeman brakes as we approach another tight curve in the road. Suddenly there is a loud bang and then a jolt as our car is struck from behind and sent spinning. Sheena lets out a yelp as the car skids to a halt and she is thrown across the back seat. I reach back and pull her up by the arm. She is shaken but unharmed. We are lucky. The car has come to a stop on the opposite side of the road: had there been any traffic in this lane, we could have been killed.

To my right I see the other police car at the roadside, with the third car jammed against it, nose to tail. The front wing of the police car is buckled where it has hit our rear. The third car must have crashed into the back of the second police car and pushed it into ours. Three policemen spring from their car and, crouching, point guns at the occupants of the third car. Beside me, the cop grabs his gun from beneath the brake pedal and orders Sheena and me to stay put as he flings open the door and runs to join his colleagues. As they shout at the people in the third car, I recognise the young woman in the driver's seat: it is the record company girl whom the police brushed aside at the airport. I call to the policemen, imploring them to lower their guns and explaining that this woman works with us.

The cop who was driving our car signals for calm and helps the woman out of her seat. She and her female passenger are shaking with fear and dazed by the impact of the crash. When I walk across the road to them, they are sobbing hysterically. I suggest that perhaps we should take them to a hospital, and the policeman agrees.

With traffic now backed up in both lanes, the police check the damage to their cars. The dents are superficial, and within a few minutes we are continuing our journey with the two weeping girls squeezed into the back seat next to Sheena, their car abandoned at the side of the road. Sheena cuddles the record company girl and tells her in a soothing whisper not to worry about our little drama. By the time we reach the hotel, she has both girls laughing. Even the cop driving the car is smiling. It is only when we are safely inside her hotel suite that Sheena pulls up her shirt to reveal the bruising on her back. She says she will be fine, and I leave her to rest while I meet the promoter in the bar.

Here, he explains why the police had been so tense and so quick with their guns. Yesterday they had discovered a plot to kidnap the singer who is sharing top billing with Sheena at the festival. I agree to allow Sheena to stay in the city and perform at the show on condition that we have a twenty-four hour armed guard both at the hotel and at the stadium.

The show passes without incident, and despite her injuries, Sheena delights the audience with a spirited performance. As we board the flight back to LA, I thank our police team for taking care of us. 'Come back soon,' one of them smiles. Once inside the plane, Sheena and I laugh at the thought of returning to Chile. This has been an experience that neither of us would care to repeat.

She has coped well with the pressure. Many stars would have panicked, cancelled the show and demanded to be put on the first flight back to LA, but as a native of one of the toughest cities in the world, little Sheena does not scare easily. She is a genuine pro, and a sweetheart. I hope it will last.

It is a year later, when she buys a mansion off Sunset Boulevard in the hills directly below the 'H' in the 'Hollywood' sign, that I sense a change in Sheena. As becomes a millionaire and superstar, the house is chic and spacious with a large, heart-shaped swimming pool, but she rarely swims, sunbathes or sets foot on

121

her tennis court. All of her free time is spent either shopping in the expensive stores on Rodeo Drive or working out for hours on end in her gym. At four feet ten in her bare feet, and with a heavy bust, Sheena has never been entirely happy with her body shape, and here in California, where the rich and famous are attended by armies of personal trainers, nutritionists and cosmetic surgeons, her insecurity becomes a virtual obsession. One afternoon, when I hear Sheena and her agent Harriet Wasserman discussing the pros and cons of various surgical nips and tucks, I fear the worst.

Her height is a major issue. Once, when she was the star guest on a live TV show in Italy, Sheena refused to share a stage with the two presenters, both leggy blondes standing six feet tall in their stilletto heels. She threatened to cancel her appearance until a separate stage had been hastily assembled at the opposite end of the studio, solely for her to sing one song. I reckon that if Sheena could have an operation to lengthen her legs she would be on the surgeon's table in a heartbeat.

In the summer of 1984, Sheena announces her engagement to Rob Light, an entertainment agent from a wealthy Jewish-American family. Handsome and elegant, with a resemblance to actor Richard Gere, Rob is a charming and likeable man, and it is hoped that this, Sheena's second marriage, will work better than her first. Not long ago, she had broken down in tears when British newspapers reported that her ex-husband had declared he was gay and was performing on Scotland's cabaret circuit, singing Sheena's hit songs while in drag. Now she is planning a fairy-tale wedding to one of the most level headed of Hollywood's major players, although their relation-ship has not always run smoothly. It comes as no surprise that on the eve of the wedding, various members of Sheena's band and touring staff are placing bets on the marriage lasting less than a year. Most predict it will be over inside six months. One of the roadies offers odds of twenty-five to one on the marriage lasting for more than two years, but there are no takers. It may sound harsh, but then rock is a brutal business. The closer you get to the top, the more people want to know you, but the fewer care about who you really are. Friends are the price that superstars pay for fame.

The wedding, on 15 January 1985, is a lavish affair held at the opulent Baltimore Hotel on the Pacific shore of Santa Barbara, California. Because Sheena is Roman Catholic and Rob is Jewish, the ceremony is presided over by both a priest and a rabbi. After the wedding feast, a band plays jazz and big band standards long into the night. In all, the party lasts for two days: longer than many had predicted for the marriage. Some weeks later, we are en route to the MTV Awards when I hear Sheena tell Rob he is not to introduce her as his wife. He must always remember that she is still Sheena Easton.

I wince, and feel a sad longing for the sweet girl I knew just a few years ago.

When she fires Deke Arlon, I lose all heart in working for Sheena. Deke, with the help of his wife Jill, had transformed Sheena from a gauche teenager into one of the most famous women in the world. It was Deke who had secured her recording contract, who had steered her to international success, and had cut the deal with the producers of the James Bond movie. But Sheena replaces Deke with Harriet Wasserman as she attempts a career makeover, reinventing herself as a bold, sexy, bad girl of pop in the image of America's fastest-rising star, Madonna.

In March 1985, Sheena has a top ten hit with 'Sugar Walls', a raunchy dance track written for her by Prince, who is currently the hottest act in the business, having bridged the gap between black and white audiences with his rock/R&B crossover album *Purple Rain*. Immediately there are press rumours of a romance between Prince and Sheena, and when she performs a show in his hometown of Minneapolis, they are inseparable. Prince requests a private room to be set aside for him backstage, decorated with purple drapes and sofa, and it is in this room that he and Sheena stay behind a locked door for two hours after the show. They certainly look like they are made to be together: they are both petite, and from behind, as they walk arm in arm, high heels clicking, they resemble a pair of twin sisters.

In June, Sheena is recording new material in Philadelphia when I receive a call from Bill Graham, America's foremost concert promoter, who is organising the Live Aid charity concert at the city's JFK Stadium. Devised by rock singer Bob Geldof as a means of raising money for famine relief in Ethiopia, Live Aid is the biggest music event ever staged. Here in Philadelphia and at London's Wembley Stadium, many of the biggest names in popular music are performing free of charge during a fifteen-hour live TV broadcast. And with an estimated global audience of two billion viewers, every musician in Britain and America wants to be seen to be doing their bit for the cause.

Geldof has assembled a stellar cast for the event: in London, the performers who have signed up to support his initiative include U2, Queen, David Bowie, Dire Straits, The Who, Sting, Sade, Elton John and Paul McCartney.

In Philadelphia the list is equally illustrious: Duran Duran, Tina Turner, Mick Jagger, Madonna, Bob Dylan, Simple Minds, Neil Young, Lionel Richie, Hall & Oates, Black Sabbath and Bryan Adams. Phil Collins is appearing at both venues, flying by Concorde from London to Philadelphia in order to play drums for the regrouped Led Zeppelin.

Bill Graham asks me to assist with stage management in Philadelphia. My responsibility is to ensure that each act is moved smoothly on and off the stage within twenty minutes, in accordance with the strict time schedule. I work for a week in advance of the show, liaising with artists and managers. I have Sheena's blessing, since she too is participating in Live Aid, although not as she would have wished. She would love to perform a set at the US show, but instead she has to settle for a supporting role as a compere, providing TV links backstage, before joining the all-star ensemble in the finale.

It is both exciting and an honour to be involved in such an historic event as Live Aid, and the day of the show, 13 July, is one that I will never forget. The same is true for anyone who witnesses it either in London or Philadelphia, or via TV screens all over the world. I rise early to watch the start of the London show on TV – British rockers Status Quo playing the aptly titled 'Rockin' All Over The World' – then head to the JFK Stadium three hours before the first act is due on stage. The day passes in a blur. My job is made easier by an extraordinary degree of co-operation between the artists and their crews. Nobody, it appears, would dare throw a tantrum on a day like this.

One of the best performances comes from Madonna. She takes to the stage in the late afternoon following an introduction by singer and actress Bette Midler, who gets a big laugh from both the audience and the people working around me when she describes Madonna as 'a woman who pulled herself up by her bra-straps'. Like Sheena, Madonna is tiny. Dressed as if from a thrift store, with heavy make-up and an unruly mass of brightly coloured hair, she looks like a naughty teenager as she smiles nervously before running on to the stage, but once out there, she commands the stage as if it is hers and hers alone. Having enjoyed a string of huge hits during the past year with 'Like A Virgin', 'Lucky Star', 'Crazy For You' and 'Material Girl', Madonna is who every young girl in America wants to be, and the audience adores her. When she skips off the stage, exhilarated and triumphant, I wonder if Sheena has been watching backstage.

By contrast, Led Zeppelin prove disappointing. In deference to Bonzo, the trio of Page, Plant and Jones is backed by two drummers; Phil Collins, newly arrived from London, and Tony Thompson, once of disco superstars Chic. Tony I had met before when Sheena worked with Chic's Nile Rodgers in New York. Nile is a funny, laid-back guy who beat me so many times at Scrabble – not especially difficult, given my dyslexia – that I insisted we play dominoes instead, a game I had mastered as a kid during those long summer evenings spent sitting outside the Mitre in Dale Road. Seeing Tony and Phil Collins playing behind Jimmy, Robert and John Paul brings back some wonderful memories, but without Bonzo it was never going to feel the same. They were right to split the band when they did.

The show's finale is chaotic. I am swamped as dozens of stars – and more than a few also-rans – fill the stage to sing, en masse, the USA For Africa anthem, 'We Are The World'. I watch as Sheena manoeuvres her way through to centre-stage and grasps the microphone from the hand of folk legend Joan Baez to sing a couple of lines before yet another artist takes over. It is her chance to perform in front of the biggest audience of her life, and she is determined to seize the moment.

After the show I am duty-bound to escort her back to the Four Seasons Hotel, where Bill Graham is hosting an exclusive party in his suite. Here, amid a blizzard of cocaine, I slip away and spend several hours at a corner table while Jack Nicholson entertains Bob Dylan and The Rolling Stones' Keith Richards with a seemingly endless stream of anecdotes. Jack is the biggest star in the room, everybody's hero, and as he flashes that devilish grin, it becomes apparent that in all of his movies, he is effectively playing himself. When I wake the following morning with a dry throat and an aching head, the thought of Jack Nicholson makes me smile, but the memory of Sheena's performance has me feeling sick inside.

Six days later, we are in New York when I tell her I am quitting. She seems surprised, but makes no effort to alter my decision. There is some sadness in our goodbye. I have shared some good times with her over the past four years, and I recall fondly the lovely girl I met at the Beverly Hills Hotel back in 1981. But it was Deke to whom I was closest, and with Deke gone, I have come to realise how little I care for the person that she has become. When I walk up to my hotel room and call a travel agent to arrange my flight home, I feel almost light-headed with relief.

12

Slippery when wet

5 OCTOBER 1986

'Hi, is that Michael Francis?'
    'It is.'
    'Michael, this is Karen at McGhee Entertainment. Doc McGhee would like to speak with you.'
    This should be interesting. Doc McGhee is one of the biggest names in the music business. He is the manager of Mötley Crüe, currently the hottest rock 'n' roll act in America, and the most notorious, with a wild reputation for drinking, fighting, taking drugs and screwing everything that moves. Two years previously, their singer Vince Neil escaped jail after crashing his Ford Pantera while drunk, killing his passenger, Nicholas 'Razzle' Dingley, the drummer for Finnish band Hanoi Rocks, and

seriously injuring the occupants of another vehicle. Mötley Crüe are trouble; but they are also big business.

'Hey, Michael,' booms a voice down the line from New York. 'Doc McGhee. I have a band I'd like you to look after. Bon Jovi. One of the guys, Richie, says he knows you from the Swan Song days. He played guitar with Messenger.'

I have a vague recollection of Messenger. They were an American band signed to Peter Grant's Swan Song label back in the seventies. People raved about Richie but not about the band. There were two priorities on Swan Song – Led Zeppelin and Bad Company. Messenger were just kids who hung around the New York office and never had a hit record.

'Richie tells me you're the best guy in the business,' Doc continues. 'Bon Jovi are coming to the UK in four weeks and we'd like you to take care of them. These guys are gonna be the biggest rock 'n' roll band in the world and I want the best for them.'

'Okay ...' I say, guardedly. The biggest band in the world? I have heard this spiel a million times.

Doc tells me all about the band. They are from New Jersey and they have made two albums, but the new record, he claims, is going to be the big one. Their latest single 'You Give Love A Bad Name' has just reached number fourteen in the UK.

It is news to me. I have never heard of Bon Jovi, but I have seen New Jersey when I have flown there, to Newark airport, en route to New York, and the place is like one huge industrial estate, its skyline dominated by huge factories and tall chimneys belching out thick smoke. I decide to pass on the band. I tell Doc that I will not be in the UK when the band arrives. He asks me to call him back if my plans change.

Later, over dinner, I ask my sixteen-year-old daughter Joanne if she has heard of Bon Jovi. Her eyes widen and her mouth drops open.

'They're going to be massive!' she exclaims. 'And the singer is gorgeous!'

'Oh,' I shrug. 'I just turned them down.'

Joanne is speechless, but her expression tells me that I have missed out on a chance to make some good money. Joanna sulks for weeks until I receive a second call from Doc's office on 26 October, the day that Bon Jovi's third album, *Slippery When Wet*, reaches number one on the American chart.

'The British tour is sold out,' Karen says, 'and we really would love you to do it.'

'That's funny,' I say. 'My other gig has just fallen through. So yes, I'll do it.'

'The guys will be really happy,' Karen says. 'And so will Doc.'

More importantly, I think, so will Joanne.

4 NOVEMBER 1986

I am at Gatwick airport to meet Bon Jovi. Their flight from New Jersey is two hours late. I stand at the arrivals gate beside bored limousine drivers holding placards inscribed with businessmen's names. A teenage boy drops his case and rushes to embrace his waiting family. Behind him, a shabby figure staggers toward me, almost bent double, one hand rubbing at the seat of his pants. He wears a calf-length leather coat and a pained expression, his hair sticking out at crazy angles. He appears to be in his forties; too old, I assume, to be in America's hottest new rock band. Then I notice the Bon Jovi logo embroidered on the travel bag slung over his shoulder.

This guy is a wreck. For a second or two, I consider bailing out, but my sense of duty wins out. I offer my hand.

'Hi, I'm Michael.'

He stops, still hunched over, and peers up at me through glazed eyes.

'Alec,' he croaks and weakly clutches my hand. 'I, uh, need the bathroom.'

I steer him in the right direction and turn to see two more guys who really do look like rock stars. The first is blond, boyishly handsome and wearing large aviator sunglasses: the second tall, dressed all in black, with long dark hair under a wide-brimmed hat. They introduce themselves as Jon and Richie. Now I understand why my daughter Joanne made such a fuss over Jon Bon Jovi. This guy could have any woman eating out of his hand. He is going to be a superstar.

Jon introduces the other two band members, Dave and Tico. Doc McGhee joins us in ebullient mood. Doc squints at the crowds around us and asks if anyone has seen Alec.

'The guy that looks like Quasimodo?' I reply. 'He's in the bathroom.'

Doc groans. 'Can you go get him?'

In the bathroom, both stalls are occupied. I knock on the first and a startled African voice snaps, 'Go away, please!' As I approach the second stall the door opens to reveal Alec, now fully upright and highly animated.

'Okay!' he exclaims. 'Let's go.'

Two silver vans deliver the entourage to the centre of London, where the band is booked into the chic St James's Club in Haymarket. As tour manager Richie Bozzet arranges for the luggage to be sent to the rooms, the band head straight for the bar. Within minutes, they are surrounded by women – a few rock 'n' roll groupies who have somehow found out where the band are staying, and also some classier thirty-year-old women in business suits. It is immediately obvious that this band is a magnet to women of all kinds. If these guys are as good on stage as Doc is claiming, they really could become the biggest band in the world.

Like every American band, Bon Jovi want to hear stories about the British artists that they have grown up idolising. Richie asks me about Led Zeppelin and Jon about Paul McCartney and The Beatles, his favourite band. As we talk, I realise that these are great guys, and close-knit, like a family. They have a sharp sense of humour, continually laughing and joking. I know we will become good friends.

SLIPPERY WHEN WET ★

Richie and Dave arrange to meet with two of the groupies later that night before we head off to Stringfellows, a famous nightclub in the heart of Leicester Square. From here, we move on to a strip club, where hundreds of pounds are spent on girls who perform erotic dances at the band's table.

As I flop into a bed at the hotel at four in the morning, too drunk to make it back to my home in Camden, I sense that this is going to be one hell of a tour – maybe the wildest time of my life.

7 NOVEMBER 1986

At the St George's Hall in Bradford, Bon Jovi begin the European leg of their Slippery When Wet tour. The venue is a small theatre in the heart of Yorkshire, a northern English county known for its mining and other heavy industries. It is not a place where you expect to find the kind of beautiful girls that would go to a show in London or New York or Los Angeles. However, as the band's bus pulls in at the stage door at five in the afternoon, we see a crowd of fifty fans: most of them are girls, and almost all are beautiful. The local promoter is amazed. He has never seen anything like it in Bradford.

Two girls in particular stand out from the crowd. One is blonde, the other brunette, and both are stunning: squeezed into tight, low-cut black mini-dresses and wearing killer heels, their hair a mass of blow-waved curls. They bounce and blow kisses to Jon as I usher the band through the door and up to the dressing room. Only when we get to the stage for the sound check do we discover the truth about these two girls. They are sisters who travelled to Bradford from London and are desperate to meet their favourite band. So desperate, in fact, that they have secured backstage passes by giving blow jobs to several members of the road crew this afternoon. Girls will do anything to meet a band, and when the crew tell the band how

133

good these girls are, I am given instructions to make sure that the girls' wish is granted.

At nine, Bon Jovi take to the stage to wild cheers. They begin with 'Let It Rock', a thumping rock anthem and the first song on the new album. I watch from the side of the stage as Jon teases the crowd and they sing every word of the song. When they play 'You Give Love A Bad Name', the crowd's response tells me that Doc McGhee is right: Bon Jovi really are going to be the biggest band in the world.

I have seen many of rock's greatest front men up close, and Jon Bon Jovi is up there with the best. There are more girls in the audience than I have ever seen at a rock show, and they adore him. Richie is the perfect foil for Jon, a stylish guitarist who gives the band a hard rock edge. Richie is the most exciting guitar player I have seen since Led Zeppelin's Jimmy Page. He also has a voice like velvet. When he sings harmonies on the Wild West-flavoured 'Wanted Dead Or Alive', he sounds a better singer than Jon.

Tico is Bon Jovi's powerhouse, puffing away on a cigarette as he batters the drums. Alec looks great on stage – a lot more impressive than when I first saw him at the airport. And Dave Bryan does his best to make playing keyboards look cool. Dave is a Jewish boy who has changed his surname from Rashbaum to Bryan. This, he tells me, is more rock 'n' roll. It must be working, because Mr Bryan disappears with the two sisters from London after the show.

The next day's performance at Ipswich Gaumont is even better – and the after-show activities are even wilder. The band's hotel is small and set in peaceful countryside two miles from the town centre. The band and entourage are booked into a group of five cottages set apart from the main hotel building. Each cottage has two bedrooms and sleeps four. This is perfect for the kind of party we have in mind.

We return to the hotel with the two sisters from Bradford and another six girls picked up at tonight's gig. Everybody squeezes into one of the cottages. Unknown to the girls, the bathroom in this cottage is overlooked by a skylight, where one of the road crew is positioned with a video camera.

In one of the bedrooms, a CD player is rigged up to two huge speakers. The Rolling Stones' album *Sticky Fingers* plays at deafening volume. Several cases of beer have been brought from the venue, the remnants of the band's backstage rider. One of the roadies opens the bottles with his teeth, the beer bubbling up and soaking the red carpet. On one of the beds, Richie is slowly undressing a young brunette.

In a break between songs on the Stones CD, I hear frantic knocking at the door. The girl with Richie pulls the bed covers up to cover her breasts as I open the door to reveal a hotel porter with a room service trolley. The porter is a fresh-faced kid of eighteen, podgy, rosy-cheeked, his sandy-coloured hair neatly combed, wearing a striped short-sleeved shirt and blue tie. Pinned to the shirt is a gold staff identity card bearing his name, Johnny.

This kid cannot believe what he is seeing.

'Johnny!' Richie yells. 'A large Jack Daniel's, my friend!'

Johnny's round face glows pink as he wheels the trolley into the room. He screws the top off a bottle of Jack Daniel's, pours a generous measure into a glass and hands it to Richie. His hand is shaking as he tries to avoid making eye contact with the half-naked girl on the bed.

I direct Johnny to a corner of the room where, gingerly, he loads a low table with the contents of the trolley; bottles of bourbon and vodka, two large buckets of ice, chilled glasses and platters of burgers and fries covered with silver domed lids. I slip a ten-pound note into his sweaty palm and he scurries from the room.

The guys grab mouthfuls of fries and pour shots of vodka as Richie takes the brunette by the hand and leads her off to the bathroom for her home-movie debut. Within fifteen minutes, Johnny is summoned once more. This time he arrives, pale and sweating at the brow, with a tray laden with two more bottles of Jack Daniel's, a bottle of vodka and a large cucumber.

Richie emerges from the bathroom, zipping up his fly. He looks at the cucumber. 'We ordered zucchini!' he cackles. Johnny looks bemused. I decide to help him out. 'A zucchini's a courgette. But this will do,' I say, patting him on the shoulder. He stares at me mutely. 'We'll call you when we need you,' I add, ushering him from the room.

The guys gather round and urge the two sisters to strip naked and lie facing each other on the bed. The cucumber is handed to the blonde, who looks up at the smiling faces around her and giggles. She takes a sip from a glass of champagne and runs her hands over the cucumber. It is certainly a prize-winning specimen, some twelve inches in length and the best part of two inches thick. She does not require any further instructions. She moistens her vagina with her fingers and eases the cucumber inside. As the guys laugh and cheer, the brunette draws close to her sister, raises a leg and slides on to the other end of the cucumber.

A knock at the door diverts our attention from the girls. I open the door to see Johnny holding a bucket of ice. 'Come on in,' I say, leading him to the bed. Between the two squirming sisters, only one inch of the cucumber is now visible. Johnny is dumbstruck.

Richie slaps him playfully on the back. 'Wanna stick around, kid?'

Johnny trembles. 'Yes, please.'

'Hey, where's Alec?' Dave asks.

I look around the room but Alec is not here.

'Maybe he's in his room.'

'Well,' Dave says, 'let's call him.'

With this, he picks the heavy, old-fashioned red plastic phone from the bedside table and places it on the bed, where the cucumber lies glistening between the two girls. As Dave dials Alec's room, the blonde takes the receiver, spreads her legs wide and pushes the hearing end inside her. Dave calls a hush in the room as Alec's voice sounds on the phone.

'Hey, what's up?' His voice sounds like deep-sea diver Jacques Cousteau doing a documentary on coral reefs.

'Alec!' Dave says. 'Come back in here!'

'Who is this?' Jacques demands.

'It's Dave!' he shouts over our laughter.

'Okay,' says the voice from the deep, 'I'll be there in five minutes.'

Cackling, the blonde girl withdraws the receiver and flings it to the floor.

Johnny's smile freezes as Richie nudges him and declares, 'Now it's your turn.' He winks at the brunette, who pulls at Johnny's shirt and drags him on to the bed. The guys cheer as Johnny half-heartedly resists her. After a brief struggle, the girl has his trousers and underpants down by his ankles. As she goes to work on him, we decide to let Johnny enjoy this moment in peace and withdraw to play a round of poker around a table in a corner of the room. Johnny is heard whimpering as the cards are dealt. Bon Jovi poker games are tense, high-stakes affairs. Momentarily distracted by the pile of twenty-pound notes at the centre of the table, I look up to see the blonde sister straddling Johnny and giving him something to remember for the rest of his life. Johnny, his face contorted in ecstasy, is oblivious to the roadie standing beside the bed, camcorder rolling.

The poker game is in full flow as the blonde rises from the bed and Johnny hastily pulls up his trousers. 'I've got to get back to work,' he stutters. The guys offer high-fives as he walks to the door, fumbling with his belt and scurrying away. I wonder what he will tell his friends the next day. Also, I wonder what will happen when Johnny next receives an order for tea and cucumber sandwiches. Will he do the rock 'n' roll thing and use the pickled one we have left behind?

★

The Slippery When Wet tour is one long party. On average, I sleep for two or three hours each night. The buzz of the band's success keeps us going. Drugs are in steady supply – mostly cannabis, cocaine and, if cocaine is unavailable, speed – but this band's chief vices are booze and women. There is none of the drug-fuelled egotism and paranoia I have witnessed around bands in the past, and I notice that Jon in particular never touches the coke. This is Bon Jovi's first taste of the big time and they are loving every minute of it. There is no arrogance about them, only excitement. They are just happy to work hard and play hard. This kind of feeling does not last forever, but for now, this tour really is the ride of a lifetime.

The British leg finishes with a five-night stand at London's Hammersmith Odeon. Every up-and-coming rock band dreams of playing here. *Slippery When Wet* is at number one on the US chart for a fourth consecutive week, but in selling out five shows at the Hammersmith Odeon, Bon Jovi are confirming their status as a truly global success. On the final night in London, champagne bottles are popping in the dressing room when Doc McGhee beckons me into the adjacent production office where we can speak privately.

Doc's serious demeanour alarms me. I wonder if there has been too much partying on the tour. Perhaps Doc fears his young stars will burn out if they continue at this pace. I have been hired to work on this tour for six weeks before the band head back to America, but maybe this is goodbye. It's okay, I tell myself. I have other work lined up when this tour finishes.

Doc smiles broadly. 'Look, Michael, I know you have other commitments when we're done in Europe, but I've been speaking with the boys and we all want you to come to America with us for the rest of the tour.'

I feel relief, then a surge of excitement.

'This is a big record and it's going to get really crazy now,'

Doc says. 'I want someone with them who can make it all run smoothly. The boys won't take no for an answer,' he laughs. 'You're part of the family now.'

I answer without hesitation. 'Okay, I'll do it.'

Doc grips my hand and hugs me. At a little over five feet, his face squashes against my chest. We return to the dressing room where Jon grins and hands me a plastic cup filled with champagne.

'Thanks,' he says. He knew what my answer would be. In a little over two weeks, we have grown close and shared some heady times. We both know there are many more to come.

Sometimes we get more than we bargain for. The first date of the European tour is 28 November. The band's girlfriends, including Jon's childhood sweetheart Dorothea Hurley, have flown to Paris from America, but when we arrive at the Zenith Theatre, we are surprised to find in the dressing room the two sisters from London, now nicknamed the Zucchini Twins. The girls are in high spirits but Jon looks like he has seen a ghost. He quickly gives me the signal to remove the sisters from the room. When Dorothea and the others girls arrive at the venue, the Zucchini Twins are busy entertaining the road crew. When the girlfriends fly back home the following evening, there is a tangible sense of relief around the band.

Wherever we travel, women are throwing themselves at Jon. I have never seen a rock star with such a powerful sex appeal. From the teenage girls pressed against the stage at the shows to the experienced groupies who check into the same hotels as the band, they all want the same thing: Jon Bon Jovi. Richie is second favourite, but all of the guys in the band get as many women as they desire.

In America, the shows get bigger and the women more beautiful than ever. Some of these women are the kind who would hang around the headline band in the days when Bon Jovi were the opening act. Back then, they wouldn't have spoken a word to the guys in Bon Jovi, but now they're telling them how much they love the band, and how they'd love to come back to the hotel to party.

The band travel from state to state in a sleek silver tour bus. Aboard this bus, sleep is not an option. There is too much fun to be had with girls and gambling. The road miles disappear during marathon games of Blind Man Poker. More often than not, Jon and Alec win all the money. Jon will go to bed drunk and we will still be playing at six in the morning when Jon will rise again, rejoin the game and clean up. Nobody complains. We know who is boss.

Occasionally we will break a long interstate journey by stopping at the roadside to blast a few rounds from an assortment of handguns stored on the bus. With a bunch of drunken rock stars spraying bullets around in the small hours, it is a wonder that nobody ends up wounded or dead.

With each passing day, the band grows richer and more famous. I have never seen a road crew happier. There are so many girls trying to get a piece of the band, the crew guys are getting laid every night. This crew have worked on many of the biggest rock 'n' roll tours of the past few years, but they have never known a rock band attract so many beautiful girls, most of whom are willing to do anything for a chance of meeting their heroes.

On 31 January, we reach Texas, where the band play seven shows in nine days. With tired minds and bodies, they need a pick-me-up, so I arrange something special to follow the gig in Houston, Texas, on 7 February. The local record company executive is a good friend of the band and suggests the Gold Star Club, reportedly the best strip bar in the state. Most of the club's dancing girls had been at the previous night's show and are only too happy to stage a performance of their own for the band. The whole of the upstairs bar is reserved for the Bon Jovi party from ten till four in the morning. At two, Jon has sunk four bottles of wine and is slouched in a chair, beaming, as twenty girls clad only in G-strings form a circle around him, waggling their arses and rubbing their silicone-boosted breasts.

The girls charge twenty-five dollars for each dance. After six hours, the bill for the girls and the band's drinks totals $23,000. The record company guy is picking up the tab. He nearly faints when he sees the bill.

At the end of the night, ten of the girls throw on their coats and return with us to the hotel, where the manager receives repeated complaints from hotel guests about the noise emanating from room 1207, occupied by a Mr J. I. Case. Wherever the band travels, the name of Justin Case always appears on the list of hotel guests included in the Bon Jovi entourage. On this list, the band members use pseudonyms to protect their anonymity. Mr Lucky Luciano is Jon, Mr Don Key Dick is Richie, Mr R. Ricardo is Tico, Lema Moon is Dave and Lord Such is Alec.

Nominally a bus driver, Justin Case does not actually exist. His room is used when one of the guys wishes to spend the night with a girl without fear of being interrupted by an unexpected call from a girlfriend back home. This extra room is always available – just in case. Over the course of the tour, Mr Case's reservations amount to a small fortune, but it is money well spent.

Richie is nicknamed Don Key Dick for good reason. The guy has a cock like a baby's arm. Girls keep coming back for more time after time. There is an unwritten code around Bon Jovi: the guys always ask a girl if she has met Richie. If she has, they move on to the next girl. Despite Richie's reputation, it is Dave Bryan who gets laid the most. This guy could bed ten women in a single day. Before the show in Detroit, he has five. After the first two, he emerges bleary-eyed from his hotel room and tells me he is worn out. I remind him that there are three more girls waiting in Mr Case's room. When he protests, I suggest that Led

Zeppelin would never refuse, and like a true rock star, he duly obliges.

From Detroit, we travel to Quebec, Canada. One hour before we reach the border checkpoint, I make a thorough search of the bus. Grudgingly, a couple of the guys give up the bags of weed they have hidden in their bunks. I order the bus driver to pull in at the side of the freeway and toss the drugs over a wire fence into a farmer's field. When travelling with a rock band, you never take drugs over a border.

In Quebec, snow lies thick on the streets. As the bus draws up at the hotel, a couple of deer amble through the car park. I suspect we have a quiet night ahead, but on entering the lobby we are greeted by three women – a mother of forty and her two pretty teenage daughters. The mother, a slender beauty resembling Jane Fonda, informs me with a smile and not a trace of embarrassment that she and her daughters have been sent here courtesy of a friend of Doc's. 'A present,' she says.

I walk the girls to the reception desk and tell the clerk, 'These ladies are with Mr Case in the Bon Jovi party. They'd like to go and freshen up in the room.'

'Certainly, sir.'

Dealing with the constant stream of girls is easy enough. If one of the guys in the band likes the look of a girl in the audience, I make sure they get a pass for the after-show party. And if the guys want to get rid of a girl, I invent an excuse to get the band out of the room and send her on her way with the minimum of fuss.

Drug dealers are a different proposition. Dealers are desperate to get close to a big rock band, not only to sell drugs but also because they love to hang out with stars. Whether we are backstage or in a club, I can spot a dealer immediately. Their body language gives them away – a predatory glint in their eye, or an occasional cocaine twitch. It is my job to make sure that the dealers do not make contact with the band.

The safe way to score drugs is via overnight courier delivery. For the best part of a decade, a travel agency in New York has maintained a lucrative sideline. The order is made in code – two tickets to New York, eight tickets to LA, and so on. The drugs are delivered to a hotel, where the package is addressed to a fictitious name. It is a clean and simple process, and one that cuts out the small-time local dealers.

Groupies and drug dealers are the flies and ticks of rock 'n' roll, but when you are the biggest band in America, everyone wants a piece of you. For Bon Jovi this means music industry faces at every show, press interviews and photos, meet-and-greet sessions with fans. On average, the band are playing five gigs each week and travelling on a tour bus for three to six hundred miles per night. The tour is getting longer and longer. Every date is selling out, so multiple nights are booked in key cities. The band have christened it The Tour Without End, and despite the good time everyone is having, that is certainly what it has begun to feel like.

After sixty shows, and with another hundred scheduled, the band are in danger of burning out, but Doc has the answer: a black Gulfstream GII jet, the Bon Jovi logo painted in large letters on the fuselage. For the remainder of the tour, the band travels in style. We set up base in a key city and fly to other cities in surrounding states. Once the show is finished, the band are delivered by limousine to an airstrip, where the GII is ready to take them back to their hotel in the key city.

The plane is staffed by two pilots and a stewardess and seats ten, the first two seats facing forwards, then two blocks of four facing over small tables. At the far end of the cabin is a toilet, kitchen and bar flanked by two long sofas. The interior is grey, the upholstery black leather. On boarding, our drinks are already placed by our seats: a glass of red wine for Jon, a large gin and tonic for me. Food is delivered from the best local restaurants – Italian, Chinese, Indian – and served mid-flight. Only a few months ago the band were grabbing every sandwich from the backstage deli tray, every bottle of beer from the ice chest, and devouring it all on the bus. Now they are living like genuine rock royalty.

When you see your band's name on the side of a plane, you know you have really made it and are making serious money. Bon Jovi are the number one act in America. Jon's face is on the cover of magazines on every street corner. Every time I switch on the radio, I hear a Bon Jovi song.

Every kid who joins a band dreams of being a superstar, but only one in a million turn that dream into reality. Jon Bon Jovi's dream – to be the biggest rock star in the world – is coming true.

13

In the line of fire

The problem with being the biggest rock 'n' roll star in the world is that for every million people who love you, there are another million who would love to throw rocks at you. Also, there are a few that would like to kill you.

On 27 March 1987, I receive word of a death threat to Jon Bon Jovi. As Jon's personal security guard, I must protect him at all cost. Therefore a threat to Jon's life is a threat to mine: if I have to take a bullet for Jon, that is what I am paid for.

The Slippery When Wet tour has reached Pittsburgh, Pennsylvania, the heart of America's steel industry. We fly into the city in the early afternoon from nearby Philadelphia, where we are based for one week at a five-star hotel. Bon Jovi's GII jet lands at a small airfield where limousines whisk the band to the Civic Arena, a cavernous sports hall much the same as every other venue on this leg of the tour. On arrival, I am summoned to the arena manager's office while the band head off to the stage for the sound check. The manager is in his forties and dressed like a car salesman. His cordial smile is brief. 'The chief of police called me earlier,' he says gravely. 'We have a major problem.'

He gestures for me to sit in a chair facing his desk and slides a fax sheet across the desktop. The Pennsylvania driver's licence of a man in his twenties is photocopied on the sheet. The man is thin in the face, with dark, shoulder-length hair. I see hundreds of guys like this in the audience every night.

'Is he our problem?' I ask.

'Yes.'

He dials the police department and briskly dispenses with the formalities before handing the receiver to me. The chief of police explains the situation. A young woman called 911 last night after a violent argument with her boyfriend. She is a Bon Jovi fan, and they had argued because she has posters of Jon all over her apartment. In a drunken rage, her boyfriend ripped the posters off the walls, struck her several times and vowed to shoot Jon Bon Jovi at tonight's show.

Jealous boyfriends are not a new problem for us. Many women think nothing of cheating on their boyfriends or husbands if it means spending the night with a rock star. At every Bon Jovi gig, backstage passes are distributed to the prettiest girls, a routine known to those crew members who hand them out as The Walk Of Shame. When the girls are led backstage at the end of the show, their partners are left to wait in the parking lot or go home. Some of the guys kick up a fuss, but there is little that they can do. Nobody can get past the security staff to reach the backstage area without official passes, and I am always present to ensure that the band members are adequately guarded at their hotels.

However, when a jealous boyfriend is known to possess firearms and has a history of violent behaviour and petty crime, as is the case here in Pittsburgh, his threat is taken extremely seriously. The police chief deploys additional officers to patrol the area outside the venue, while I co-ordinate extra security measures within the building. I inform Doc McGhee, the band's road crew, and the venue's own security staff: everyone, in fact, other than Jon and the band. If a rock star were told every time a threat was made to their life, they would end up a virtual recluse, afraid to perform in public.

Security is tightened on every entrance, and every person entering the building is subjected to a full body search. I select twelve of the venue's regular security guards as extra protection for Jon. When he is in the dressing room, they stand guard near the door. When the band is on stage, they will act as a cordon between Jon and the audience.

The guy has taken his girlfriend's two tickets for the show. We know the seat numbers, and have three men positioned near these seats, ready to grab him. At eight-thirty – fifteen minutes before the band are due on stage – a senior police officer pulls me to one side and tells me there has been no sign of the gunman. I make a final check on the crew and security staff. My orders are simple: 'You must stay focused at all times, and nobody – nobody – gets on that stage.'

As I walk to the dressing room to collect the band, I know we have done every possible thing to keep Jon safe, but I have worked in this business long enough to understand that you can never be one hundred per cent certain. Knowing that if all else fails, I must run on to that stage and act as a human shield for Jon, I say a silent prayer and open the dressing room door.

The show is among the best the band has played on this tour, but for me, the minutes pass like hours. Every time Jon stands alone at the edge of the stage, my heart is in my mouth. Something is thrown at Jon: he catches it, a rolled-up Pittsburgh Steelers football shirt, and I let out a nervous laugh. Each flash of a camera sends a shiver through me. The pyrotechnics explosions at the end of the performance ring in my head like gunshots.

After ninety minutes, I have scanned every face in the first few rows hundred of times: I know each and every one of them. As the band link arms and take their bows, the house lights illuminate the entire arena. I stare at the mass of smiling faces, people cheering and applauding. It is the gunman's last chance ...

And then it is over. I run on to the stage, throwing a towel across Jon's shoulders and holding him tight to me, shielding him, and almost lifting him off his feet as we rush off the stage.

★

I leave the band in the dressing room swigging champagne, and find the commanding police officer in the adjacent production room. He shares my relief, but has some bad news.

'There's two feet of snow outside,' he says. 'You won't be leaving Pittsburgh tonight.'

'We have to,' I reply bluntly. 'We're not staying here while that guy is on the loose.'

I contact the pilot at the airfield. The runway is iced over and he has been advised not to take off.

'This is an emergency,' I tell him. 'Can you get us out of here?'

He says he can. The police chief orders an escort of six squad cars to deliver us quickly and safely to the airfield. Two limousines are waiting for us in the load-out bay at the rear of the building. As the limousines reach the top of the ramp leading out to the back lot, Jon sees the flashing red lights of the police cars and asks me what is happening.

'They're just making sure that we catch our flight on time.'

'Okay,' he says, easing back in his seat.

At the airfield, we drive across a soft carpet of snow to the clear tarmac, where engineers are clearing ice from the wings of the GII. Jon and the other guys are not unduly worried: they are all drunk on champagne, and a pair of pretty girls are entertaining them as the engineers finish defrosting the wings and we are cleared for take-off.

As the plane taxis to the runway, I find myself muttering another little prayer. I glance to my left, where Jon is slumped, half-asleep, as if only the seatbelt is holding him up. Oh well, I think to myself; you've got to die sometime, and if it has to be now, I might as well go with the biggest rock star in the world.

The engines roar and the plane races away. I feel the wheels skidding beneath us, my knuckles whiten as I grip the armrests, but quickly the plane rises. Through tiny crackles of ice on the window, I see the lights of the city glowing yellow and orange, a thousand feet below. Thank you, Pittsburgh, and good night.

August 1987 sees Bon Jovi acclaimed as superstars on both sides of the Atlantic. On 22 August they return to Britain to headline the Monsters Of Rock festival at Castle Donington before an audience of eighty thousand. Staged at a motor racing circuit in Leicestershire, this is the biggest annual rock event in the UK. But before then, they play eight major arena shows in their home state of New Jersey and in neighbouring New York State. All 130,000 tickets for these shows are sold within hours.

1 August is the first date of three at New York City's Madison Square Garden, the most prestigious stage in the finest city in the world, and the venue for many legendary performances and events. The greatest names in popular music have played at the Garden: Elvis Presley, the Rolling Stones, Frank Sinatra, John Lennon, Led Zeppelin, The Who, Bob Dylan, Stevie Wonder, Elton John, David Bowie, Bob Marley & The Wailers, Pink Floyd.

Bon Jovi have played here before, but as relative unknowns when they opened for Kiss in the early eighties. Now they are returning as all-conquering local heroes, joining the new elite of superstar acts that have graduated to the Garden's stage: U2, Prince, Madonna, Van Halen, Def Leppard. In 1978, the year that Jon Bon Jovi became a teenager, Bruce Springsteen, New Jersey's greatest rock 'n' roll hero, performed on the Madison Square Garden stage for the first time. Now the pupil is following in the master's footsteps. As he sits in a dressing room backstage, Jon wonders aloud if The Boss also used this room before his first night at the Garden, or if Muhammad Ali waited here in the moments before he walked out to face his old foe Smokin' Joe Frazier back in 1971.

This is a special night for everyone connected with Bon Jovi. Thirty minutes before the band take to the stage before an audience of 20,000, they greet their families and friends in a reception room. At one end of the room stands a bar and a hotdog stall, where a man in a red and white striped apron and white hat grills Italian sausage and onions under a sign reading, 'Doc's Hotdogs'.

Doc McGhee makes a brief speech congratulating his boys on their first number one album, which is now certified four times platinum. He then presents to each band member a silver pendant shaped like the Superman logo but with a double 'S' taken from the tyre-track design of the Slippery When Wet cover artwork. Each pendant is inset with fifty tiny diamonds representing the individual states of America. As the families and friends applaud, Jon turns to me with a sixth pendant in his palm, and places it around my neck. I am, he says, officially a member of Bon Jovi's 'Jersey Syndicate'. I feel a lump in my throat as I thank him.

After the show, hundreds of people are waiting backstage to meet Jon. The glitterati of the New York entertainment industry are gathered to pay their respects to rock's brightest young star. Record company people are hovering. The band is invited to dozens of parties, including one at the Hard Rock Café.

In the dressing room, Jon has just showered. I tell him about the crowd waiting for him along the hall.

'I want to be on my own for an hour,' he says with a shrug. 'Can we just go out and get a beer?'

I tell him I will have a limousine ready in a few minutes.

'No,' he smiles. 'We'll walk.'

I think about saying no. After the threat to Jon's life in Pittsburgh, I have been wary of anyone who approaches him, and it was here on the streets of Manhattan, just a few blocks from the Garden, that John Lennon was shot dead less than seven years ago. But there is also the issue of Jon's sanity. If a rock star is cut off from ordinary people and becomes a recluse, as happened to Elvis Presley, they can lose their grip, their humanity, and in Jon's case, the common touch that has made his songs so popular all over the world. Ultimately, no one is going to hurt Jon while I am at his side.

'What do you fancy doing?' he asks.

I tell him the salt beef sandwiches at Carnegie's deli are good.

'Okay!' he smiles. 'Get me out of here!'

Jon ties his hair back and pulls on a baseball cap, and we sneak along a corridor unnoticed. An elevator takes us down four floors and a fire exit leads us out to the street next to Penn Street station. We walk quickly for two blocks and get a table at the back of the deli.

It is just past midnight. We order the salt beef sandwiches and two beers. As we talk I glance up at the mirror on the wall above Jon's head and see a guy coming towards us. He pauses when I turn to face him, and I immediately recognise him as Bill Medley from the Righteous Brothers. I had seen him earlier this evening at the show.

'Jon,' he says, 'I had to come over because my daughter is your biggest fan.'

Jon laughs. 'Bill, sit down. Shit, man, you're a legend!'

'No,' he says, 'you're the legend – what a show!'

Jon signs a menu for Bill's daughter and they speak for a few minutes. Bill thanks him and goes away happy.

We linger over our beers for an hour. Jon reflects upon how far he has come in such a short time. Just a few years ago, Bon

Jovi were playing to a hundred people at the Stone Pony club in Asbury Park, New Jersey. Now they have headlined at Madison Square Garden, but Jon is already thinking bigger: on the next tour, he wants to play at Giants Stadium, a venue four times the size. This is typical of Jon. In the twelve months that we have spent together on the road, I have seen Jon develop into a global star, but still ambition burns within him. No matter how good he is and how successful the band, Jon always wants to be better; always.

'Enjoy the moment,' I say. He pauses with a bottle of beer at his lips and listens intently. 'This is the best tour I've ever done,' I tell him. 'But don't keep thinking about the future. Make the most of this time while it lasts. It can get bigger, but it might never get better than this.'

In September, the Slippery When Wet tour finishes after fourteen months and 160 shows, although both the band and the crew have come to believe that if Doc McGhee had his way, it truly would be The Tour Without End.

The final dates are in Japan. We arrive in Tokyo in the last week of September for five shows at the famed Budokan theatre. The Bon Jovi entourage fills the thirteenth floor of one of the city's most luxurious hotels. Above us, the penthouse suite is occupied by Michael Jackson, who has just begun a world tour in support of his new album *Bad* with a performance at the 38,000-capacity Korakuen stadium.

On the afternoon of Bon Jovi's first Budokan gig, Jon is summoned to Jackson's suite. I accompany him to the penthouse, where two huge security guards stand on duty at the door. Inside an opulent living room decorated in an elegant Japanese style, Jackson greets us with a soft hello and a weak handshake. I leave Jon talking to him in private and return to the entrance hall to speak with his security men.

Jon reappears after fifteen minutes, beaming excitedly. On the way back to his room, he tells me that Michael has accepted his invitation to join Bon Jovi on stage for their last night at the Budokan. He has agreed to sing one song with Jon at the end of the show. I am sceptical, since there is no written agreement, only a verbal acceptance in the course of a conversation. But during the next five days I liaise with Jackson's people in arranging extra security at the venue, plus a dressing room for Michael and two additional rooms for a small number of his 250-strong entourage.

When the night arrives, the band is one hour from going on stage when word is received from Jackson's camp that Michael will not be showing. I had tried to warn Jon that this might happen given Jackson's well-publicised eccentricity, but he and the other guys in the band are bitterly disappointed.

The after-show party is at the Lexington Queen, a rock club at the heart of Tokyo's Roppongi district, where many Western tourists socialise. Richie Sambora invites a group of high-profile European models to drink sake with us in the roped-off VIP area. We return to the hotel at two, boisterous and still pissed off at Michael Jackson for letting us down at the last minute.

Congregated in the hotel bar, we elect to teach Jacko a lesson. A call is made to Jackson's personal trainer, who cares for the star's pet chimpanzee Bubbles when they are on tour. The guy is a Bon Jovi fan who attended the previous night's gig at the Budokan. When we call he is asleep, but as soon as we tell him that Jon wants to come up to his room to see Bubbles, he perks up and says, 'No problem'.

I lead a party of four to the room. Once inside, I explain that the plan has changed: we are taking Bubbles to the bar to meet Jon. The guy panics and pleads with us not to do it, but as I am backing him into a corner, Tico is scooping Bubbles into his arms and scurrying from the room.

The guy calls after us as we follow Tico to the elevator. Calmly, I turn to face him.

'Tell Michael if he wants to see Bubbles again, he can come to the bar and get him.'

In the bar, we place Bubbles in an armchair. He is a friendly little fellow and a star in his own right. Clad in a red and grey-striped romper suit, he accepts bananas from us, which we order with our drinks. For two hours, we are expecting a visit from Jacko's security staff, but nobody comes. Eventually, we come to the conclusion that Jackson's personal trainer is too scared to let anyone know that Bubbles has been abducted. So we are stuck with him: or to be specific, I am stuck with him. I take the chimp to my room and watch over him for three hours before returning him to the bodyguards outside Jackson's suite. They shake their heads in disbelief as I walk towards them with Bubbles waddling at my side, his hand in mine.

'Don't ask,' I say sleepily, patting my little friend on the head and walking quickly away before any questions can be asked. As I roll into bed, I laugh at the stupidity of our prank. Fourteen months on the road can drive anyone crazy.

At last, we are going home. I am longing to see my family again, but it is tough saying goodbye to the guys in the band, to my friends in the road crew, to Doc, and especially to Jon. I have never felt so close to someone I have worked with. We have shared so much, and next year we are going to do it all over again.

I have never had so many good times on the road with a band. It really is like a family on tour, with Doc as the father and Jon his favourite son. The band members are as close as brothers. Success and fame can ruin the relationships within a band, but these guys have not argued or fought with one another even though they have been living out of each other's pockets for more than a year.

They began this tour as rising stars and ended it as the biggest rock band in the world, and through it all they have stuck together as a family should. They have survived by adhering to Doc's two golden rules: always give one hundred per cent on stage, and never let the backstage madness get out of hand.

The tour's final gross is an astonishing $28.4 million. The band has broken attendance records in major arenas all over the world, and on top of the ticket price, fans have bought tour programmes and T-shirts by the truckload. One of the shirts – white, one size fits all, and featuring a full-length picture of Jon – would sell out as fast as we could get them out of the boxes. Jon hated the design when he first saw it, but this particular shirt made so much money, it became known as 'White Gold'. At numerous shows, the merchandise stalls were doing such good business that we delayed getting the band on stage until the stalls had cleared.

It is hard to believe that when this tour started, even though they had a number one album in America, the band were staying in cheap hotels and travelling in a tour bus. Now they are richer than they could ever have dreamed. Jon, certainly, is a millionaire. And he even made money off me during the tour. Not only did he beat me at poker countless times: whenever we spent a free evening at a bowling alley, we would all gamble and I would end up losing to Jon. Mostly, our bowling nights coincided with visits from the band's girlfriends. Partying was off limits, so we would dine out and then go bowling. We competed for a trophy, a big tin cup that Richie would drink brandy from if he won, which was often. One night in Atlanta, Georgia, Jon had already taken two hundred dollars off me when he challenged me to a final game: double or quits. I accepted the challenge and promptly lost. Emptying my wallet, I counted out $281.

'You're a hundred and nineteen bucks short,' Jon sniffed.

'Here,' I said, pulling off my shirt and handing it to him as the other guys looked on, laughing. 'You've taken everything else, so you might as well have the shirt off my back.'

Jon delights in reminding me of this as we sit drinking beer at a hotel in Shizuoka, Japan, before I fly back to London alone, and the band head home to New Jersey.

After two or three beers, I check my wristwatch and with a heavy sigh, I rise to leave. Embracing Jon, I feel like I am leaving one family for another.

'Well,' he smiles, 'we made it.'

I return to London physically and mentally exhausted. On a cold and grey October morning, a black taxi delivers me to the door of my home in Camden Town. I find my hands shaking as I turn the key in the lock. June runs to greet me and throws her arms around me. We stand there in the open doorway, holding on to each other for minutes on end, before she lets out a joyful laugh and leads me into the kitchen.

We drink tea while exchanging news. She tells me about the kids, how they are doing at school and how they are looking forward to getting home tonight and seeing their old man. My mother and father will be visiting us tomorrow. I begin to tell June about the tour, but I am so weary, my sentences trail off unfinished.

'Go to bed,' she says. 'We can talk later.'

I sleep for six hours. It is four in the afternoon when I wake, but my body clock is in another time zone altogether. I feel as if it is show time. I sit upright in bed, adrenaline coursing through me and overriding my fatigue.

This strange sensation is one I must get used to: coming off a long world tour is like coming off a drug. Sleep comes in fits and starts and unexpected bursts of nervous energy come like nicotine cravings. After fourteen months of hyperactivity – in which gigs, flights, hotels and parties pass in a blur – adjusting to a normal home life is a long process. In addition, I feel detached from life in Camden Town. It is almost as if I am getting to know my loved ones all over again. I have missed several family milestones – Joanne's eighteenth birthday, Mum and Dad's fortieth wedding anniversary, my own eighteenth wedding anniversary; not to mention my sons' school sports days, always a favourite of mine.

I am well aware that the job I do places a strain on the relationships I hold dearest, but I can't imagine doing anything else. The truth is it was never about the money. I love the life. The buzz is incredible. Touring is like a drug, you get addicted. Sometimes it could be tough and you couldn't wait to get home again, back to the welcoming heart of family life. But once you'd been home a while you'd get itchy feet; you begin to fret to be out on the road again. To give it up is unthinkable.

Sometimes I'd try to conceal how much I was looking forward to going; or I would tell June that a tour was only scheduled for six months, even though I knew that it was likely to be longer. But Bon Jovi are set to record a new album in the first quarter of 1988, and already I know I will be away for another year or more.

14

What's up, Doc?

On 25 April 1988, late at night, I receive a call from Jon Bon Jovi. He has bad news: Doc McGhee has been convicted on drug trafficking charges pertaining to the seizure of 40,000 pounds of marijuana by the United States Drug Enforcement Agency in North Carolina back in 1982. The timing of the conviction is significant, with American forces poised to invade Panama under the banner of President George Bush's 'war on drugs'. US press reports suggested a link between Doc's offences and the activities of Panamanian leader Manuel Antonio Noriega, whose influence in the smuggling of narcotics into the United States had previously been overlooked in return for assistance in co-ordinating America's covert action against the socialist regime of Nicaragua.

It is with a mixture of amazement and relief that Jon details Doc's punishment. He is sentenced to a five-year suspended

159

prison sentence, plus an extensive programme of community service and a fine of $15,000. Further indiscretions notwithstanding, he will remain a free man, able to continue managing Bon Jovi's affairs. It appears that, all things considered, Doc has got off lightly.

★

Bon Jovi release their fourth album, *New Jersey*, on 1 October. Within two weeks, it has topped both the UK and US charts. The 'Jersey Syndicate' tour begins in Dublin on Halloween. Every date on the European tour sold out months in advance. We are back in business.

With one or two exceptions, the Bon Jovi entourage remains unchanged, and everyone clicks smoothly back into the touring routine as if we had never stopped. Doc, too, is unchanged. Some men would have been humbled by a conviction for drug smuggling, but Doc is a tough character who has shrewdly turned the situation to his advantage. Having been ordered by the law courts to undertake community service duties, Doc has offered to set up a rock festival with an anti-drugs message. The chosen venue is Moscow, where Doc's star acts, including Bon Jovi and Mötley Crüe, will perform free of charge. All proceeds will help fund charities for victims of drug and alcohol abuse. The event is to be the biggest ever staged in the Soviet Union and will generate huge media interest, therefore guaranteeing a healthy increase in revenue for McGhee Entertainment Inc.

Small wonder that Doc is smiling happily as we fly from Helsinki to Moscow on 29 November to announce the date of the festival – in August of 1989 – and to launch a charm offensive on the Russian media. A press conference is conducted via interpreters with some difficulty, and then the fun begins. At a radio station's studio, vodka flows freely as members of local rock band Gorky Park join Bon Jovi in playing a selection of blues standards. Then we are treated to a midnight sleigh ride through the streets of Moscow. I sit beside Jon in the second of four horse-drawn sleighs. We are all drunk and I want to be close to Jon to ensure that he does not do anything stupid like jumping off the sleigh as it speeds along the snow: a broken limb would force the cancellation of the forthcoming British and American tours, and jeopardise my job. The ride is exhilarating and we pass around a flask of brandy to take the edge off the freezing air that is rushing into our faces and bringing tears to our eyes.

After the sleigh ride, the bar of the Intercontinental Hotel offers welcome warmth, and we continue drinking vodka throughout the small hours and into the dawn. Sometime after seven, our Russian guide suggests a tour of the Kremlin. He leads Jon, Doc and me out into Red Square. A fresh layer of snow has fallen and the temperature is approaching twenty degrees below freezing. We trudge unsteadily across the square. I squint as pale sunshine reflects off the snow. Jon, a true rock star, is wearing sunglasses beneath a black stetson, and is wrapped in a pale brown sheepskin coat.

At the entrance to the Kremlin, two soldiers stand guard, dwarfed by the building's tall, dark walls. Our guide approaches the soldiers and attempts to persuade them to admit the world famous rock star Jon Bon Jovi, but he is as drunk as we are, and the soldiers wave him away. We are too cold to protest, and return to the hotel to get a little sleep before our flight leaves for Glasgow and another sell-out show.

March 1989 brings Bon Jovi back home to America's East Coast. While playing shows in New York State, New Jersey, Pennsylvania and Connecticut, the band is based in New York City at the Plaza Hotel and makes round trips by plane to perform in the surrounding cities.

On 9 March, the band enjoys a night off before the following evening's show at Nassau Coliseum in Uniondale, New Jersey. Jon has been invited to dine at one of the oldest and finest Italian restaurants in New York City, and is filled with nervous excitement as he and his girlfriend Dorothea join several other guests and me in the Plaza's lobby. We drive by limousine to Little Italy, the heart of the city's Italian community. The limousine pulls up at the kerbside between a gleaming red Ferrari and another black limousine outside the restaurant. There is no sign above the door. A popular haunt for mobsters since the 1930s, this place is one of the city's best kept secrets.

Jon straightens his black dinner jacket before stepping from the limousine, affecting cool, but his smile is stiff, betraying his nerves. Dorothea follows, elegant in a long black coat, her dark hair drawn back in a pleat. Three of the couple's friends are with us, plus a friend of mine, Paul Spires, a 71-year-old multi-millionaire who owns half of Palm Springs.

Inside the restaurant, it is like a scene from *The Godfather*. There are twelve tables with red and white checked tablecloths and a softly lit bar at one end of the room. As our party is welcomed and led to a table, four guys seated in one corner of the room nod to us. Sharply dressed and with Mediterranean complexions, these guys look like they belong here.

Although our reservation is for seven people, I count eight chairs at the table. As I gesture to a waiter to remove the extra chair, the restaurant's owner, Vinnie, introduces himself and sits with us. Vinnie looks like a young Al Pacino. 'You guys are going to have a good time tonight,' he smiles.

No menus are offered. Vinnie simply tells us what his wife is cooking in the kitchen downstairs. 'Five dishes,' he says. 'I'm going to bring you some of each. You're gonna have some chicken and there's a great linguini sauce tonight, perfect.'

Two bottles of vintage red wine arrive at our table courtesy of the four guys over in the corner and we all give a little nod of thanks.

During the course of the evening the bottles keep coming – at least two bottles sent over from each of the twelve tables. By midnight, Jon announces that we are, indisputably, not white toast. We are Italian. And we are very drunk.

Once the meal is finished, the centre of the room is cleared of tables and chairs, the jukebox is turned on and we dance the night away to classic songs by Frank Sinatra, Tony Bennett, the Ronettes, Marvin Gaye, Smokey Robinson. The other diners are up and dancing with us. It is an incredible night. When we leave at two, stumbling into the limousine, Jon has almost lost the power of speech.

We return to the bar of the Plaza Hotel and one of our guests is sick on the carpet. Silently, I thank God it didn't happen in the restaurant. Paul Spires is reeling drunk, having barely touched alcohol since he was a teenager. He tells me he needs to get back to his hotel. I lead him by the arm out to the street, hail a passing cab and help him on to the back seat. Handing a twenty-dollar bill to the cab driver, I ask him to make sure that Paul gets inside his hotel.

The bar is now closing, but Jon is not done. He wants to go to Central Park. There are four of us, Jon, Dorothea, myself, and Margaret, Jon's personal assistant. Jon asks a waiter to bring us eight bottles of wine, which we slip into our coat pockets. Jon decides we should all go ice-skating, as you do when blind drunk at three in the morning.

The park is a dangerous place to be at night; muggings and murders are commonplace, but we are all too far gone to care. The most famous rock star on the planet is walking through Central Park at night, drunker than the winos slumped on the park benches, and the only protection he has is me. And I am drunker than he is.

A winding path lit by tall lamps brings us to Wollman Ice Rink. The gates are locked, so we climb up over the fence, taking care not to drop the wine bottles. We slip and slide on the ice, laughing and tumbling over. Suddenly, flashlights are shone in our faces, leaving us dazed and blinking.

'Don't move, we're the police!'

Peering out into the gloom, I can see ten or fifteen policemen at the fence. We are surrounded.

'Jon,' I say. 'For God's sake – we're in trouble. Tell them who we are.'

It is at this moment that I regret telling Jon stories of British gangsters Ronnie and Reggie Kray, who ruled by fear in the East End of London during the 1960s. On this tour, Jon and I have been checking into hotels as Ronnie and Reggie. Now is not the time for jokes.

'We're Reggie and Ronnie Kray,' Jon shouts, 'and we own this goddamn place!'

One of the cops, a tall, powerfully built black guy, stares at us with contempt. This guy really wants our asses.

I hiss at Jon, 'Calm down and get us out of this!'

Jon shrugs and turns to the black cop. 'Officer, I'm Jon Bon Jovi and I'm the biggest rock star in America!'

The cop laughs, 'And I'm fucking Martin Luther King!'

As we are led off the ice, Jon and Dorothea are handcuffed.

'Excuse me sir,' I protest. 'I'm this man's bodyguard, and where he goes, I go.'

'Oh,' he smiles, 'don't worry about that, my friend!'

They throw us in the back of two squad cars and drive us to Central Park's very own police station, reputedly the smallest in America. As he drives, Martin Luther King is laughing his head off. 'Jon Bon Jovi? Kiss my ass!'

At the station there is one female officer on the front desk. As we are marched to the desk, she looks up from her typing and shouts, 'Oh my God – it's Jon Bon Jovi!'

Now, perhaps, they will believe us. We are instructed to sit on a row of red plastic chairs beside the desk. Under harsh strip-lights, I am slowly sobering up and coming to terms with the predicament we are in. I must get Jon out of here, but at this time of night, who can I call? Who will get out of bed and come to the station to post bail for us?

I decide on Paul Spires. He is asleep when my call is put through to his hotel room. And he is still drunk.

'Paul, you've got to come down here right away, and bring some ID.'

'Okay,' he says, half-heartedly.

Thirty minutes pass. Jon produces a bottle of wine from his coat, but I tell him it would be best if he did not drink it here. Instead, I get four cups of weak coffee from a vending machine. I suspect that Paul Spires has fallen asleep again, and ask if I can make another call.

'No,' an officer grunts. 'You only get one call. You'll have to go to the cells.'

'You're kidding!' Jon protests. 'I've got a show to do tomorrow night!' But there is no bargaining with New York City cops, not even if you are a world famous rock star. I look at Jon and shake my head: there is nothing that I can do. We are led along a narrow corridor and down a flight of concrete steps to a heavy, barred iron door. The officer unlocks the door, waves us through and locks it behind us. Jon and I are placed in the first empty cell, Dorothea and Margaret in the second. Each cell is sparsely furnished with a steel wash basin and two metal-framed beds with thin mattresses and a single sheet and blanket. I remove my boots and jacket but keep the rest of my clothes on as I ease myself into the cold bed.

'Don't worry,' I say to Jon. 'We'll be out of here in an hour.'

Exhausted, I am soon asleep. At eight, the grille in the cell door is snapped open. 'Someone's come to get you out,' a policeman says, unlocking the door.

Jon and Dorothea huddle together, hung over and half-asleep, as we are taken upstairs. Paul Spires is waiting for us, bleary-eyed, his grey hair sticking upwards as if he has put his finger in an electrical socket. 'Sorry, Michael,' he groans. 'I thought I was dreaming when you called me.' It wasn't until he woke up, he explains, and heard on the early morning news that Jon Bon Jovi had been arrested in Central Park that he realised it was true.

As Paul fills out the forms to post bail for the four of us, the female officer on the front desk watches a sheet of paper curling from the fax machine beside her.

'Listen to this,' she says. 'You're never gonna believe it.' The fax is a hand-written note from Donald Trump, the Wall Street mogul who also owns Wollman Ice Rink. 'If you arrest Jon Bon Jovi for breaking into my property,' the message reads, 'my daughter will never speak to me again.' Nevertheless, we are each charged with trespassing and fined $300. The morning air is cold as we file out of the station and into a waiting limousine. As we head back to the hotel, Paul rubs his tired eyes and utters a disbelieving laugh. 'What are you guys doing to me? You've got me drunk for the first time in fifty years and you end up in a police station! When I left, you said you were going to bed!'

'I'll explain everything later,' I reply with a shrug.

Jon sits opposite me, his face half-buried in the upturned collar of his coat, his eyes glaring.

'You prick!' he snarls. 'They arrested me! I'm a wanted felon!'

'Oh well,' I sigh. 'At least you're not white toast.'

In the last week of March, the tour reaches the heartland of the United States. We have a night off in Indianapolis on 27 March, so I arrange for the band to dine at St Almo's, an old and celebrated restaurant that has entertained numerous American presidents during its lengthy history. I visit St Almo's every time I am in the city. I know the manager and gave him tickets and passes for Bon Jovi's show at the city's Market Square Arena the previous night.

St Almos is not in the most fashionable area of town, but the atmosphere here is amazing. The décor is evocative of the Prohibition era, with one long bar staffed by two barmen in white aprons and bow-ties. The corridor leading to the dining area is panelled in dark wood and lined with pictures of all the presidents who have enjoyed St Almo's hospitality. It feels like this place has been here forever.

The manager has reserved a private dining room for the Bon Jovi party. With wood panelling on the walls and door, the room is like a cocoon. The table seats twelve. As we order wine, two seats at the table remain empty. Richie is due to arrive with the new woman in his life – the movie star and music icon Cher. None of us has met her before. As the waiter pours the wine, I notice that everyone is dressed a little smarter than usual. Nobody is saying as much, but this is a special night.

When Richie and Cher enter the room, I catch my breath. Cher is extraordinarily beautiful, with large, dark, almond-shaped eyes, smooth skin and long, glossy curls. She also has an aura about her, the like of which I have not experienced since meeting Elvis Presley. A beaming Richie introduces her to everyone. I gently offer my hand.

'Are you the straight one?' she asks. For a second I am speechless. Everybody else is laughing. I realise that Richie must have told her that Jon and I use the names of Ronnie and Reggie Kray when checking into hotels. I return her smile. 'Call me Reg,' I say.

We linger over the meal for hours. Cher is charming company, witty, with a very British sense of irony. She can also mix it with the boys, and no subject is taboo.

When Richie and Cher leave us, the party moves next door to the Canterbury Hotel, favoured by rock 'n' roll bands for many years. Twenty glamorous girls are waiting for the band in the hotel bar. These girls are serious groupies. Many of them have booked rooms at the hotel in the hope of bedding a rock star.

While I am ordering drinks at the bar, I meet the owner of the famous Indianapolis racing circuit. He tells me that girls like these have been coming to the Canterbury ever since the first Indy 500 automobile race. For this reason, the race drivers always leave their wives at home when they compete in the Indy.

I buy him a drink and listen to his tales of the great Indy races, and of the debauchery that goes on behind the scenes. It sounds a lot like the business I am in. He asks me about Bon Jovi and the other rock stars I have known and worked with. When I tell him about Elvis, I find myself thinking about Cher, and smiling. It isn't just that she's beautiful, poised and charming. She's more than a singer, an actress. She has that something extra, an indefinable quality that marks people out as special. She is a star.

15

Fairytale in New York

It is one o'clock in the morning in Kansas City. Jon Bon Jovi sits facing me in the lounge area of my hotel room, opening a bottle of fine Italian red wine. Two empty bottles are on the table between us. Earlier, we shared another two over dinner in an Italian restaurant. We are both very drunk. As he fumbles with the corkscrew, Jon sways to the music playing from a ghetto blaster: Prokofiev's *Romeo and Juliet*.

This is a typical night off for Jon. We are approximately halfway through the Jersey Syndicate tour, and wherever we are in the world, there is nothing that he likes more than a quiet dinner, followed by a couple of bottles of wine in his hotel room. We sit, just he and I, talking and listening to classical music or opera.

Tonight, however, is a little different.

'Reg,' he says, lighting a cigarette, 'I'm going to tell you something and you can't say a word to anyone else – not Doc, not Richie, nobody.'

'Sure,' I reply. 'What's up?'

'I'm getting married next week,' he smiles.

For a second or two, I sit back in my chair chuckling, before rising unsteadily to my feet to embrace him.

'Congratulations,' I say, clinking my glass against his.

'We've booked a chapel in Vegas,' he says. 'But remember, you can't tell anyone.'

I understand his need for secrecy. As rock 'n' roll's number one sex symbol, Jon Bon Jovi is a fantasy figure to millions of women, and he wants to keep that fantasy alive. To do otherwise could amount to career suicide. Many of the teenage girls who scream at Jon every night know that he has been dating Dorothea since the couple were at high school, but they might cool towards him if they knew he was married, and find another favourite band.

For this reason, Jon aims to keep the wedding out of the news. He and Dorothea will travel alone to Las Vegas ahead of Bon Jovi's show in the city on 24 April and get hitched at the Graceland Chapel.

'It'll be just the two of us,' he says. 'No family. We're saving that for later. If we were taking anybody else, you'd be the best man.'

I smile again. 'Just let me know if there's anything you need.'

Ten days later, the morning after Bon Jovi have played at Irvine Meadows in Los Angeles, I meet Jon and Dorothea in the lobby of the St James Club Hotel, an elegant art deco tower on Sunset Boulevard. We ride by limousine to the airport, where I escort them to the departure gate and wish them good luck. They walk off to the plane holding hands. I return to the St James Club to breakfast with Doc. He asks me what Jon is doing today and I tell him that he and Dorothea have gone shopping. It feels awkward lying to Doc, but my first loyalty is to Jon.

In the early evening, I am in my room when I receive a call from Jon. 'We did it, man,' he laughs.

He and Dorothea are waiting to greet me at the hotel's roof terrace bar, where we share a bottle of champagne under a starry sky. The air is cool, so we walk across the street to a restaurant fashioned from an old railway carriage. We eat hotdogs and drink bottled beer. 'Reg, you've got real class,' says Jon. Then I walk the couple back to their room.

I kiss Dorothea lightly on the cheek and whisper in her ear, 'Goodnight, Mrs Bon Jovi.'

'What are you smiling about?' Doc calls to me as I walk out to his table on the roof terrace.

'It's a secret.'

In the morning, Doc calls my room. 'So they got married?'

'Did he tell you?'

'No,' Doc snaps, 'I heard it on the fucking radio!'

'Oh well,' I laugh. 'That's showbiz!'

Eight days after the wedding, the band throws a surprise party for Jon. The guys were shocked when news of the wedding broke, but they understood his need for privacy. The party is their way of telling Jon that there are no hard feelings.

We are in Salt Lake City, Utah, where alcohol is prohibited by strict Mormon law. However, as any major rock band knows, Salt Lake City offers the best groupies in America: straight-laced, clean-living, well-bred and God-fearing Mormon girls who love nothing better than to screw a rock star. We hire the VIP lounge on the top floor of the Hyatt hotel. A mini casino with card tables and roulette wheels is set up for the entertainment of the band, crew, assorted friends and music industry players, and dozens of girls. During one game of poker, twenty thousands dollars sits at the centre of the table. I take a sip from a gin and tonic and look to one side of the room where two naked girls lie on a long leather sofa, performing cunnilingus on each other. A few feet behind them, one of the road crew is banging another girl, oblivious to the onlookers.

171

Jon observes this vision of Sodom and Gomorrah with a mixture of amusement and discomfort.

'Come on, Reg,' he says, rising from the poker table, 'let's go find someplace a little quieter.'

On 6 August 1989, Jon and Dorothea celebrate their wedding in a style befitting a rock star who, less than one month previously, had performed before a crowd of 100,000 at New Jersey's Giants Stadium. The venue for what the couple are calling their 'Post Elopement Extravaganza' is South Street Seaport in Manhattan. The top floor of this five-storey dockside building is covered by a high dome and encircled by a roof garden terrace offering spectacular views of the Statue of Liberty, the World Trade Center towers and the Hudson River.

After such a low-key wedding, Jon and Dorothea want to treat their families and friends to a special night. Money is no object: each bottle of pink champagne costs more than my entire wedding did twenty years ago.

To co-ordinate security, I hire ten former policemen I befriended when visiting New York with Led Zeppelin in the Seventies. With two hundred limousines arriving at the venue via a network of narrow streets that pass through the fish market, the cops' experience in keeping traffic flowing proves invaluable. They also make a complete sweep of the building, checking all exits and entrances, before the first guests arrive at six.

Within the hour, the roof terrace is filled with men and women in evening dress, drinking champagne cocktails and watching the sun set below the Manhattan skyline. The band members arrive separately, Richie without Cher, who is in Los Angeles rehearsing for an upcoming tour. I check with the maitre d' that all the family members are present before he invites the guests to enter the main hall under the dome, where long tables are arranged in lines parallel to the head table. When

Post-Elopement Extravaganza!

Sunday, August 6th, 1989

at seven in the evening

Bridgewaters

South Street Seaport

New York, New York

Dorothea and John

Semi-formal attire

Formal invitation to the most talked-about party in Manhattan ...

everyone is seated, I lead Jon and Dorothea into the room to cheers and applause.

Dorothea wears a classic white lace dress with a plunging neckline and long tassled sleeves, her dark hair flowing over her bare shoulders. Jon, ever the rock star, wears a jacket of turquoise silk over a white vest top, black jeans and cowboy boots. As I take my seat on the head table, there are tears in my eyes. They are two special people, childhood sweethearts who have been through so much together, good and bad. I feel as proud as if it was the wedding of one of my own sons. I am pleased, too, that Jon is pledging his future to Dorothea, a strong and beautiful woman who fell in love with him long before he was a rock 'n' roll star.

As I watch them talking and laughing together, I see them staying together for a long time, having children. Jon has always wanted kids and taken an interest in mine. During those nights on the road when we sit up all night drinking wine and talking about our lives, I have told him about my own family: how tough it was raising children with little or no money, and how every sacrifice you make for your family is worth making ten times over. I remember telling Jon, as we emptied a bottle of wine costing three hundred dollars, that the first thing that goes out of your supermarket trolley and back on to the shelf is the very thing we were drinking. I remember also the card that Jon enclosed in a case of wine he presented to me last Christmas: 'To Reg – just in case'.

After we have dined on seafood and pasta and toasted the couple with more champagne, the tables are cleared from the floor and Mink Deville, one of Jon's favourite bands, performs from a small stage. The group's singer, New Yorker Willy Deville, is dressed up like Elvis Presley and delivers a selection of Fifties rock 'n' roll standards with panache. Everyone in the room is singing and dancing, and there is wild cheering when Jon jumps up on the stage to duet with Willy on a couple of his favourite Elvis tunes.

Mink Deville bow out at a quarter to eleven in time for Jon and Dorothea to lead their guests out to the terrace for the evening's big surprise, one that I have arranged with the help of my friends from the New York Police Department. State law does not permit private vessels on the river at certain times, but a few strings have been pulled to allow a barge to pass the South Street Seaport at the designated hour. Once a team of waiters has recharged everyone's champagne glasses, a call is made to the captain of the barge and the night sky is lit up with fifty thousand dollars' worth of fireworks, explosions of red, gold, white and green. With the Statue of Liberty illuminated in the background, it is an amazing spectacle, and the perfect end to a wonderful night.

★

I wake the following afternoon to find an envelope tucked under the door of my room at the Plaza Hotel. Inside is a request to call Cher's management company in Los Angeles.

In the four months since I first met her in Indianapolis, Cher has visited Richie on several occasions while we have been on the road. At one of the shows, a gang of female fans, jealous of her relationship with Richie, hurled insults at Cher and threw chewing gum in her hair. Since then, I have made sure that she is well protected whenever she is with us, and in the time we have spent together at concert halls and hotels and aboard the band's jet, we have struck up a warm rapport and a solid friendship. On one occasion, when we sat backstage waiting for Jon and Richie to change out of their stage clothes, she asked if I would work for her when Bon Jovi finished touring. I was flattered, and replied that I would think about it.

The past two years have seen Cher's star rise to its highest since the early seventies. She has become one of Hollywood's leading actresses, appearing opposite Jack Nicholson in *The Witches Of Eastwick* and scoring two more huge box office hits

175

with *Moonstruck* and *Suspect*. Also, her music career is back on track. Her 1988 album, simply titled *Cher*, produced a top five US single in 'I Found Someone', and a second hit with 'We All Sleep Alone', a track co-written and co-produced by Jon and Richie. And her new album *Heart Of Stone* is already riding high in the American charts.

I dial the number in Los Angeles and speak to Bill Samuth, Cher's manager. He makes a formal offer to employ me as Cher's personal bodyguard, beginning in the autumn of 1990. The terms are generous. I tell him I will call him back when the Bon Jovi tour is finished. I am so close to Jon and the band, it feels almost disloyal to think about working with anyone else. But I know that in this business things can change in the blink of an eye, and I guess it makes sense to keep my options open.

16

From Russia with love

From an airstrip in Newark, New Jersey, a Boeing 747 climbs up to 30,000 feet en route to Russia and the Moscow Peace Festival. The plane carries six of the biggest acts in rock 'n' roll – Bon Jovi, Ozzy Osbourne, The Scorpions, Mötley Crüe, Cinderella and Skid Row – plus members of each band's road crew and assorted record company representatives, management staff and a small number of American diplomats. At least half of the people on board, including a pair of diplomats, are wearing custom-issue black leather jackets, embroidered with the festival logo: a metallic American eagle over the Russian hammer and sickle and the CND peace symbol incorporating Russian, American, British and German flags.

The festival has been organised by Doc McGhee as part of a

deal he struck with law enforcement officers following his conviction for drug trafficking offences in April 1988. It is to be one of the largest live music events ever staged, with an audience of a quarter of a million people over two days. All money raised will aid the Make A Difference Foundation, described in the publicity releases as 'a non-profit organisation dedicated to combating drug and alcohol abuse among the youth via a pro-responsibility message.'

Publicly, officially, the Moscow Peace Festival is a mission of salvation. In press interviews leading up to the event, the artists express their desire to help save young lives and bring rock music to a nation starved of Western pop culture. Privately, rivalries between the bands are intense. Mötley Crüe were once Doc's golden boys and the biggest rock band in America, roles now assumed by Bon Jovi. For guys as arrogant as Mötley Crüe, being upstaged by former apprentices is a bitter pill to swallow. The tension between Bon Jovi and Skid Row is even greater. In 1987, Jon Bon Jovi received a Skid Row demo tape from the band's guitarist Dave 'Snake' Sabo, a childhood friend from Sayreville, New Jersey. Jon informed Doc McGhee that the band had potential. Doc's younger brother Scott became Skid Row's manager, and in return for songwriting advice, Jon signed them to a publishing deal with his and Richie Sambora's company New Jersey Underground Music. In their naivety, Skid Row agreed to a deal that ceded a large proportion of their future earnings to this company. Skid Row have now sold millions of records but have yet to see most of the money.

The remaining three acts have no axe to grind. Ozzy Osbourne is a friend of Doc's who has agreed to perform in Moscow as a favour to Doc. The Scorpions, Germany's most successful rock band, are old pros who have seen and done it all in a career that stretches back to the early seventies, and have recently signed to McGhee Entertainment. And Cinderella, a four-piece hard rock band from Philadelphia, are indebted to Jon Bon Jovi, who saw them performing in a club in their home town and persuaded Bon Jovi's record label to sign the young band. Cinderella have now sold a million records, but they know their place.

Within minutes of taking off, the party starts. The 'fasten your seat belts' signs are still illuminated, but Skid Row's hyper-active singer Sebastian Bach – a lean, rangy kid of twenty-one with straight blond hair down to his ass – is prowling the aisle and swigging from a bottle of vodka. The scene resembles a school outing as various rock stars and crew guys pass bottles over the seats, cracking jokes and slapping high-fives. For those who want it, mounds of cocaine are emptied on to tray tables from polythene bags. Using the sharp edges of credit cards, the coke is arranged into six-inch lines and snorted through hundred-dollar bills.

Ozzy is the grand old man of rock 'n' roll excess. He has been loaded for the best part of twenty years. Ozzy is idolised by the younger bands, who try to impress him by guzzling vodka as if it were water. They are like children vying for their father's attention.

The guys in Mötley Crüe are completely out of control. I have never known a band so despised by other bands and by people in the industry. Every band loves girls and drugs, but the Crüe are constantly trying to outdo everyone else. Most bands do drugs because they enjoy them. These guys do drugs because they think they have to. Mötley Crüe make a lot of money for Doc, but nobody I know of has any liking or respect for them.

Halfway into the eight-hour flight, I close my dry, tired eyes to sleep. Seconds later I wake with a jolt as members of Cinderella and The Scorpions strike up a medley of Beatles and Led Zeppelin songs, accompanied by acoustic guitars. Rubbing at my eyes, I see two of the diplomats edging past Sebastian Bach as he stands in the aisle, draining a bottle of Stolichnaya vodka. There is an expression of horror on the diplomats' faces.

Sebastian is still standing as the captain announces twenty minutes till landing, the cue for frantic activity from everyone who has not finished their drugs. Nobody contemplates testing the vigilance of Russian customs. As the plane descends, rattling as it encounters air turbulence, lines of coke are noisily snorted and joints are greedily sucked down to their bitter last.

This is some anti-drugs mission.

The first day of the festival, 12 August, is a huge success. The enormous concrete bowl of the Lenin Stadium, scene of the 1980 Olympic Games, fills with a capacity crowd of 140,000, but backstage there are problems. Throughout the day, I hear road-crew members complain that amplifiers and guitars have gone missing. In the catering hall, the staff – flown in from America – are bewildered as first food, and then an oven, disappears. A division of the Russian army is controlling security at the stadium. We suspect that the soldiers are stealing from us, but they are heavily armed and we feel powerless to protest.

Plus there is a bigger drama developing backstage. Mötley Crüe are unhappy with their lowly position on the bill and are arguing with Doc. On the previous night, Doc held a meeting in his hotel suite, where he gave an assurance to all six acts that there is to be no special treatment of any one band. There is, he stressed, no formal billing at this event. On both days, each act will perform at the same time: first Skid Row, then three Russian bands – Nuance, Brigada S and Gorky Park – followed by Cinderella, Mötley Crüe, Ozzy Osbourne and The Scorpions. Bon Jovi will close the show. Bon Jovi's was the first name on the tickets before any other acts were booked, so the headlining slot is rightly theirs, although they are not billed as such, partly in deference to Ozzy, who is by far the most popular artist with this audience. This delicate arrangement satisfies the egos of all parties, with the exception of Mötley Crüe, who hate being upstaged by Bon Jovi.

Doc also makes a promise to Mötley Crüe that Bon Jovi will not be using pyrotechnics or any other fancy tricks to steal the show. The Crüe are particularly sensitive on this point. Doc keeps his word and the first day's show passes without incident, but on the second day, 13 August, this so-called Peace Festival turns into all-out war.

The audience again numbers over 100,000 and Doc is smiling broadly as he strolls around the backstage enclosure. He might not enjoy watching his superstar acts performing for free, but it beats going to jail. Moreover, with American television crews here to record the event, the Moscow Peace Festival provides the best kind of publicity – international exposure, and all in the name of a good cause.

With a conspiratorial wink, Doc ushers me into Bon Jovi's dressing room. After last night's performance, Jon Bon Jovi told me he wanted to make a spectacular entrance on the second night, to do something truly special that will make the Russian people remember Bon Jovi as the stars of this event. Doc has a plan. It is, he stresses, top secret. The other bands, Mötley Crüe especially, are not going to like it. Doc has authorised Bon Jovi's crew to set up enough fireworks for a Fourth of July celebration, and has enlisted the help of the commanding officer of the Russian army division in plotting Jon's big entrance.

At eight, the sun sinks from view behind the stadium's high walls. As The Scorpions are playing their final song, the Bon Jovi crew are working at high speed on the other side of the revolving stage, ready to swing into action. I lead Jon Bon Jovi from the band's dressing room beneath giant concrete arches. Jon wears a heavy Russian army greatcoat over his stage clothes, medals clinking at his chest, a dark towel draped over his head for disguise. He bounces on his soles as we walk through the backstage area. Here we are joined by four armed guards, who follow us down a flight of steps to a gate at the foot of the stage that leads out to the arena. At the gate are ten security men in black bomber jackets and fluorescent bibs. We pause here for a minute as I gaze out into the darkness to survey the audience. The first row of people is no more than ten feet away, but nobody sees us. Everyone is looking up at the stage, cheering and applauding as The Scorpions take their bows.

We move quickly. The gate is opened a fraction and we slip through, first two of the guards, then Jon and myself followed by the other two guards. Jon keeps his head down. My right arm is around his shoulders, steering him. The guards lead us around the edge of the arena where the audience thins out a little. Every few paces I look to each side and behind. My heart is racing and I can feel Jon shaking at my side. All around us are smiling faces, some of the people a little drunk, everyone in high spirits. One teenage lad bumps into the leading guard and laughs a drunken apology as we press on. When we reach halfway around the perimeter, we turn ninety degrees and move towards the very centre of the arena. Our progress slows as the crowd becomes ever more densely packed. I grip Jon tightly as we weave left and right and step over little circles of people sitting on the grass. At last we reach the centre, where steel barriers ring an enclosure one hundred feet square. Here, on a small stage six feet high, road crew technicians control the sound mix and onstage lighting using large, flat mixing consoles. Several security guards are positioned beside the barriers. I pull the access-all-areas pass from inside my shirt. One of the guards shines a pocket torch to check my pass before unhooking two of the connecting barriers and waving us through. Our armed escorts nod to me and stay outside the barriers, facing the audience. I lift Jon up on to the soundboard stage and he hunches down out of sight as I climb up beside him. So far, so good – but now comes the tricky part. He lifts the towel from his head and smiles up at me. 'This had better work,' he says.

Bon Jovi's intro tape begins, a loud drum pattern punctuated by chants of 'Hey!' – the start of 'Lay Your Hands On Me'. Under flashing lights, the revolving stage turns to reveal the band's logo on a backdrop behind Tico's drum kit. A deafening

Res;
Thanx
for not lettin
anybody grab me!
Richie
Look at that
mustache ehe!!!

Guarding Richie Sambora in Brazil. Richie is holding
on tight to his famous cowboy hat – the one he wore in
the video for 'Wanted Dead or Alive'. Fans will grab
anything they can.

Lay your hands on me: Jon gets up close to his
fans at Rock in Rio. Wherever he went, he knew
I would never be more than a few feet away.

Dad with Frank Bruno, training in Arizona before
the Tyson fight in 1989.

Ringside at the world heavyweight title fight between Mike Tyson and Frank
Bruno at the Las Vegas Hilton in February 1989, one of the most memorable
weekends of my life. Left to right: me, Jon Bon Jovi, Richie Sambora, Alec
John Such, Elvis Presley's manager Colonel Tom Parker, and The Greatest
himself, Muhammad Ali. Note the chicken's foot hanging round Alec's neck.

Beach party at the start of The Lost Week, November 1989. From left: Tico Torres, Jon Bon Jovi, me, Alec John Such, Richie Sambora. Reg was my nickname, after gangster Reggie Kray.

The Lost Week tennis match. Jon and I are laughing because Doc is trying to play without a racket. Incredibly, he has just won a point with his hands.

A pensive moment in Guadalajara, Mexico, 1990, during the riots which soured the end of the New Jersey tour.

High jinks with
George Michael
(second left, in
baseball cap)
and friends at
LAX.

With my new best
friend – the tennis
machine – at Cher's
home in Malibu.

A night to
remember: with
Frances Ford
Coppola and
Cher backstage
at New York's
Paramount
Theater.

The Kiss A Team at the end of The Farewell Tour. From left: tour manager Tommy Thayer, Ace Frehley, Peter Criss, manager Doc McGhee, Paul Stanley, tour accountant Paco Zimmer, Gene Simmons, me.

A surreal moment in Japan. Seconds before I escort them onto the stage, three seven-foot aliens try to wedge themselves into a very small lift.

Kiss fans come in all sizes. Gene with a young admirer – also called Gene after her parents' idol – in Melbourne, Australia.

Boarding Kiss's private plane in Chicago. From left: Dave 'Snake' Sabo from support act Skid Row, Ace Frehley, me and Peter Criss.

Costume is integral to the Kiss experience. These boots and the legs inside them – belong to Paul Stanley.

Doc backstage in the dressing room with a bevy of good-looking Kiss fans.

Kiss un-masked. From left: Gene Simmons, me, (kneeling) Peter Criss, Tommy Thayer, Paul Stanley. Tommy has replaced Ace Frehley on guitar.

Watching you watching them: the art of security is to be ready for anything.

roar surges out of the crowd around us. Crouching, I lead Jon to the front of the soundboard stage. Stretching out before us is a path ten feet wide, bisecting the audience and leading one hundred metres to the foot of the stage. Lining each side of the path are two hundred uniformed Russian soldiers. Some of the fans close to the path are looking back towards us, wondering what is about to happen. Jon stands up, straightens the great-coat and places a general's cap on his head. I jump down to the path and turn to face him.

Suddenly, Jon is illuminated with two spotlights beamed from positions high up on the sides of the stadium. He thrusts his arms aloft and punches the air. Every face in the crowd turns to see him. The ground beneath my feet shakes with the noise of the crowd. Jon leaps down beside me, then dashes from one side of the path to the other. People strain to reach him as he runs his open palms along rows of outstretched hands. I move off ahead of him, staying low to avoid blocking the view of the television cameras trained on Jon from front and back, and scanning both sides of the path for that one lunatic who might try to get over the barrier and get to Jon. There are so many people and all of them so close to the star – so much potential for danger.

Jon safely reaches the front of the stage in two minutes. It feels like ten, fifteen. Exhilarated, relieved, adrenaline coursing through me, I give Jon a shove in the backside and he springs up on to the stage. He struts out to centre-stage as the band plays the heavy metal riff to 'Lay Your Hands On Me'. I run along the pit area directly below the stage, past security guards, photographers and TV cameramen, and scale a steel stairway to take up my position at side of stage. Sweating heavily, I feel a hand tug at my elbow. I turn to see Doc beaming up at me. He rises on the balls of his feet and yells toward my ear, 'Best entrance I've ever —'

'BOOM!'

Three flash-bombs explode simultaneously on either side of the stage, sending a shock wave through the stage boards under our feet and filling the air with hot white smoke. Momentarily deafened, I see Doc rocking back on his heels, laughing. I turn away to watch Jon, as always. He is at the very edge of the stage, holding his mike-stand out and cupping one ear as the audience roars its approval.

As the song climaxes, Jon walks back towards me, slipping off the greatcoat and flinging it into my arms. Gathering up the trailing coat tails, I look up to see Mötley Crüe's Tommy Lee, a blur of long hair and black leather, running full-tilt at Doc. With a single punch to the chin, Lee lays Doc flat on his back. Lee stands over Doc's prostrate figure for a second, yelling 'Motherfucker!' so loud I can hear it from twenty feet away over the sound of the band. Then he disappears as fast as he came. One of Bon Jovi's road crew makes a grab for Tommy's arm but is brushed aside.

I help Doc to his feet and lift my T-shirt to wipe a little blood from the corner of his mouth. Within seconds there are people all around us. I tell two of the people to take Doc to the medical room and return to my position to watch over Jon. Dave Bryan has seen the commotion and offers a puzzled expression as he continues playing. I shake my head and mouth the words, 'It's okay', but I know for certain that it is far from okay. This could get very ugly.

After a great performance, the Bon Jovi guys are buzzing as we board a bus and drive back to the hotel with a police escort. Only then do I tell them about Tommy knocking Doc on his ass.

'What the hell for?' Richie asks.

'Because you had pyro and they didn't,' I reply.

Jon is furious. One of the guys suggests we should get hold of Tommy and teach him a lesson.

'I don't think that's such a good idea,' I say. My repeated

pleas for calm are ignored. Mötley Crüe's cocky attitude and stupid drunken pranks have pissed off a lot of people. Now these people have an excuse to give the Crüe a few lumps. I don't care if these idiots get whacked, but Mötley Crüe's tour manager Rich Fisher is an old friend of mine. Keeping my thoughts to myself, I elect to help him out.

When our bus arrives at the hotel, the band members head straight for their rooms to shower before reconvening in the bar. When everyone has had a few drinks, the trouble will really start. In my room, the telephone's red message light is blinking. Rich Fisher has posted a voice message.

'Michael, you saw what happened with Tommy and Doc. I've got to get the guys out of the hotel tonight. Come to room 705 at eleven-thirty.'

I have forty minutes. I shower and walk down to the bar. The hotel is a hollow circular tower with the bar at the centre of the ground floor, overlooked by balconies that service each of the twenty floors. When I arrive, the bar is crowded and noisy. Every member of every band is downing shots of vodka and speaking in animated tones about Tommy's attack on Doc. I take one of twenty or thirty shot glasses arranged on the bar, tilt my head back and swallow the vodka in one. I wince a little and run the back of my hand across my lips as Sebastian Bach re-enacts Tommy Lee's punch to anyone who will listen. As Sebastian swishes the air with his fist, the people around him are looking up to the balconies – hoping, perhaps, to catch sight of Tommy.

Tico and Dave Bryan are arguing over what action should be taken with Tommy. Emotions are running high and my attempts at mediation prove unsuccessful. I sink another vodka shot and slip away from the bar to find Rich Fisher in agitated mood. He opens the door, beckons me into the room and hurriedly resumes a conversation on the phone. Rich has booked a private jet to fly Mötley Crüe back to America tonight. Now all we have to do is get the band out of the hotel before the restless mob in the bar comes looking for them. I check the service elevator while Rich collects the four band members. They flinch when they see me at the elevator door, but Rich assures them that I am here to help. We squeeze into the elevator, descend to the basement and walk through the kitchens, surprising the staff, before a fire exit leads us to a waiting van. Rich thanks me. The band members do not. Tommy Lee is still drunk and belligerent and yelling obscenities as I walk around the building and through the front entrance. Loud voices ring out from the bar as I take an elevator up to my room. It has been a long day and I have had enough, but as I slide the key card into the door lock, I hear noise from a nearby room, thuds and yells – the sound of a fight. The door to the adjacent room is ajar and I step inside to see an American promoter kneeling on a bed with a pretty young hotel maid before him on all fours, her dress bunched up around her waist. They are oblivious to my presence. I quickly realise that the only sounds in this room are the couple's groaning and panting, and the rattling of the bed frame against the wall. The fight is in the next room.

I step lightly from the first room and find another open door. As I enter, a scream of rage brings me to a sudden halt. I see two men grappling on the floor between two beds. The man on top is Dave Bryan. He has a heavy black telephone in one hand and is bringing it down hard on the other guy, once, twice, three times.

'Dave!' I shout.

For a second he turns to me, breathing heavily, his face red with exertion. Then he continues his assault. I jump on to the nearest bed and grab him around the waist. It takes all my strength to prise him off his victim. As I lift Dave kicking and screaming on to the bed, I look to the floor to see Tico, his nose bloodied and a clump of Dave's hair extensions in his fist.

'What's all this about?' I ask.

Their expressions are blank. It is just a stupid drunken fight caused by an argument neither can recall. This kind of thing has happened before and will happen again. I drag Dave off the bed and to my room. He stands over the wash basin, tugging at what is left of his hair and splashing water in his face to cool off. We walk to the bar and drink a couple of vodkas.

I leave Dave talking to Richie and head upstairs. I check on the room where the fight happened and find Tico slumped on one of the beds, still dressed and snoring loudly. At last, there is peace.

The following afternoon, we fly to the UK for another sell-out show on 19 August at the 50,000-capacity National Bowl in Milton Keynes. The flight is quiet. Dave and Tico share a joke about the fight. Everyone is tired and hung over. Skid Row are with us – they are one of the support acts for the Milton Keynes gig – but even Sebastian Bach has to sleep some time.

Two days before the show, Bon Jovi conduct an in-store signing session at Tower Records in Piccadilly Circus, one of London's busiest and most famous tourist sites. Fans queue around the block to meet their heroes. The band sit in line behind a long table, exchanging a few words with awestruck fans while autographing their record covers and jackets. Some of the girls get a kiss from Jon or Richie. Others lift up their tops for the guys to scrawl their signatures across their breasts.

The band are scheduled to leave the store at six, but a few minutes before the hour, there are still hundreds of fans waiting in a line stretching up Piccadilly. There is not enough time to meet all of them, but Jon does not want the fans to go away disappointed. He asks me if he could play an impromptu performance on the roof of the store, as U2 did in the video for their hit single 'Where The Streets Have No Name'. The store's manager leads me to the jazz department on the second floor. The room has large windows overlooking the street, and only two customers are browsing the aisles. I take the band up to the room while Richie's guitar technician retrieves two acoustic guitars from the tour bus parked in a nearby side street. The windows are opened and Jon leans out to wave to the people below. The pavement is quickly jammed with excited fans. Jon and Richie play three songs to the delight of the fans before a police officer taps me on the shoulder.

'Are you the group's manager, sir?'

'No, but I can help.'

The officer says he will arrest us for public disorder if the performance does not stop immediately. The crowd is spilling out into the road and blocking the traffic. People could get hurt or even killed. I apologise to the officer and tell Jon to finish the third song quickly and say goodbye to the fans. The police escort us to the bus and we return to the band's hotel. We have three hours to freshen up and enjoy a few drinks in the bar before we head to the East End for a party to celebrate my thirty-ninth birthday, which was yesterday. The George is one of the most famous pubs in London, a genuine old-fashioned cockney boozer. Its customers have included many of the most notorious East End gangsters and villains. Tonight, the renowned pub piano player Jack Appleton, dressed in Union Jack suit and matching bowler hat, performs a selection of cockney folk songs and wartime favourites, both English and American.

The pub is packed with my family and friends from Camden and the East End, Bon Jovi, Skid Row and their road crews, even Doc McGhee's mother and father. Everyone is drinking warm English beer and singing rowdily as Jack Appleton leads us in renditions of 'The Lambeth Walk', 'Land Of Hope And Glory' and 'Knees Up Mother Brown'. As Jon stands swaying with his arm around Skid Row's Dave Sabo, trying to sing songs he has never heard before, a few of the pub's regulars watch him from the bar, smiling and wondering who the hell these daft, long-haired Americans are.

The pub's doors are locked at eleven so that the party can

continue uninterrupted. At midnight, Jon calls a hush and hands me a large parcel wrapped in green and gold paper bearing the logo of the upmarket department store Harrods. As my guests look on expectantly, I tear the paper off to reveal a butler's uniform: black tailcoat, grey waistcoat with brass buttons, white shirt, black bow tie, pin-striped trousers and black bowler hat. Everyone is laughing, Jon especially. We have a long-running joke on this tour. Whenever we share a hotel suite, Jon will introduce me as Reginald, his English butler.

'Come on, Reg!' he smiles. 'Try it on.'

I can hardly refuse. I walk to the toilet with laughter ringing in my ears and emerge to loud cheers in full butler regalia. Jackie reprises 'Knees Up Mother Brown' and I sing it solo, tipping my hat for added comedy value. It is four in the morning when we stumble out of the pub into the cool twilight. I am still wearing the butler's outfit when I fall into bed at my home in Camden Town.

I meet Jon at the hotel on the following afternoon for our daily jog. Normally we run at eight in the morning, but not today when we are both nursing hangovers. Carrying small bottles of water, we run through Regents Park in two circuits, six miles in total. There are hundreds of people in the park, sitting on the grass in sunshine, but nobody recognises Jon, who wears a Lonsdale boxing top, red shorts and his hair tied up beneath a baseball cap.

As per usual, Jon goes off like a rabbit and comes home like a donkey. I start off like a donkey and catch him up with a mile to go. The sweat is pouring off us as we slow down on the return to the hotel. There is something I need to ask Jon. For weeks, we have been talking about staging a party to celebrate Bon Jovi's status as the biggest band in the world. Jon wants it to be the kind of party that Led Zeppelin threw in the seventies.

Perhaps he senses, as I do, that when this tour finishes, when the band go home and count their money, that everything will change. Money changes everything and everybody. A party like the one that Jon is talking about will never happen again.

'This has got to be the most notorious week in rock history,' he says between swigs of water. 'It's got to make us legends.' Money, he says, is no object. Everything will be charged to his platinum credit card. 'But,' he tells me, 'it's got to be money well spent.' He turns to me, smiling. I have calls to make.

Back in Jon's hotel suite, I shower, then leaf through the band's tour itinerary. On Halloween we arrive in Australasia for eight shows, finishing in Auckland, New Zealand, on 18 November. The next gig is in Portugal on 31 November. This is perfect. On the schedule, these twelve days are set aside for promotion and the possibility of additional gigs in Australia. I make two calls; the first to the band's Australian promoter, the second to Big Lou, an old friend of mine who owns most of the strip bars in Sydney.

'We need a place where we can have a week-long party with twenty-five beautiful women,' I tell the promoter. 'And it's got to be someplace where nobody will know who we are, and where nobody will find us, not even the wives and girlfriends.' He knows just the place. Club Mirage is a resort hotel on the semi-tropical Great Barrier Reef coast, a little paradise hidden away from the world.

Big Lou knows the kind of girls we are looking for. Australian girls are renowned for liking a good time. Every model, stripper, hooker or groupie who parties with the band on the Australian tour will be told about Club Mirage. With such a prize on offer – a week in one of the most beautiful places on Earth with the biggest rock band in the world – all of the girls will try that little bit harder. Each girl will be awarded marks out of ten, and those with the highest marks will come to Club Mirage.

I finish talking with Lou and tell Jon that the party is on.

'Reg,' he grins, 'you're a star.'

All through this tour, we have been calling Jon 'white toast'. Now he is putting his money where his mouth is, and it is up to me to keep my end of the deal. Seven days in paradise with the best drugs, booze and women that Australia has to offer. This is going to be the ultimate rock 'n' roll party. In anticipation of the fun ahead of us, I name it 'The Lost Week'.

17

The lost week

Bon Jovi's private jet descends through thin cloud cover to reveal Australia's Great Barrier Reef coastline. On the plane are the five members of the band, myself, Doc McGhee, Patrick, the head of our Australian security team, and Ira Sokoloff, who handles the band's merchandising. Below us miles of silver sand stretch between the deep blue ocean and the rich green tropical forest. Jon Bon Jovi turns to me with an approving smile. The Lost Week has begun.

Upon landing we are greeted on the tarmac by a fleet of limousines ready to deliver the band to the Club Mirage. In each limousine, bottled beer is on ice. The journey passes quickly. Within thirty minutes, Jon is excitedly pointing to the white-walled hotel and the secluded crescent beach below.

We have six villas booked: three for the band and their entourage and three for the girls, who are arriving after us. Each villa has five bedrooms. I have a room in the main hotel building, overlooking the villas. In this room, dubbed Mission Control, I can watch over the band and any other guests who are staying at the hotel. I must ensure that anything happening here remains private.

Doc leads the band to the bar while I meet with the hotel manager to explain what we need. Each villa is to be stocked with the best pink champagne and the finest red and white wines. We will require a separate dining area, and one member of the hotel staff must be available twenty-four hours a day to take care of the villas. The manager agrees with a gracious smile. I ask if he would welcome our other guests on arrival. He nods. I cannot wait to see his face when he sees who it is Big Lou is bringing with him.

The 'fun bus' arrives within the hour. The hotel manager and two young porters stand beside me in the lobby. Big Lou is first to emerge wearing a loud Hawaiian shirt, his broad, bearded face creased in a grin. Knowing that Lou understands what is needed to make a great party, I realise that this one is going to start with a bang.

Over Lou's shoulder I see the girls walking off the bus. Some are tall, some short, some blonde and some brunette, but they all have one thing in common: their breasts barely move as they skip towards us. I turn to introduce Lou to the hotel manager, whose jaw is down by his shoes. The porters' eyes are almost out of their sockets.

The manager's face flushes as he leads us through the lobby and out to a patio, where a golf buggy stands ready to take the girls to their villas. Except that this is no ordinary golf buggy. It belongs to the hotel's owner, an associate of Lou's, who is allowing us to use it for the duration of our stay. The buggy is painted gold and customised to look like a miniature Rolls Royce, with twelve seats, a stereo and a cooler in the back filled with champagne. The manager takes the wheel and drives the first dozen girls to the villas. Big Lou sits up front beside him. The buggy disappears over a ridge to the sound of girlish laughter and popping champagne corks.

By sunset we are ready to eat dinner, but no separate area has yet been prepared for our party. Instead, the manager invites the band to dine in the hotel's sumptuous five-star restaurant. Our table is in the centre of the room. This is a bad move. When the first group of girls arrives it is obvious they have all been shopping at the same store. All are wearing pink hot-pants with matching tank tops and big hair. Most of the other guests are honeymooning Japanese couples who look on in horror. And with each new bottle of champagne, the noise at our table grows louder.

The hotel manager hovers at my shoulder and whispers in my ear. 'Mr Francis, you were right. Let's meet in the morning and make other dining arrangements.'

The dinner is wonderful. We feast on giant lobster – three feet from claw to tail – soft-shell crab and the best Australian wine. With all these amazing girls around us, anticipation fills the air. And this is just the beginning. If the first night is anything to go by, we may never come back to earth.

After dinner we retire to the villas. At midnight I am back at Mission Control, organising the next day's yacht trip to the Great Barrier Reef, when there is an urgent knock at the door. My good friend the hotel manager is ashen-faced. The front desk has received several calls complaining about the noise coming from a room along the hall from mine. This room is also booked under our group reservation. As we reach the door, we hear a girl squealing over loud rock music. The manager knocks but there is no reply. He opens the door using his pass key and I enter first to find one of the Bon Jovi road crew standing naked at the foot of the bed as a redhead lies spreadeagled beneath him, her firm breasts sitting up like melons. She is handcuffed to the bedposts and squirming with pleasure.

'Please!' the manager begs. 'You must stop this right away!'

The crew guy looks crestfallen as I reach past him to turn the music off. The redhead pouts like a schoolgirl who has had a candy bar taken from her.

'Mr Francis, there is another problem,' the manager says, leading me to the window and opening the curtains with a dramatic flourish. 'There!' he yells, pointing to the Blue Lagoon in the hotel courtyard, a twenty foot-high mini-mountain with waterfalls cascading on to many different levels. To my astonishment, it is crawling with naked bodies.

On the topmost level of the lagoon is the pot-bellied Ira Sokoloff, a bottle of champagne in one hand, his ponytail flapping from side to side as he humps one of the girls. It is like a scene from a human rodeo. Ira's pink face lights up the whole lagoon. This is a respected businessman and a friend of ex-President Jimmy Carter, and at the age of fifty he is discovering what rock 'n' roll is all about.

In a pool directly below Ira, two sisters are performing oral sex on one of the crew. All told there are sixteen bodies on the rocks, with the rest of the entourage cheering every move. Sadly, I must break up the party. The hotel manager fears he will lose his job.

Once the lagoon is cleared and the revellers have returned to the villas, I am invited to the manager's office, where we come to a mutually beneficial arrangement. Between our villas and the lagoon, hotel staff will erect a cabana, a big blue-and-white striped open-sided tent with a long table set for forty people. Two chefs and two waiters will be specially assigned to our party. We will be as far away from the other guests as possible. This way, nobody gets hurt.

196

22 NOVEMBER

A luxury yacht glides across the ocean towards the Great Barrier Reef. On board, fifteen guys, twenty-five girls, ice chests filled with food, beer, wine and champagne, plus a two-ounce bag of cocaine and some of the finest weed in the Southern Hemisphere. All of the girls are naked.

Two hours out to sea, we drop anchor. All four of the yacht's bedrooms are in use as the vessel comes to rest. One of the crewmen, Brad, is a typical surfer dude; blond, lean and tanned. Today he is living a life that, previously, a kid like him could only dream of. He asks for a volunteer to help catch some small fish, which we will use as bait for bigger fish to barbecue on the yacht. Jon Bon Jovi says he will go with Brad, which means that I, as his security guard, am going too. We swim four hundred metres to a group of rocks. Using snorkels and spears, we hunt for fish. Within thirty minutes Brad catches fifty.

We are halfway back to the yacht when Brad calls out to us. I am ten metres ahead of Jon. Brad is another twenty metres back. I turn to see Brad holding one of his two spears out of the water. There are no fish left on it. Something big has taken the bait.

I might be Jon's security guard, but my contract applies to dry land only and says nothing about sharks, which will eat you whether you are a rock star or not. If there is a shark around, you are not supposed to panic or splash about. I panic. I splash about. I am swimming like Mark Spitz. I do not climb on the boat. I fly up there.

Now Jon is panicking but everyone on the boat is cheering and throwing bits of bread in the water. They think it's hilarious. I breathe a huge sigh of relief as first Jon and then Brad make it back safely. Shaking, I light up a big spliff and knock back a glass of champagne. I sink into a chair, close my eyes and hope that Jon will forgive me for leaving him for dead.

The party continues on the yacht for another six hours. Led

Zeppelin and Bob Marley songs play as we empty the bags of pot and coke and sail slowly back to shore. Brad barbecues the few fish he had left on one spear.

The boat docks at ten and we head for the cabana. In the middle of the table is a huge silver bowl, three feet in diameter, filled with sangria. Joints are ready-rolled on the table, courtesy of one of the hotel's waiters. Shattered, I bid everyone good-night and collapse alone in my bed.

23 NOVEMBER

I am woken by the phone ringing. It is 4 a.m. Tico tells me we have a problem. I am still half asleep when I enter one of the girls' villas and see chunks of long dark hair all over the tiled floor. This beautiful girl, probably the prettiest of all of them, has passed out and been shaved bald. And not just on her head. There is not a hair left on her entire body. Worse, the girl is a stripper who returns to work in a few days. She slowly regains consciousness and I lead her to the bathroom. She bursts into tears when she sees her reflection. I roll a joint as she sits sobbing on a bed. The joint does the trick. Within a few minutes, we are all laughing. The poor girl looks like she has just walked out of a shop window but at least she has got a story to tell when she is drunk. Nobody will admit to shaving her, but we each have our suspicions. I know who has a bald fetish, but I am not about to tell.

As the days pass, we develop a sense of what makes these girls tick. Most groupies are used for one night and then discarded, but here we learn about their lives. Gina, the redhead who was handcuffed to the bed, is a pastry chef who lives with her parents and has a boyfriend back home in Melbourne. In fact, only fifteen of the twenty-five girls are strippers; the remainder are fitness instructors, nurses, secretaries. These girls have careers, partners, normal lives, but for these seven days they are living a fantasy existence.

198

25 NOVEMBER

The Lost Week is drawing to an end. The guys have been playing pick and mix, but as we reach the final few days they realise there are combinations they have not yet tried. Nobody wants to end up sitting alone in a hotel room next week thinking, Shit – I never had Sally the nurse and the girl with nipples like strawberries.

Out here, there are no inhibitions whatsoever. Whenever the girls are summoned to the guys' villas, they are ready for action, whether it is with one of the guys or with one another.

Tonight, Gina and two blonde sisters are performing a show for all of us in the main villa. Twenty people are in the room, and the three girls are getting bigger cheers from the other girls than from the guys. The show lasts for two hours and proves highly educational. For the first and only time, we are late for dinner.

As we eat, the girls thank us for a wild time and for an incredible new experience. Most of them have never had sex with another girl before, and it is an experiment they are eager to repeat.

'There's a whole other world out there,' Gina smiles.

26 NOVEMBER

The Lost Week Tennis Tournament, and a prize of $10,000 to the winners. The action begins in the early evening. A champagne bar is set up on one side of the court. Eight ladies are helping out as ball girls. Wearing just the bottom half of their bikinis, they are not exactly dressed for Wimbledon.

The matches have been competitive and now it is time for the final: Jon and myself versus Doc and Patrick. Ira is umpiring, but Jon and Doc have been arguing so much during their previous games that all the ball girls have fled. Now Doc has a problem. He can't find his tennis racket and suspects that Jon has hidden it. Jon says he hasn't and insists that we start the match, so for the first fifteen minutes, Doc is playing with only his hands.

'That piece of shit!' Doc spits.

The game is tight. Jon is so pumped up, it is like he is entering a world title fight, but unless he is on stage, he has no co-ordination whatsoever. He is losing us every point.

'Jabba the Hut!' he yells at me. 'Come on, you fat fuck!'

Ira calls a close decision in Doc's favour.

'You blind cunt!' Jon chides him.

The next call goes Jon's way.

'You're off the tour!' Doc yells at Ira.

'Fuck this,' Ira says, and leaves. Now it is just the four of us.

The sun goes down and the floodlights com on. We are in the final set. A waiter brings a tray of beers on to the court, plus a glass of wine for Doc. He could not survive ten minutes without a drop of wine. And by now, he has realised that winning this game will cost him much more than $10,000 in the long run. Jon will be so pissed off if he loses, he might even cancel the extra tour dates that Doc is planning, and Doc will end up losing a fortune.

It is past eleven when, at match point down, Doc volleys weakly into the net. Game, set and match – Bon Jovi and Francis. Jon is beaming.

We never see the ten grand.

27 NOVEMBER
The hotel manager produces our bill from a large red envelope. I can almost smell his pleasure. This is his moment: payback.

'Would you care for a drink, Mr Francis?'

'I'll have a large G and T, thank you.'

The bill resembles *War And Peace*. $15,000 for champagne alone. The girls must have been bathing in the stuff. They have also blown $10,000 on clothes from the hotel's boutiques.

200

But what's this? $20,000 for the golf cart? 'Come on!' I shrug. 'We only hired it for a week!'

'It has gone missing, sir.'

'Well, we don't know anything about it and we're not paying for it.'

'Mr Francis,' he says gravely. 'The last time our golf cart was seen was the night before last, at sunset, with six members of your party heading towards the ocean.'

As I plead innocence, I have a picture in my head of Big Lou and Tico driving the golf cart towards the beach with four girls in the back, laughing and waving champagne bottles. I know that the cart is now somewhere out at sea, but there is no way that Tico is going to cough up twenty grand.

We make a deal on the golf cart: $8000.

Two hours and five gin and tonics later, our negotiations are completed with the manager $70,000 down on the original fee.

Our last night in paradise. Everyone is at the beach savouring the sunset as I tiptoe around the villas making a thorough inspection of the girls' rooms, checking for evidence that might embarrass or incriminate us in years to come. We will all remember the Lost Week for the rest of our lives – and I have a bag filled with videos – but what happens out here must stay out here.

I have a nice surprise for the guys. They think that we have run out of drugs, but I have tucked away a little stash. The guys' faces are like kids on Christmas morning as I arrive at the beach carrying a silver tray laden with big lines of charlie, fat joints and a dish full of pills.

'Here comes The Chemist!' Richie Sambora cackles.

The Lost Week ends with the whole party getting drunk and stoned under the palm trees. For the last time, couples pair off, but at the end of the night, all of the guys are back in their rooms, alone. We want to be gone by the time the girls wake up.

28 NOVEMBER
Five tired, hungover and rather sad-looking rock stars board the fun bus parked outside Club Mirage. The drive to the airport is quiet, but once aboard the chartered jet, champagne is poured and our spirits lift. As the plane taxis to the runway, everyone is laughing and joking and recounting stories from the past week. The stories get longer and longer. We tease Tico about the golf cart but he refuses to admit that he was the one who drove the damn thing into the sea. The smiles say it all. We did it. The Lost Week: the longest and wildest party in the history of rock 'n' roll.

As the plane takes off, a cheer goes up. Only one person is not cheering. Jon Bon Jovi sits between Doc and myself, his hands clasped together in prayer and looking to the heavens.

'Please, God,' he whispers. 'Just let me get away with this and I promise I will never sin again.'

18

Running on empty

The Lost Week may be over, but both the band and I still have work to do. December 1989 sees Bon Jovi return to Europe and then go on to finish the Jersey Syndicate tour in South and Central America.

Originally, Doc had intended to follow the Australian tour with more dates in the Pacific Rim territories of Malaysia and South East Asia, but I had other plans. I had not seen my family since August and I was desperate to spend Christmas at home in London. I suggested to Jon that we should return to the UK because there had been such a buzz about the band after their big outdoor show at Milton Keynes in the summer. Jon liked the idea and so did Doc. Dates were booked in Spain, Portugal, Holland, France, Germany, Finland, Sweden, Ireland and the UK, with two nights at Birmingham's NEC and four at Wembley Arena. All of the shows sold out within hours.

We fly into London from Frankfurt on 23 December. Jon goes shopping in Harrods to find presents for my children, and I spend Christmas Eve with June and my mum and dad at the Mitre in Dale Road, where we have shared so many memories. On Christmas morning, I hand out gifts collected from around the world: a Japanese kimono for Joanne, and toys for Daniel and Grant from FAO Schwarz in New York. Later that day, June prepares Christmas dinner for fourteen people. In addition to me and the children, there are my parents, my brother Simon, all the band except for Dave Bryan, who has his own commitments, Jon's wife Dorothea and last but not least, Doc.

We squeeze around the table to enjoy a traditional Christmas feast of roast turkey and a small mountain of vegetables. A dozen bottles of Jon's favourite red wine are soon finished. Before the kids go to bed, Jon gives them each a personalised Bon Jovi tour jacket in brown leather with their names embroidered on the chest. By midnight, we are drinking brandy and smoking cigars when I tell Jon about the beautiful cemetery in Highgate, just a few miles from Camden, where Karl Marx is buried.

'Let's go see it!' Jon exclaims.

'It's the middle of the night,' I explain. 'The place is closed.'

'We can get in,' Jon insists.

I remind him of the last time we got drunk and broke in to someplace, in New York back in March, when we ended up sharing a cell for the night, but Jon is adamant.

'Come on,' he winks. 'Let's do it!'

The limousines deliver us to the gates of Highgate Cemetery and we clamber over the black wrought-iron railings. For fifteen minutes we stumble around in the darkness, guided only by starlight, until by chance we come across the statue of Marx raised on a huge stone plinth. We sit at the foot of the tomb, passing a bottle of brandy, while Richie rolls a joint. We stay for an hour, laughing, joking and swapping ghost stories. At two we return to the limos, tired, cold, drunk, stoned and happy. I spare a thought for the chauffeurs – driving a posse of drunken stars in the small hours of Boxing Day.

As the first limo drops me at my door, Richie says, 'Reg, your wife is a beautiful woman and a wonderful cook.'

Too far gone to reply, I pat him on the head and wobble away in the direction of my bed.

In the second week of January Bon Jovi end their UK dates with a fund-raising show at Hammersmith Odeon in aid of Nordoff-Robbins Music Therapy. Jimmy Page joins them, at my behest, to play on couple of numbers. The band then have a few days off before the last leg of the tour. But while they make the most of some much-needed relaxation, I am en route to Rio de Janiero. Under instruction for Doc, I must make special security arrangements for the band before they fly in two days later.

Rio de Janeiro is one of the most dangerous cities in the world, where rich tourists reside in luxurious hotels on Copacabana beach not far from the city's sprawling slums. Crime and corruption are rife, abduction and murder commonplace. Life is cheap. When bringing a rock band to Rio, security is paramount, and I am taking extraordinary measures to ensure Bon Jovi's safety.

On arrival in Rio, I meet with Marcel, the Brazilian tour promoter who works with Bon Jovi and other international rock acts. He looks older than when I last saw him, his once-dark hair now grey. As he drives to his house in the hills overlooking the ocean, he tells me that two months before our arrival, he was kidnapped and held to ransom for two weeks. He was only freed when police stormed the kidnappers' hideout and shot dead all four of his abductors. He himself escaped unhurt, but the episode has left him badly shaken. I sympathise: I remember all too well how it felt with Sheena Easton when we were in Chile, even though our 'kidnap' turned out to be a false alarm.

Over dinner, we discuss my requirements for additional security both at the band's hotel and the venue, the famous Maracana foot-ball stadium. I feel confident that we have everything in place. I meet the four security men who will operate a rotating twenty-four-hour armed guard for the duration of the band's stay and share a drink with Marcel in the hotel bar, then retire to my room and watch TV for an hour before the phone rings.

'Two gentlemen are here to see you, Mr Francis.'

'Okay, send them up.'

Paolo and Freddie are brothers I use whenever I am in Rio. Tall and lean, they are ex-policemen who now work as a specialised security team. We meet in the privacy of my room because they are bringing me a gun. We agree that Paolo and Freddie will be with me at all times, starting from tomorrow when the band arrives. I pay them in cash and arrange to meet them at the airport in the morning. When they leave, I place the gun in a drawer and ease into bed. I am shattered. Within seconds of my head touching the pillow, I am asleep.

In the morning, I slip the gun inside my jacket and take a cab to the airport in bright sunshine. The promoter has paid the airport police to allow the band to come straight off the plane and into waiting limousines without passing through customs. As the plane taxis towards us, I feel a hand on my shoulder. Two policemen stand beside me. One of them gestures with a sub-machine gun as the other speaks to me in broken English.

'I work for Bon Jovi,' I say, showing my laminated tour pass and glancing around me, searching for Paolo and Freddie. A handcuff is snapped around my wrist and I am led away to a small cell in the basement of the terminal building. Sitting on a wooden chair in the cell, I try to remain calm, telling myself that Paolo and Freddie will soon get me out of here. As the minutes pass, my heart sinks. Nobody saw me being led away by the police. I could be here for hours.

When the cops reappear at the cell door, a third man is with them, a stocky guy, also in uniform, his light brown shirt stained with sweat at the armpits. I rise from the chair as they step inside the cell.

'Passport?' the stocky guy hisses, looking me up and down.

'I don't have it with me,' I reply. 'It's at the hotel.'

I reach for my wallet but he pushes me hard in the chest, slamming me into a wall. The two cops grab my arms and twist me around. As they hold me, my face pressed into the rough cement of the wall, the other guy whacks me twice in the back. I feel a searing pain in my kidneys. This bastard knows what he is doing.

I am pushed down into the chair and handcuffed again. The three men leave and lock the cell door. For two hours, maybe more, I sit wincing at the pain in my sides. Thoughts race through my head. I wonder if the band has made it to the hotel safely, and whether somebody has raised the alarm. They will know that something is wrong because I am not at the airport to meet them. I wonder why the police are holding me: if all they want is a back-hander, they could have taken the money from me hours ago. I would love to return the compliment to the guy who whacked me, too, but right now, what I need most is to get out of this cell and back to the hotel.

At last, the two cops return without the third man and lead me up several flights of stairs towards an office. As we reach the door, I hear a voice call my name from along the corridor. It is Paolo. I have never been so pleased to see him. He and Freddie confront the policemen. The conversation, in Portuguese, is heated. Paolo remonstrates with them to remove the handcuffs, which, grudgingly, they do. Inside the office, I am presented with a fine of two thousand American dollars for breaching a restricted area of the airport. Paolo tells me to pay so that we can leave without further incident. I pay in cash and curse under my breath as we walk out of the office and through a fire exit into the main terminal hall. Only when we are riding back to the hotel do I feel the weight of the gun in my jacket pocket as I lift my T-shirt to show the bruises on my back to Freddie. Had the police found the gun, I dread to think what might have happened to me.

At the hotel, I meet with Doc. He arranges for a physician to look over my injuries – fortunately, I have sustained only bruising – and suggests that we keep the incident to ourselves for fear of alarming the band. I swallow a handful of painkillers and accompany Doc to the Maracana, where the band is sound checking ahead of tonight's show.

Shortly before the band goes on stage, I hand the gun back to Paolo, both for my own safety and for those around me. After what I have been through today, I feel like plugging anyone who gets in my way; although my misanthropy subsides in the course of the show as the painkillers kick in and a warm sedative glow washes over me.

The fourteen-month Slippery When Wet tour was a test of our stamina and sanity, but the current tour is now in its fifteenth and final month, and all of us are feeling the pace. Morale within the band is at its lowest since I have been working with them. The Lost Week was fun, but it was a brief respite from the daily grind of the road. Perhaps it would have been smarter to end the tour in Australia. Every show since then has been sold out, but the band is now running on empty. Tico and Dave came to blows in Moscow, and now there is tension between Jon and Richie. Jon has always been the star, Richie his sidekick; but now that Richie is dating Cher, it is he and not Jon who is on the covers of magazines and in newspapers' gossip columns. Bon Jovi will always be Jon's band, but since Richie and Cher became rock's most famous couple, I have sensed some resentment in Jon. The sooner this tour finishes the better.

The end comes in Mexico. On 16 February we journey to Guadalajara, four hundred miles west of Mexico City, for the

231st and 232nd shows of the tour. This is the last stop on the road. In the afternoon, while the band checks in, I go with the crew to the venue, yet another football stadium. As soon as we arrive I sense trouble. The local crew offer no assistance as our guys unload the band's equipment from two trucks. I walk around the stadium and see a crowd of two or three hundred gathered at a perimeter fence. These are not fans: they are young people chanting angrily and jeering the Bon Jovi crew. Some are wearing red scarves over their faces. This is a riot mob.

I search for the promoter in the backstage area and meet with blank expressions until, finally, I am directed to an office where his assistant greets me with a sweaty handshake and explains what is going on. The stadium, he says, is owned by the university, which takes a cut of the revenue from each show that is staged here. For reasons the assistant is unable, or unwilling, to explain, the promoter has not paid the university its share of profits from two previous concerts. If the university doesn't get paid, classes will close for lack of funds and the students will lose their education. This is why they are collected in a mob outside the stadium.

I return to the hotel at noon to find Doc and the band watching television reports of the student protest at the stadium. An interpreter explains what is happening as irate students yell at the cameras. Jon's expression is one of nervous exhaustion mixed with anxiety. He says little but it is apparent that he would prefer to be anywhere but here.

Tour manager Paul Korzilius arrives with fresh news, all of it bad. Two hundred riot police are at the stadium, facing the protesters. The road crew have been ordered to leave the area. All of the band's equipment, including Richie's prized double-necked guitar, remains in flight cases in the backstage enclosure, unprotected. Negotiations between the promoter and the student faculty are ongoing.

Jon is feeling claustrophobic and asks if we can go out for lunch, just to ease the tension a little. Two policemen accompany Jon, Doc and me to a restaurant two blocks from the hotel. The policemen wait outside while we eat. Jon is tense and picks at his food, but three glasses of wine help him to relax. When we are finished, Jon gives his credit card to a waiter, but after five minutes his card has still not been returned. I walk to the back of the room, ducking through a tiny archway to see the waiter swiping the card and processing a roll of blank credit slips. I snatch the card from his fingers and grab him by the throat. A second waiter and a chef jump to his assistance. I warn them off, but the chef is shouting at me and brandishing a large kitchen knife. I loosen my grip around the waiter's neck and call though to Doc to alert the policemen. As the chef takes a step towards me, the policemen rush in with pistols drawn. The knife clatters to the tiled floor and I withdraw from the kitchen, followed by the policemen, who walk us back to the hotel.

Paul Korzilius has more news for us. The promoter and students have come to an agreement of sorts, but it is now too late to set up the equipment for tonight's show. As a result, we have a new schedule: tomorrow, the band will play twice, in the afternoon and then in the evening. The fans with tickets for the first night will be admitted to the afternoon matinee.

Next day at noon, we ride to the stadium escorted by four police cars. Our bus passes through a throng of fans and students to the gates at the rear of the stadium, where another bus stands gutted and blackened by fire, its windows smashed. Our interpreter, employed by the promoter, informs me that students wrecked the bus thinking it belonged to Bon Jovi. This, I tell him, should not be relayed to the band.

The first show is at four and passes without incident. The stadium is half-full. A few small groups of students loiter at the fringes of the crowd, but they are wary of the heavy police presence and restrict their protests to chanting between songs. The band plays for an hour before returning to a shabby dressing room deep below ground level. Here we must wait for five hours before the second performance. I cannot take the risk of driving the band out of the stadium and then back in again, past a mob that is growing rowdier with each passing hour. I have two armed guards positioned in the corridor outside the dressing room, with orders not to allow anybody through.

The band members kill the time drinking whiskey and margaritas. By a quarter to ten, they are drunk, desperate to get the show done and get the hell out of Mexico. I lead them up a wide concrete staircase to ground level. Lining the path to the stage are a hundred policemen in full riot gear: black body armour, shields and helmets with visors pulled down over their faces, three-foot-long batons at their waists, their fingers twitching over the handles. Clearly, these guys are ready to kick ass. The audience has swelled to near full capacity and by now many of them are drunk, fans and students alike. Firecrackers explode in the hot night air. The atmosphere is heavy with menace.

The band plays fast and loose, trying to get the job done as quickly as possible. The audience reaction is frenzied, exciting the police, who repel crowd-surfers with a shove or a whack of the baton. Sensing the need for calm, the band plays a couple of slow numbers back to back. Jon, wobbling from all the tequila he has drunk, serenades the fans with an impromptu rendition of 'Guantanamera'.

With an hour gone, a hail of bottles and stones is thrown from the crowd. Few of them reach the stage: most strike the police ranked along the crash-barrier in front of it. The police react swiftly and brutally, pulling people over the barrier and laying into them mercilessly with fists, boots and batons. Jon is appalled and turns to me at the side of the stage.

'Do something, man!' he yells in my ear. I race to the edge of the stage and jump ten feet to the ground in between the foot of the stage and the barricade. Immediately a riot-stick cracks into my back. Pain shoots up inside me but I stay on my feet. I turn to the policeman who struck me, holding up my palms and pleading with him to stop hitting out. As he pauses, one of the road crew appears beside me and is felled by a blow to the skull.

I drop to the ground to attend to him and a space clears around us. The policeman who whacked me helps to drag the guy to safety under the stage, where we prop him up against one of the steel-pole supports. He is bleeding at the temple from a deep cut, but conscious. We carry him out behind the line of police and through a gate at one side of the stage, where a medic rushes to help us.

Now that our man is safe, I must act quickly to get the band out of danger. A full-scale riot could erupt at any second. People could get killed, and I have to make sure that Bon Jovi are not among them.

I run around to the back of the stage and up a ramp to where Doc and Paul Korzilius are in agitated conversation. Doc draws a finger under his throat and points to Jon. 'Get them off as soon as this song is over!' he yells to me. Dashing behind the drum riser to the other side of the stage, I grasp the pocket-torch hung on a cord around my neck and signal with two flashes to the crew guys and the band members.

The song finishes. Jon shouts 'Goodnight!' And we are off and running to the bus, which is backed up to the ramp at the rear of the stage, its engine revving. I count the band members on to the bus, plus Doc and Paul Korzilius, then slam the door shut behind me. 'Go!' Doc roars. A cordon of police stands guard at the gates, holding back a smattering of students who hiss and yell as the bus edges past, joined at the front and rear by armoured police vehicles. Downtown Guadalajara is a blur of yellow street lights and neon signs as we speed back to the hotel. High on adrenaline and fear and all the booze they sank in the dressing room, the band members laugh and joke: all except Jon, who hunkers down in his seat, deep in contemplation, saying nothing.

Doc's suite fills with the band and crew. Beer and tequila are served, but the mood is sombre. The end of a tour should be a celebration, especially when that tour has proven a spectacular success for the biggest rock band in the world, but the toasts proposed by Doc are token gestures. Everyone in the room knows that this tour has gone on too long, and that after what has just happened we are lucky to be alive.

'Where's Elvis?' Doc enquires. I look around the room for Jon, but he is not with us. I step out of the suite and walk up to Jon's room. He answers the door in a bathrobe, his hair wet from a shower.

'Is everything okay?' I ask him. 'Do you need anything?'

'Reg,' he sighs, 'I'm done.'

I place a hand on his shoulder. He offers a thin smile. His eyes are empty.

'Call me half hour before it's time to go,' he says. I turn and leave the room.

On the following morning, I fly to New York with Richie and Doc, then on to London alone.

As I sink back into my seat en route to Heathrow, a glass of gin and tonic at my side, I think again of Jon in his room in Guadalajara last night, looking like a man with the world on his shoulders, distant, and tired of the whole circus. A sense of loss comes over me, as if something special has been misplaced somewhere out on the road during these past fifteen months.

Brotherhood, Jon calls it. On the Slippery tour, the band was tight, like a family. They were different from other bands: they had a genuine love for each other, and on stage there was a wonderful chemistry between them. On this tour, they have shared some great times – Jon's wedding, The Lost Week, the Bruno fight, getting stoned at Karl Marx's tomb – but cracks have appeared, and in Mexico, I could sense the brotherhood coming apart. Everyone was burned out, but Jon's face betrayed more than simple fatigue. Even his relationship with Richie was strained, and this was the most important relationship in the band.

Several times during the past year, Doc had asked Jon if he

wanted a break. Jon refused: the band was selling out everywhere and he wanted to keep it going. Like James Brown before
him, Jon proclaimed himself the hardest-working man in show
business. In America, touring was smooth, like clockwork, but
in Guadalajara, the pressure on Jon had been brought to a head.
When rock stars are exhausted at the end of a long tour, they
need to be pampered even more than usual, not forced into
performing two shows in one day while riot police struggle to
control an angry mob. Mexico was a step too far.

I reflect on whether the band can survive this rocky period,
especially since Jon has been writing songs for a solo album, the
soundtrack for a new Western movie, *Young Guns II*, starring
Jon's friend Emilio Estevez.

I am reminded of the night that Jon and I sat in a New York
deli in August 1987, after Bon Jovi's show at Madison Square
Garden. His boyhood dream had come true: after years of
struggle, his band was on top of the world. Moreover, the guys
were united.

I remember what I said to Jon that night, that it might never
get better than this.

The next time I hear from Jon is near the end of 1991. His solo
album has proven a huge success, producing a number one
single in America with 'Blaze Of Glory'. Richie has also released
a solo record. For months, it has been rumoured that Bon Jovi
have broken up. I am in London with Cher on her European
tour when Jon's call is put through to my hotel room. He is
buzzing with excitement as tells me that the band has regrouped
and is working on a new album, then his voice hardens.

'You're gonna hear some rumours, Reg,' he says, 'but let me
just tell you, whatever happens, I'll never tour without you.
Things between us will never change, you're still part of the
family. But I've fired Doc today.'

'Okay,' I reply, too stunned to say anything else. The band of brothers lives on, but the father figure is gone, ousted by the favourite son. This is a pattern as old as history, but somehow I never thought it would happen to Doc. After all, without him Bon Jovi would never be where they are. He turned them from wannabes into superstars. Now Jon wants to take control, and the balance of power is shifting. All of a sudden, everything feels different.

19

The gilded cage

Ten miles west of downtown Los Angeles, Malibu is home to many of the world's richest stars. One hour's drive from LAX airport along the Pacific Coast Highway, it offers luxurious and secluded houses, private beaches and clean air; a beautiful environment for beautiful people.

Point Dune is one of Malibu's most famous beauty spots, where wooded mountains slope gently to the ocean and a steep-sided promontory divides the white sands of Zuma beach. The Point itself is a nature reserve where bramble, tall grasses and small trees grow wild. Where the point juts into the sea, there is a sheer drop one hundred feet to where the waves crash and foam, and sea lions cluster on the rocks.

On either side of the headlands, sandy cliffs rise from the beach. Elegant houses are spread from here up the mountainside, linked by a narrow road that dips and bends with the contours of the land. Where the road takes a gentle curve through pine forest, a short driveway leads to a massive gate of solid, heavy oak, seven feet high and set into a cream-coloured stone wall. The wall encircles a two-storey Spanish-style villa, its cream walls, oak beams and terracotta tiled roof partially visible beyond tall palm trees.

It is a cool March evening in 1992 when I enter this house for the first time. I am to live here with Cher. 'Come for three months,' she told me. 'If it works out, you can stay for as long as you like. I want you to be happy.'

She greets me at the door with a smile and a hug. Dressed simply in faded blue jeans and white T-shirt, she looks stunning. She leads me through to the living room, a huge space dominated by a gleaming black grand piano. Arranged on the piano are three silver-framed photographs; of Cher with Nicolas Cage, her co-star in the movie *Moonstruck*; with *Moonstruck* director Francis Ford Coppola; and with Richie Sambora. None, I note, with her ex-husband Sonny Bono. Beside the photographs stands the golden Oscar statuette she received as Best Actress for *Moonstruck*.

At the centre of the room sits a huge broken stone bought from a museum in Cairo. Cher is fascinated by the history and myths of ancient Egypt, hence her pet name 'Cleo'. Encircling the stone are four long white sofas. Dark oak beams run the length of the ceiling. The floor is polished wood. The cream-painted walls are decorated with religious icons, including one hundred crucifixes, collected on her travels around the world. The house and interior décor are of her own design and exude the kind of subtle class that only serious money can buy.

She is clearly enjoying herself as she leads me on a tour of the property. French windows open on to a sun deck and swimming pool, where a narrow path winds up a gentle slope through tropical gardens to a green-surfaced tennis court.

'Do you play?' she asks.

I nod.

'That's good, because I don't. Someone should.'

She laughs. 'Let me show you your room.'

We walk back inside the house and up a flight of stairs. There are three rooms on the top floor of the house; Cher's bedroom, the guest bedroom, where I will sleep, and a gym. My room is huge, with an en suite bathroom. The walls are natural stone and lined with gold and platinum discs commemorating her millions of record sales. One is for a Sonny & Cher album.

The frame of the king-size bed is cut from the same stone as the walls. Opposite the bed is a top-of-the-range hi-fi, TV and VCR system. On a ledge running the length of one wall are more framed photographs of Cher, some stills from her movie career, others glamour shots used to promote her albums. In all of them, she looks wonderful.

I feel a million miles from Dale Road in Camden and the house where I grew up with three families.

'It's beautiful,' I tell her.

She smiles. 'You must be tired after your flight. Let's get you a drink and something to eat. Come and meet Andy.'

Downstairs, a maid is lighting dozens of scented candles in the living room, the warm fragrance of vanilla sweetening the air. The kitchen is the most homely room in the house, spacious, with a breathtaking view of the ocean. Seated at a large wooden table is Andy, a chef who worked at the Four Seasons Hotel in Los Angeles before Cher hired him. He offers a glass of Long Island Iced Tea from a pitcher. It is the best I have ever tasted.

We sit at the table and Andy produces a sandwich of grilled chicken on Italian bread. As I eat, Cher speaks excitedly of a new movie script and her plan to meet Richie Sambora for a romantic break in Europe. Andy has a dry wit that I warm to instantly. When he leaves at sunset, Cher asks me to check that the doors are locked. Returning to the kitchen, I sense a change in her mood. She shifts in her seat, her face tightening and her voice hardening as she begins to explain why she has brought me here.

Two weeks ago, an intruder broke into this house. He entered via the kitchen and carried with him a samurai-style sword. The alarm was raised by a female guest who woke at 2 a.m. to find the man standing at the foot of her bed in a ground floor bedroom. Her screams alerted a security guard on night duty at the house and woke Cher, who was asleep upstairs. As Cher called the police, the guard found and over-powered the intruder. Her guest was unharmed. The police arrested the intruder, who was subsequently charged with unlawful entry and possession of a dangerous weapon. The man had a history of mental illness and is believed to have stalked other celebrities in the Malibu area. He remains in police custody but may soon be released with a suspended sentence. Cher is frightened.

'I want you to take care of me, Michael,' she says.

'Okay,' I nod.

A few minutes earlier I had been feeling slightly fuzzy with the effects of jet lag and Andy's cocktail. Now my senses are sharp. I ask Cher to show me the rest of the house and gardens; the gym and the office beneath; several more rooms including one shelved from floor to ceiling with thousands of video tapes of her favourite movies; and most importantly, her bedroom.

The bed is an ancient Egyptian fantasy. Ten feet long by eight feet wide, its frame is carved from stone, with a sphinx figure-head on each corner post. The whole fantastic creation is draped in white silk. The stone walls are decorated with dozens more crucifixes and family photographs.

Adjacent to the bedroom, two large bathrooms, white tiles sparkling, and a walk-in closet with clothes rails stretching for thirty feet. Below are arranged two hundred pairs of shoes. It is the stuff of fairy-tale princesses, the kind of room that every little girl dreams of.

As we leave the bedroom, she lifts a pillow from the bed to reveal a heavy black semi-automatic handgun. She notes my surprise but says nothing. We walk back to the living room, where I pour another drink from the pitcher Andy has left in the refrigerator and we settle on facing sofas. We talk for an hour, mostly about Bon Jovi's surprise decision to sever their ties with Doc McGhee. Cher cannot believe it and neither can I.

At ten o'clock, she stifles a yawn with her hand and rises to go to bed. I kiss her on the cheek, we hug, and she walks upstairs as I begin snuffing out the candles. I make a check on the entrances to the house. I check the alarms are on and the windows are secure. I check the views of the garden from the house and also assess the view of the house from the garden, noting the bushes and other places in which an intruder could hide. This is to be my nightly routine: for tonight at least I am satisfied that all is as it should be. Closing the door to my bedroom softly behind me, I breathe a sigh and flop onto the bed without undressing. After years of touring the world, my body has built up a resistance to jet lag, but my mind is racing. Cher's home is a paradise but she is a prisoner within it. No amount of money can buy peace of mind. I realise how lonely and vulnerable she must feel.

I wonder if she is asleep. I wonder if she can sleep at all.

I wake to the sound of breakers crashing on the beach, the barking of sea lions and the dawn chorus of birdsong. It is six o'clock. The sun is pale yellow in a soft blue sky. I find a T-shirt and shorts from my trunk.

Cher's bedroom door is ajar. She is sleeping. I walk downstairs, drink a glass of water and slip out through the gate at the foot of the garden to stroll along the beach. The sand feels cool under my bare feet. I see two other people; a man walking a dog and a surfer paddling out to sea on his board. The man with the dog smiles as I pass and nods, 'Good morning'. He looks like Tom Cruise. I rub my eyes and take a second look over my shoulder. It is Tom Cruise. I laugh to myself, 'Welcome to Malibu.'

The sounds of the ocean and the beauty of the scenery ease away the worries of last night. The air is salty and fresh. The sun warms my skin. I continue walking to the next point, then turn back. Tom and his dog are gone. The surfer glides in to shore on a small wave. I find myself smiling. I could get used to this.

I arrive back at the house at eight as members of Cher's domestic staff begin quietly setting about their work. The pool cleaner skims a net across the water. A team of four Mexican gardeners, aged between twenty and fifty, are watering the lawns and shrubs. One of her several cars – a black Porsche, her favourite – is being waxed and polished.

I walk up to the gym for a light, thirty-minute workout. The gym room offers the best views of the ocean and the Point through floor-to-ceiling windows. I shower, then join Cher for breakfast at nine-fifteen. She is seated at the kitchen table, talking and laughing with three women.

One I recognise immediately. Angie Best is the ex-wife of the legendary Irish footballer George Best. George is a renowned playboy, drinker and womaniser whose long hair and pop-star looks had him dubbed 'the Fifth Beatle' in the late sixties, when he played for Manchester United's European Cup-winning team. Angie is a beautiful blonde with an amazing figure. She has a healthy glow and the look of a survivor. Having lived with George, she would need to be. Angie is Cher's personal trainer.

Paulette Betts is another beauty. A little taller than Angie at five feet ten, Paulette has wavy red hair down to her waist. She was formerly married to Dickey Betts, a guitarist in the Allman Brothers Band, whose leader Gregg Allman married Cher in 1975, four days after her divorce from Sonny Bono. Allman and Cher's stormy on-off relationship finally ended in divorce in

1979. The couple had one child, a son, Elijah Blue, in 1977. Allman and Betts clashed when the former, under threat of indictment before a grand jury, testified against the group's road manager John 'Scooter' Herring in a drug trafficking trial which resulted in a seventy-five-year jail sentence for Herring. Their wives remained close. Paulette is Cher's best friend and confidante. If anyone knows Cher inside out, it is Paulette. Some women have a weakness for musicians and Paulette is like Cher in this respect. She is currently dating Bruce, the guitarist in Cher's band.

The last woman at the table is Cher's assistant Debbie Paul. Debbie has worked for many years as the link between Cher and her management, her record company and her movie agent. To get to Cher, you go through Debbie Paul. She is a tough-talking woman with a sharp sense of humour. It is like a scene from *Absolutely Fabulous* as the girls gossip excitedly and attack the small mountain of mail that arrives daily; movie scripts, tapes of new songs, letters from charities and fan mail. The crank mail is separated by Debbie beforehand and forwarded to a security firm.

Cher wears no make-up, tight black sweatpants and a baggy T-shirt with her own face on it, a faded souvenir of a previous tour. She does not need a Versace dress to look like a superstar. Her breakfast is vegetable juice and a cocktail of thirty vitamin tablets. The other girls eat fresh fruit with home made granola prepared by Andy the previous evening.

Paulette has news of a major movie producer's drug-taking and sexual deviance, as exposed by a notorious Hollywood madam. Lurid details are discussed and jokes fly across the table. I realise that I must be on my toes to keep up with these girls.

My thoughts turn to work and last night's conversation with Cher. I take another walk around the property to see what improvements might be made to secure the house. I speak to each member of staff and stress the importance of following a strict security code. If they notice anything out of the ordinary, no matter how trivial it might seem, they are to report to me immediately.

At ten, a beauty therapist arrives to treat the Ab-Fab girls to a full manicure, pedicure and wax, which they enjoy every second day. Then it is workout time, as Angie Best leads them through a two-hour gym session. Angie is a little tyrant, barking orders as she puts each of the others through their paces. This is when the house truly comes alive. The noise in the gym is deafening, with Angie shouting over the whirring of life-cycles and rowing machines and the thump of Cher's favourite songs; Bon Jovi's 'Bad Medicine', Aerosmith's 'Love In An Elevator', Van Halen, Guns 'N' Roses and more. The music stops for thirty minutes as the girls watch *Oprah* on a giant video screen while jogging on running machines. Then Bon Jovi's 'Livin' On A Prayer' signals the start of a forty-five minute period of step aerobics.

Throughout the two hours there is laughter. Here with the girls, looking out over the ocean, working up a sweat and singing her favourite songs, Cher is free of her anxieties. As she finishes, her adrenaline is running high. She frees her damp hair from a headscarf, runs a hand across her brow and pulls at her sweat-darkened shirt with an expression of mock disgust. She is happy.

I hand her a towel and she vanishes into her bedroom to shower. She emerges in jeans and a Bon Jovi T-shirt to run through scales in a daily singing lesson. Cher has a powerful voice and the body of a woman half her forty-five years, but she works hard at both.

The girls reconvene for lunch at one o'clock on the sun terrace. Andy brings out a large bowl of salad with cous-cous, Cher's favourite, and bottles of Canadian mineral water. She drinks nothing else. The talk quickly turns to men, musicians. Cher teases Paulette about Bruce. He must be good in the sack, I think to myself, because it is clearly not his guitar that is the attraction. But Bruce is a great guy and I feel for him as Cher and Paulette compare notes.

After lunch, I accompany Cher on a shopping trip. She loves to shop and has the money to buy anything and everything she wants. I do not drive, so she takes the wheel of the black Porsche and zips through the mountains to the mall in Pacific Palisades, pointing to the homes of her famous neighbours as we pass. Sting's house is especially beautiful.

When we park, I walk around the car to open the door for her, glancing around me for anyone who might approach. But this is Malibu. People here are accustomed to seeing celebrities. A pretty teenage girl notices Cher and nudges her friend. They smile as we head for the place that Cher always visits first, a frozen yoghurt shop. She orders two vanilla yoghurts. She certainly loves her vanilla. She produces two coupons from her bag and hands them to the girl behind the counter.

'You get two free yoghurts when you spend twenty-five dollars,' Cher smiles. The cashier is as surprised as I am. Cher is worth millions and she collects coupons to get free frozen yoghurts. We exchange a laugh and stroll through the mall, sipping our freebies. I hold her cup as she tries on a pair of shoes in a chic clothing store specialising in one-off items. She takes the shoes and two casual tops. The sales assistant feigns nonchalance as she swipes Cher's credit card to the tune of two thousand dollars. Cher is beaming as the shoes and clothes are neatly packed into a single bag. I take the bag in one hand, still holding the free yoghurts in the other.

Next stop, a lingerie store. She holds up a brassiere and matching panties, red silk with a lacy black trim. I feel a red flush warming my face.

'What do you think?' she asks mischievously. This, I sense, is a test. A little game to make certain we are on the same wavelength.

'Very nice,' I reply, stumbling a little.

'Can you get them for me? Here's my card.'

A smiling cashier wraps the new purchase and swipes the

card. One bra and a pair of drawers cost more than any suit I have ever bought. Cher signs the paper slip and turns to me, all girlish exhilaration. She is a true shopaholic.

We return at five o'clock to an empty house. Cher dashes upstairs with her shopping bags. I wonder whether she is trying on her new undies as I make an inspection of the house and gardens. Andy has prepared dinner, a salad of turkey breast and fresh green vegetables, which he leaves in the refrigerator. I bring the food to the terrace where Cher sits with a glass of water. I have a bottled American beer. Cher rarely touches alcohol but does not object to others drinking despite the messy scenes she has witnessed over the years with rock stars and hangers-on getting wasted on booze and drugs.

The sun sets over the Pacific as we eat and talk. Cher is a great talker and storyteller, and she does not mince words. She speaks of her life with Sonny in the early seventies, the fabulous parties they held at their home, where George Harrison and Ringo Starr would mix with Neil Young and other rock royalty. As the night turns chill, we move inside the house and talk for another hour or so before Cher retires to bed just after nine, clutching a book on Roman history. I go to bed and watch TV with the sound turned low. My thoughts turn to home, to Camden, to my wife and family. This house feels very big with just Cher and myself in it.

A month passes before I truly feel comfortable living with Cher. For much of my adult life I have lived with rock stars on the road, but to experience the home life of a superstar like Cher is something else entirely. A world tour with Bon Jovi could last for more than a year, a whirlwind of constant travel, partying and fan hysteria, but I would always have a home to go to, an escape from the madness. Now my home is a mansion in

Malibu, where a world famous pop star and Hollywood icon sleeps in the next room. It is not a bad life, but it takes some getting used to.

I am Cher's constant companion. It is my job to keep her company and keep her alive. We are growing close. She speaks to me constantly about Richie; and when I recall my childhood and the trouble I had at school, she surprises me by revealing that she too suffered a mild form of dyslexia as a child. For someone who spends so much of her time reading, it is astonishing. Reading is her passion. The walls of the house are lined with volumes on history and religion, and she rarely goes to bed without a book in her hand.

Like many dyslexic kids, she developed a sense of humour about her condition. When you are young, it feels better to have people laughing with you about it. That way they're not laughing at you, and you can feel part of the crowd.

I make other friends within Cher's social circle. If Bruce is visiting with Paulette, we will leave the girls to talk in the house and ride out on his Harley Davidson to a secluded beach, where we get stoned under the stars. If Andy stays late, we sit and chat and drink Pina Coladas on the terrace. One evening I persuade him to cook us a chicken curry. Cher joins us to eat and spends the whole night raving about the curry and swapping stories of life on the road. Our experiences of touring are very similar. I am mindful of revealing too much about Bon Jovi's touring habits and Richie's in particular, but there is little that I can say that will shock her. Even the sanest people do the weirdest things when they are on the road. It is what you do to survive. If you didn't enjoy it, you couldn't do it.

Here in Malibu, my life has fallen into a set pattern. The day begins at seven o'clock with a check of the security system, followed by an hour-long workout in the gym. Then I take a walk on the beach, pausing to rub the Oscar on the piano before I go; a stupid little ritual, but it always brings a smile to the face of a poor boy from North London. My walk along the beach

227

takes me past the homes of Anthony Hopkins and record company mogul David Geffen. Sometimes it feels like I am the only person in this place who is not rich and famous.

The days are spent bantering with the AbFab girls and shopping with Cher. She gets such a kick out of spending money, but most of the clothes will be worn once and then left hanging in the closet.

In the evenings, it's just the two of us. After dinner, we watch a movie together, or if Cher is tired and wants to read alone in her bed, I will watch TV in my room. Sometimes we go out to dinner or a movie. When we return to the house, Cher will read film scripts or play new songs sent to her by music publishers. She is always in bed by ten.

At night the house is eerily silent. From eight in the morning when all the staff arrive it's like Piccadilly Circus, and then on the stroke of six, everyone leaves and it's suddenly dead quiet. It's as if we're in Cinderella, and the ball has to end each day. After a while the inactivity gets to me, as all the days begin to blur into one. At first it is hard to be bored in paradise, but there's only so much paradise you can take. Fridays at six for me have their own special air of sadness: from the Friday night until Monday morning, often we never see another soul. Our highlight most weekends is a cinema trip on the Saturday night or maybe an antique market on the Sunday morning.

One evening Ray Liotta comes by to take Cher out to dinner. They met at a Hollywood premiere and have spoken frequently since. Cher has been busy completing a new album, but now she is free to accept his invitation. All day she has been as excited as a teenager, discussing with the AbFab girls which outfit she should wear. At seven, an hour before he is due to arrive, she summons me to her room, where shirts and tops of various colours are spread out on the bed. She holds up two lacy tops, one black and one white.

'Well?' she grins

'White,' I say.

'Thank you, Michael. Ray is due at eight. Could you wait for him downstairs?'

I nod and depart with a smile.

Ray arrives at eight on the dot. He wears a beautiful green silk shirt and a brown suit with the jacket slung over one shoulder. He says that Cher has told him all about me and my father and we discuss boxing as we wait for her to come down. I warm to Ray instantly. He is naturally funny and knows his boxing. When Cher appears she looks radiant in the white lace top and blue jeans, a tiny cross at her neck. Ray rises from his seat and she kisses him lightly on one cheek. They look wonderful together, and clearly there is a spark between them. I find myself hoping that maybe this could be the start of something special, but it is not to be. Whatever the reason, they elect to remain good friends, and nothing more.

Only rarely will a guest stay the night at the house. During my second month here, Michelle Pfeiffer arrives to accompany Cher to a movie screening at a nearby theatre. Cher had told me she has a date but said nothing more. When I answer the door to Michelle Pfeiffer, I am stunned. She wears a white shirt, blue jeans and flip-flops. She is so beautiful, it is difficult to keep from staring. They drive off in Michelle's car and I am left alone in the house. Half-heartedly watching a sports channel, the time passes slowly. The girls return in high spirits and settle on the white sofas for a heart-to heart. Michelle is sleeping over, so I retire for an early night.

One week later and we have another visitor in Sharon Stone. Andy stays late to cook a simple meal of chicken and rice, which we eat in the kitchen. He opens a bottle of the finest red wine and we leave the girls to talk in private. I sit with Andy beside the pool, sipping Pina Coladas, watching the moon's reflection glittering on the Pacific and assuring each other that, yes, we have just eaten dinner with Sharon Stone.

Cher calls out to us when Sharon is about to drive home.

'If Michael were single, we'd be a match made in heaven,' Cher says.

I am still smiling when I wake the next morning.

★

Not all our time is spent in Malibu, however. One overcast afternoon, Cher and I are at London's Heathrow airport en route to LA at the end of a brief promotional visit. Twenty-five pieces of her luggage have been passed through to the baggage hold and another ten pieces are on a trolley I am wheeling past bored security men. As I load the cases on to the conveyor belt for x-ray screening, an official peers intently at the video image and selects one case for inspection.

'Is this yours, sir?'

'Yes,' I lie. The bag is Cher's, but she will not want to watch as a man she has never met before picks through her underwear. When you work for a star like Cher, you do everything for them, whatever the potential for embarrassment.

'Can we open it?'

'Of course. No problem.'

As the bag is unzipped, Cher stands mutely beside me in coat, scarf and sunglasses. The official pulls out some T-shirts and a skirt and lays them gently on the counter. Rummaging around, he uncovers what appears to be some kind of sleek dark plastic item, possibly electrical. A hairdryer, I think. He tugs at it and, to my horror, an enormous vibrator emerges from the bag. This thing is a monster; a good nine inches from base to tip.

Glancing up at me, the official is almost as red-faced as I am. I would feel sorry for him if I were not so embarrassed myself. If this was anything else – a pair of knickers, stockings, whatever – I'd say it belonged to me, but not this.

I turn to her with a pleading expression.

'It's okay,' she tells the official, 'it's mine.' With a sigh, she places the vibrator back in the bag. Handing the bag to me, she glides towards the duty free shops, unruffled. Struggling behind her, I can't push that trolley quick enough.

On arrival at LAX, we are greeted by Cher's assistant Debbie Paul and a chauffeur-driven limousine. We reach the house at dusk. Cher heads upstairs to soak in a bath and Debbie calls me into her office. She has some bad news. The police have told her the stalker has been released with charges pending. We decide to keep this information from Cher to avoid worrying her unecessarily, but I double-check every entrance to the house before going to bed.

Next morning, I receive a call from the Malibu police when Cher is working out. The stalker has been spotted nearby. A squad car calls at the house and we drive out to an intersection, where one of the officers points to a shabby figure seated at a roadside café.

'That's the guy,' he says.

Thickset, with long, lank grey hair and beard, he looks like a wino, the kind of dropout who lives in a car. I take in every detail of his face. I want to know exactly what he looks like. The cops inform me that there is a restraining order preventing him from entering the area within a mile radius of Cher's home. His present location is right on the edge of that one-mile exclusion zone. This guy knows what he is doing.

We drive back to the house where I ask the officer to drop me off outside the gate. I do not want Cher to see the police car. She and the girls are chatting in the kitchen. I say hello and walk upstairs to my room. In a drawer beside the bed is the gun given to me by Cher's former security guard. I check that it is fully loaded.

'Michael!' Cher calls from the kitchen. 'Paulette wants to know what the guys at Heathrow found in your bag.' The girls are cackling loudly, but I don't feel much like laughing.

I place the gun back inside the drawer and force a smile as I walk downstairs.

20

Keep the faith

A bright, clear morning in Malibu. Cher and the girls are in the gym when the phone rings in the kitchen. Debbie Paul is in Hollywood attending a business meeting, so I answer and smile when I recognise a familiar voice on the line.

'Reg, it's Richie.'

'Mister Donkey Dick! Where are you?'

'We're in LA for rehearsals. How are you?'

'Good, thanks. Cher's working out upstairs. I'll just get her.'

'No, man, I wanted to speak with you.'

For months I have been expecting a call from Richie or Jon regarding the next Bon Jovi tour. Since they dispensed with Doc McGhee, the band has been managing its own affairs. This week they released a new album, *Keep The Faith*, which entered the UK chart at number one and the US chart at number five, a triumph for a band who have been inactive for two and a half years – a

233

lifetime in the rock business. In addition, the rise of grunge music – led by Pearl Jam and Nirvana – has effectively finished the careers of numerous eighties rock stars, but Bon Jovi have survived better than many expected, perhaps better than the band themselves dared to hope.

In these circumstances I expect Richie to sound upbeat, but his voice is dry, and falters as he explains, 'We had a band meeting today and your name's not on the list for the tour. What's going on?'

For a few seconds I am too shocked to answer. 'I don't know,' I tell him. 'Nobody's told me about the tour. I've been waiting for Jon to call.'

'I'll ask around,' Richie says. 'If I hear anything, I'll let you know.' He gives me his number at the Bel Age hotel in Hollywood. 'I'll see you soon.'

'Okay,' I reply and place the receiver back in its cradle. I feel numb as I walk out to the sun terrace and slowly breathe in the sea air. My emotions are mixed. I wonder whether Jon has simply forgotten to call me. Perhaps Richie is mistaken. I think back to the end of the last Bon Jovi tour in 1990, to the riot in Guadalajara. Everyone was exhausted and tense back then, Jon more than most. I have not seen him since. I did not work with him when he released his solo album in the summer of 1990, but there is no bad blood between us, none that I can recall. But Doc is gone, and I cannot help thinking that maybe I am next.

Jon calls me two days later. His tone is light, friendly. I do not mention Richie's call. Jon expresses his delight at the success of the new album and invites me for lunch at his home on the following day. Jon has a house on the beach, just around the Point.

The next day, he arrives at noon in a black jeep wearing faded blue jeans and a black T-shirt, his hair shorn to collar-length in a more fashionable cut. For an hour he chats to Cher and me over coffee in the kitchen. He checks his watch and says that Dorothea will have lunch ready soon. On the twenty-minute drive back to his house, Jon asks me about my family and how I am enjoying life in Malibu.

His beach house is built on stilts and reaches out over the water. The entire structure is wooden, the interior decorated in a simple, homely style. The day is warm and Dorothea serves lunch on a terrace overlooking the calm ocean. We eat pasta and drink red wine. The conversation centres on family. As Jon pours me a third glass of wine he reminisces about the Christmas dinner that June cooked for him and the band in Camden Town, and the drunken pilgrimage to Karl Marx's tomb which followed. I laugh and forget the previous days' anxieties.

At five, I tell Jon that I must get back to Cher's house. I am accompanying her to a movie screening this evening. I thank Dorothea for a wonderful meal and kiss her on the cheek. Only when I am stepping up into the passenger seat of Jon's jeep do I think again of the conversation I had with Richie. Jon speaks little during the journey, while rock songs play quietly on the radio. As he pulls up at the gate to Cher's house, he turns to me with a solemn expression.

'Reg, you won't be coming with us on this tour.'

Despite Richie's warning, I am too stunned to reply.

'This is out of my hands,' Jon shrugs. 'We've changed management, and they don't want you on this tour. It's not personal, it's business.'

I cannot believe what I am hearing from a guy who has been so close to me for so long: someone I have worked with, drunk with, laughed with, and risked my life to protect. Someone who told me a few years back that he would never tour without me. Someone who just a few hours earlier had told me how he will always cherish the memory of eating Christmas dinner in my home. Jon is the boss, he makes the decisions, and he can have whomever he wants on the tour. This is bullshit and we both know it.

I am too proud to plead for my job. I wrench open the jeep's door and Jon calls after me, 'Reg, you'll be looked after.'

More bullshit. I walk through the gate and head for the house. I do not look back. After five years, it is all over in a matter of minutes.

If he wants to move on, then fine, I think, fixing myself a large gin and tonic as soon as I get inside. But he should have done it like a man, and not tried to soften me up before telling me. I finish my drink, pour another and walk up to my room to call home. As I wait for an answer, I wonder how to explain this to my kids. They idolise Jon and think of him as part of the family. June is woken by the call. She is sympathetic but sleepy, and I am drunk. I tell her I will call again in the morning.

As I roll into my bed, I remember something my brother Billy told me just a few weeks ago. Billy works with Sting. Sting met Jon recently at the Four Seasons Hotel in LA, and Jon had described me as he would describe a brother. A bitter smile passes my lips. I have worked in this business long enough to know that you should never get too close to anybody you are working for. If you do it will always end up hurting you.

In the morning, Richie calls again.

'You were right,' I tell him.

We meet at lunchtime at his hotel. In a quiet corner of the bar, we drink beer and talk over old times.

'It's all bullshit, politics,' concludes Richie.

After two hours, he drains his glass and rises to hug me.

'It won't be the same without you, Reg,' he says.

21

Love hurts

On 16 August, my birthday, I am woken by a telephone call from June. She tries to sound upbeat, but there is sorrow in her voice. It is a difficult conversation that leaves me feeling desolate as we say our goodbyes. A walk on the beach does little to clear my head or lift my mood. At noon, Cher and Paulette Betts take me for a lunch of grilled fish and chilled Californian wine at a beachfront restaurant. A warm breeze ruffles the canopy over our heads. It is a perfect Californian summer day, but as the girls talk, I find myself drifting out of the conversation, gazing out over the Pacific and seeing instead the streets of Camden Town.

We return at four to the sweet smell of a cake that Andy has baked for me. The cake is decorated with a single candle. I blow out the flame and make a wish.

'What did you wish for?' Paulette asks.

'It's a secret,' I reply. I wish I could be home with my family.

'Come outside,' Cher says, tugging at my arm. 'I have a surprise for you.'

Cher leads me to the tennis court. Paulette and Andy follow with a bottle of champagne. On one side of the court stands a huge square shape, five feet high and four feet wide, covered in pink wrapping paper. I tear off the paper to reveal a tennis trainer machine. Designed for players to practice alone, it is programmed to fire balls from the opposite side of the net. Now, on the weekends when only Cher and I are at the house, I will have someone – or rather, something – to play tennis with. These machines are not cheap; they retail at around five thousand dollars. Touched by her generosity, I thank her with a kiss.

The following afternoon, I find myself talking to the machine as it sends services fizzing towards me. If it would only answer back, I might feel less like leaving.

Summer blends imperceptibly into autumn, and a smiling Debbie Paul brings some good news. The stalker who had broken into Cher's home carrying a samurai sword has finally been jailed. I feel some of the tension ease from my shoulders before stepping into my room and checking that the gun is still in its drawer. As my father instructed me in the boxing ring, you should never drop your guard. But also I can't help thinking that now the immediate danger is over, the ties that are keeping me here are not as binding as they were.

At the end of November I am woken again by a phone call from my wife. She cannot conceal her distress. Her breathing is laboured and her speech comes in rapid bursts. There has been an attempted break-in at our house in London. She opened the curtains of the french windows that lead to the garden to find a man on the other side of the glass in the act of trying the door.

'I want you back here now,' she sobs. 'Enough is enough.'

This time I know she means it. She has never delivered an ultimatum before. I put the phone down and sink back on the bed with a sigh. All this time I have been so concerned for Cher's safety and now my own wife is feeling under threat. I have yearned to get back to London, to June and the kids, so why am I still here? Is paradise more important than the love of my wife and family? Of course not. I just haven't had the guts to tell Cher that I'm going, not when she is feeling so alone. Only now I have no choice. If I do not go home now, I will lose my marriage.

I take a slow walk on the beach thinking of how I will break the news to Cher. The surf crashes loudly on the shore. I know she will understand my reason for leaving, but that doesn't make it any easier to say. I return to the house to find Cher and Debbie in the kitchen. Cher immediately senses my unease. She asks Debbie to call a record company executive in New York and sits opposite me at the table.

'What's up?' she frowns.

I tell her about June's call. 'I have to go.'

She nods. 'Okay.'

We sit in silence until Debbie returns.

'Michael needs to get back to London,' Cher explains to Debbie. 'Try and get him on the first flight out tonight.'

Debbie hurries back to her office and Cher turns to me.

'Do you think you'll be back?'

'I don't know.'

'You know you can come back any time you want,' she tells me.

We rise and embrace. As we part, there are tears in her eyes, and in mine.

'Go on,' she says. 'Pack your things.'

My steps are heavy as I climb the stairs to my room. I fold my clothes into two cases and linger over the view past the palm trees and out over the glittering ocean. I know I will not return. Perhaps Cher senses it too. This is difficult for us both. I am not just a bodyguard. I am her friend and companion. She feels safe at night with me here. She is a wonderful person, warm, funny, intelligent, caring. The best person I have met in the twenty-five years I have worked in the entertainment business. But this is a strange world that she lives in. It feels like a movie, not the real world.

I remove the gun from the bedside drawer and walk downstairs to lock it inside a safe. I think of the gun under Cher's pillow and the panic room. I think of Cher going to her bed tonight, feeling for the gun before laying her head on the pillow to sleep.

Debbie calls to me from the kitchen. 'I've got you on the Heathrow flight at five.'

I see past her to the terrace, where Cher stands alone, her head tilted towards the Point, where gulls circle high over the cliffs. I picture June at the window of our bedroom, looking out over the sloping slate roofs of Camden Town.

I feel sorrow but also happiness. I am going home.

For the next two years I continue to work with Cher whenever she is in Europe. In April 1993 she travels to Armenia, the place where her father was born. She is on a mission, sponsored by the United Armenian Fund, to raise awareness of the terrible suffering of the country's orphans and refugees. With her she has her hairdresser, her best friend Paulette Betts, and me.

Armenia is east of Turkey on the borders of Europe and Asia, and is in conflict over territory with neighbouring Azerbaijan, a conflict which flared up in 1991 when both nations gained independence from the Soviet Union. The fighting has left many thousands dead, crippled, widowed, orphaned and impoverished. Visiting Armenia proves a sobering and humbling experience for us all.

We fly to the capital, Yerevan, in a cargo plane loaded with ten tons of food and medical supplies. Upon landing, we are greeted by police and given a motorcycle escort to our hotel. It is summer but the skies are grey over a bleak cityscape of slum housing and dirty streets. The hotel is the best the city has to offer, but has neither electricity nor hot running water. We have been told what to expect and have packed our cases with bottled water, toilet rolls, fresh fruit and chocolate.

Leaving Cher to unpack, I meet with two police officers in the hotel lobby. Given the poverty of the city's people, their desperation and the crime that this desperation breeds, the police fear an attempt to kidnap Cher, and advise me to carry a gun for the duration of our stay. With a rising sense of unease, I accept their offer of a small police-issue pistol, which I slide into the inside pocket of my jacket. I thank them and walk back up to Cher's room, wishing she had simply made a donation to relief charities or made an appeal via the American media instead of coming to a place which is feeling more dangerous with each passing hour. But I have confidence in the team assigned to us, provided they are on our side. It is my job to ensure that they are.

Cher and Paulette have lit their hotel room with candles. When I ask for a chocolate bar, Paulette looks at Cher, who shrugs. She has given everything to the hotel maids, save for a handful of apples and bananas. The maids, she says, have not seen a chocolate bar in years. I smile. This is typical of her. I retire to an adjacent room to sleep, the gun within reach on a bedside table.

In the morning, we are greeted by four policemen and driven to one of Armenia's largest orphanages. A cameraman from the US news channel *60 Minutes* is with us. Cher wants the American people to see for themselves the full extent of the problems in Armenia.

The orphanage is an imposing red-brick structure surrounded by a wire fence twelve feet high. Many of the windows are boarded up. It resembles a prison and evokes painful memories

241

from my past. As soon as the heavy black doors swing open to the entrance hall, the smell is overpowering. I gag, then pinch my nose and take deep breaths through my open mouth as I try to regain my composure. Cher covers her nose and mouth with her scarf, but removes it before we enter the first room where she is to meet some of the children. The scene inside the room is both horrifying and heartbreaking. In a space sixty feet by forty, there are fifty children aged between five and fifteen. Some are disabled. Most have their heads shaven. Their dirty clothes hang off their bony frames. Some of the younger kids are huddled together under thin blankets, four or five to a bed. None of the children speak, but their eyes all say the same thing: they just want someone to hold them and love them. It is a sight I will take to my grave. There are so many kids and so few of us, I feel powerless to help. Cher is led to another room filled with silent, pleading faces. She struggles to raise a smile for the children, but there are tears at the corners of her eyes. I excuse myself and walk outside to the courtyard, where a small group of older children kick a tin can in the dust in a crude game of football. I sit on the stone steps and wait for Cher to return. I have seen enough.

Cher's face is pale and drawn as she receives thanks from the governor of the orphanage before we leave. We drive for ten minutes to a hospital for children, passing through the city centre and a park where all that remains of the trees are stumps. Our guide informs us that the trees have been cut down for firewood during recent winters.

The conditions at the hospital are no better than the orphanage. The generator breaks down repeatedly, forcing the staff to work without electric light or much of the vital, life-saving machinery. Anaesthetic and other materials are in short supply. Draughty corridors are lined with tables fashioned into makeshift beds, where children lie scratching at bedbug bites.

In the wards, the young patients are confined to outsized beds with heavy iron box frames and barred sides. Cher speaks to some of the children in rudimentary Armenian. They do not know who she is. They are just happy to be spoken to, and to feel that somebody cares. When she climbs the stairs to the fourth floor and the mental ward, I find I cannot bear to go inside. I stand at the door and speak to one of the only two doctors working in the hospital. He tells me how he hopes to see glass put into many of the empty window frames before winter arrives. After four hours at the hospital, we return to the hotel. The journey is silent.

The next day, we visit an eight-year-old girl named Christina, who suffers from cerebral palsy. Christina's parents had written to Cher to ask her help in finding treatment for their daughter. Cher has arranged for Christina to fly to the United States where she will be treated privately at Cher's expense. We drive to the family's home, a tiny, sparsely furnished apartment on the outskirts of the city. Christina's mother serves tea in chipped china cups. A wedding present, she tells us proudly. Christina asks Cher if she will take her to Disneyland when she comes to America. Cher nods and says that if Christina is strong enough, she and her mother can come to stay at her home by the ocean when her treatment is completed. The little girl's courage has a profound effect on Cher.

On the following afternoon, we fly home. At the airport I hand the gun back to the police officer, relieved that I did not need to use it. Cher is saddened by what she has seen in Armenia, but determined to make whatever difference she can to these children's lives. As she speaks of her plans, I wonder what she can realistically achieve. Cher could give fifty million dollars to Armenian children's charities, but in a war-torn country of such crippling poverty, would the money be sure to reach the children who need it most? In America her charity work has a tangible effect. After starring in *Mask* as the mother of a facially deformed child, she campaigns on behalf of similarly afflicted children and performs benefit concerts to raise money for their care. When she was forced to cancel a

New York concert after losing her voice, she invited the kids to her suite at the Plaza Hotel. A room was filled with balloons; hamburgers and ice cream were delivered on room service. Cher could only whisper to the kids, but they all left happy.

For the sick children and orphans of Armenia, there appears to be little hope. All through the flight back to London, I cannot erase their faces from my mind.

In the last week of April, I accompany Cher on a short tour of Europe in order for her to promote a new album release. She is excited about the trip because it offers a chance to catch up with Richie Sambora, who is touring Europe with Bon Jovi. Cher and Richie have been dating, on and off, for four years, but when Bon Jovi are on the road, Richie is easily led astray, tempted by the beautiful girls who gravitate towards a big rock band.

Richie is great fun to be around, the complete rock star, and he loves to live his life in the fast lane. He always has two or three girls in his life at any one time. He has two rooms in every hotel and two limousines on call, one for the girl coming in and one for the girl going out. Perhaps Cher suspects he plays around on tour; and in Madrid, Richie finally, inevitably, comes unstuck.

Bon Jovi are here to play an open-air gig at the Vincente Calderon stadium, the home of the city's second biggest football team, Atletico Madrid. As our flight from Italy touches down at Madrid airport, Cher tells me she wants to surprise Richie by showing up unannounced at the band's hotel. I know from experience that this is not a good idea, but who am I to spoil his surprise? I am sure that Jon will be surprised too when I see him.

We arrive at the hotel in Madrid at 1 p.m. The Bon Jovi party is not checking in until the evening. The penthouse suite is reserved for Cher, but she is too excited to bother with unpacking. In a limousine provided courtesy of the hotel, we head straight for a beautiful square in the heart of the city, where Cher spends hours happily flitting between the most expensive stores in Madrid, spending a small fortune on clothes. At ten, the limo driver drops us off at the best restaurant in the city and delivers Cher's mountain of shopping back to her suite.

It is midnight when we return to the hotel. In the bar, Jon Bon Jovi is huddled at a table with New Jersey's biggest rock hero Bruce Springsteen. Jon is all smiles as he jumps up to greet me. He hides his embarrassment well and asks why I am in Madrid. The answer is right behind me. As he recognises Cher, his smile freezes for an instant. I pat his shoulder, savouring the moment.

Cher says a brief hello to Jon and Bruce and we settle at another table. Within a few minutes, Cher's manager Bill Samuth appears, handing her a slip of paper with Richie's room number written on it. She smiles and rises abruptly, smoothing her dress before hurrying off to surprise him. There is no time for anyone in Bon Jovi's entourage to send a warning to Richie's room.

I excuse myself from the table and dash to an elevator. This could be a messy scene. I am concerned for Cher and intrigued to see if Richie can wriggle his way out of this one.

When I catch up with Cher, she is standing outside his room and banging loudly on the door.

'Maybe he's out somewhere,' I say with a shrug, but there are noises, muted whispers, from the other side of the door. I am about to suggest that we go up to Cher's suite when the door slowly opens to reveal Richie, clad in only a towel wrapped at the waist, his hair wet, smiling sheepishly like a naughty schoolboy who has been caught stealing candy.

'Hey!' he exclaims and moves to kiss Cher. It is not a convincing performance. Behind him, a naked young woman scampers to the bedroom.

Without another word, Cher brushes past Richie and heads after the girl. Richie turns to me, panicking. We stand together in the doorway, listening intently as Cher, in clipped tones, asks the girl to leave. Snatching a T-shirt, she rushes past us, her bare feet pattering as she runs out of the room and along the hall. Cher grabs Richie's arm as he tries to escape to the bathroom. Silently, I back away and close the door behind me.

I take the elevator back to the lobby, and join the Bon Jovi party as they jump into a fleet of limousines en route to a club, where dozens of preening, olive-skinned Spanish girls chatter excitedly and queue for admittance to the VIP room. Only the prettiest get past the velvet rope to drink champagne with the band, record company big-shots and senior road crew members. One beautiful girl with glossy long hair and shining dark eyes remembers me from a previous Bon Jovi tour.

'Where is Richie?' she asks with a smile that suggests they have met before. She is certainly his type.

'He's back at the hotel,' I reply, picturing Richie in his towel, pleading with Cher and sweet-talking her.

I leave the club for the hotel at 5 a.m. As far as I can tell, Cher is still with Richie. Maybe his charm has worked. To my knowledge, it rarely fails.

In the morning I am leaving the hotel's gym when I see the girl who was in Richie's room dragging a bag towards an exit, sullen faced. Amid the drama of last night, I had not noticed how closely she resembles a younger Cher. Over breakfast in Cher's suite, she tells me I missed a very interesting night's conversation. She jokes about the incident, but I sense sadness behind her smile.

For the next two nights, Richie stays with Cher in the penthouse suite, but this is the end of their relationship. On the morning of 31 April, before Bon Jovi depart for their next show in San Sebastian, I drink a beer with Richie in the hotel bar. He does not appear upset. Perhaps the novelty of dating someone more famous than he is has worn off. And with the choice of women that he has waiting in every city, it is hard for even a woman like Cher to compete.

With Richie gone, Cher consoles herself with a two-day

shopping spree before flying home. She buys numerous pairs of shoes, antique furniture and several crucifixes for the walls of the house in Malibu. On our last night in Madrid, I accompany her to dinner at an Italian restaurant, where she speaks philosophically of her break-up with Richie.

It must be difficult, I say half-jokingly, to say goodbye to the guy we call Mister Donkey Dick. She gives a wry smile.

'It's not the quantity that counts,' I say. 'It's the quality.'

She sniffs. 'Only guys with small dicks say that.'

End of conversation.

On the flight back to London, Cher is in a subdued, contemplative mood. I leave her to her thoughts. After all the years I have been working with Bon Jovi, perhaps I know Richie better than Cher does. Clearly they care about each other; but I have always believed that the age gap is a problem. She is thirteen years older than he is. Richie is no saint and Cher has known that all along, but I think she always believed she would be the one to change him, that they might marry and raise a family together. Now we both know the truth.

Wrapped in her thoughts, she seems more alone than ever. She is beautiful, rich and a superstar, and has such a big heart. She has more talent for friendship than almost anyone else I know. She surely deserves to be happy. But Cher is the loneliest person I have met.

22

Send in the clowns

In 1995 a familiar face comes back into my life. Doc McGhee invites me to work with him again, managing a fresh crop of young rock bands. Doc has lost many of his big name acts – Bon Jovi, Mötley Crüe and Skid Row – and is searching for new talent. McGhee Entertainment Inc. opens a London office, conveniently located in Camden Town, in Royal College Street, two doors from the house where my father was born. From here, I am to act as Doc's eyes and ears in the UK. There are hundreds of bands in cities all over Britain, desperate for a break. My job is to find the bands with genuine potential. It seems like the perfect opportunity. I need some time with my family. I will remain involved in the business I love, but instead of disappearing for months on end, I can return home almost every night.

In reality the job is more difficult and frustrating than I could ever have imagined. I watch a succession of struggling bands in sweaty clubs and crumbling backstreet venues. Yet in bands that are playing in pubs, I meet guys with egos bigger than Jon Bon Jovi's. And when I do find a band with promise – Face, featuring Ringo Starr's son Zak Starkey on drums and football manager Terry Burton's kid Danny on vocals – not even Doc's influence can get them a record deal.

After eighteen months, all my efforts have come to nothing. So when Doc asks me to join the Kiss world tour instead, I jump at the chance. June's initial reaction is one of disappointment and yet, deep down, I sense that she's relieved. Over the years she has got so accustomed to daily life without me; it hasn't been easy for her to adjust to having me under her feet.

Kiss is not a band I have taken seriously before. With their clownish make-up and outlandish glam-rock costumes, they have always struck me as more of a circus act than a genuine rock band. But back in the seventies they were America's biggest band, derided by critics yet adored by millions of fans: Jon Bon Jovi included. To the multitudes of the Kiss Army, they were comic-book superheroes come to life. Each of the four band members had a fantasy alter-ego: frontman Paul Stanley was 'The Starchild', bassist Gene Simmons 'The Demon', guitarist Ace Frehley 'The Space Ace', and drummer Peter Criss 'The Catman'. They played pop-oriented hard rock and staged the most spectacular shows ever seen in the rock arena. Peter's drum-kit rose on a platform thirty feet above the stage. Ace's guitar belched smoke and fired pyrotechnic 'rockets'. Paul strutted and pouted like a New York streetwalker. And Gene dribbled fake blood from his obscenely long tongue before 'flying' on wires up into the rafters during his signature song, 'God of Thunder'.

By the turn of the eighties their record sales had dwindled as fashions in music changed and a new generation of post-punk bands moved on without them. But on stage they could still fill arenas around the world with sell-out crowds of dedicated fans, and when first Peter and then Ace quit the group, Gene and Paul continued with an ever-changing cast of sidemen. In 1983 the band shocked its fans by unmasking, and four years later the wheel turned full circle when they enjoyed their biggest UK hit with the single 'Crazy Crazy Nights'. Kiss remained a major act into the nineties, but by then the serious money was in a reunion. What their public wanted was Gene, Paul, Ace and Peter back together in make-up, the full nostalgia trip. And this is precisely what Doc is delivering in 1996.

As soon as I join the tour it is clear that the band is split into two camps. Gene and Paul are two of the smartest rock stars I have met. Together with Doc, they are the engine that is driving the whole multi-million-dollar operation. Gene is teetotal and Paul rarely drinks; neither of them takes drugs, nor ever has. They are complete professionals and shrewd businessmen; but above all, they are a pleasure to be around, witty and hugely knowledgeable about music. Ace and Peter, meanwhile, are archetypal rock 'n' roll casualties, guys who have blown fortunes on booze and drugs, parties and fast cars. Peter has his quirks – the first thing he does in every hotel room he stays in is seal the curtains closed with gaffer tape – but Ace is on another planet entirely. He acts as if he is still hung over from the seventies. In fact in an industry littered with those who succumbed to the fatal allure of the rock 'n' roll lifestyle it is a miracle he has survived into his late forties. There are three kinds of rock stars: those like Gene and Paul – although they are rare – who never get into substance abuse in the first place; those who can give it up when the glamour wears off and live to enjoy a fit and healthy old age; and those who can't. Ace cannot function like a normal person. He can't even walk in a straight line, hence his nickname, 'The Crab'. Even the stage make-up cannot conceal the scars of his crazy life. His skin is heavily pockmarked, and his nose is pitted and cratered like the surface of the moon. Ace's drinking was one of the reasons he left the band in the first place more than twenty years ago. Gene and Paul remain sceptical of his ability to hold himself together for the duration of a tour, but business is business, and they need him: without Ace, a Kiss reunion would have no real pulling power.

Gene and Paul's relationship with Ace and Peter is that of parents and their delinquent adult children. There is still some affection between them – they still speak fondly of the days they spent rehearsing together in a cold loft in their home town of New York. But they seldom socialise with one another, and almost the only time you see all four of the band together is when they are on stage. Kiss is now Gene and Paul's show, with Ace and Peter the minor players. They are paid a fee for each show that they play, just like the ever-changing line-up of musicians who replaced them when they quit in the early eighties. Gene and Paul even own the rights to their characters' make-up. I am reminded of Peter Grant's offer to promoters of Led Zeppelin shows: ten per cent of Led Zeppelin is better than one hundred per cent of nothing. Likewise, Ace and Peter understand that it is better to have a small slice of the revenue from a Kiss tour than to return to obscurity, and so they must play by Gene and Paul's rules.

I join the Kiss tour in Europe, where they are headlining Germany's Rock Am Ring festival before an audience of 70,000. It seems ridiculous that a bunch of guys nearing fifty are still billing themselves as 'The Hottest Band In The World', but the show is amazing. Musically, Kiss are no Led Zeppelin, but visually they have to be seen to be believed. This is not just a rock gig but an event. Kiss use so much pyro – fireworks, flash-bombs and great jets of flame – that the band members and anyone working on or around the stage operates to a well-drilled routine to avoid getting blown up or burnt to a crisp. A four-man team travels with the band solely to arrange and produce the pyro. Safety is paramount: at every venue at 4 p.m. there is a stringent fire check with the local fire department and the venue's own safety officer. Some countries are stricter than others. In Japan, for instance, we are likely to get permission for ten per cent of the pyro we can get away with in America.

Gene and Paul run the show on stage as tightly as they do off it. Gene stomps around in thigh-high boots with seven-inch stack-heels, flicking his tongue as he leers at the girls in the first few rows. The girls are all dreaming of riding The Big Monster – and it is his tongue they lust after since, as he himself frequently jokes, he is hung like a second-grader. Paul works tirelessly, always on the move, a shameless poser and a great rock front man. A lot of Paul's moves are familiar to me: they're the same as those that are used by Jon Bon Jovi. He tells me that when Bon Jovi supported Kiss way back in 1984, Jon would be at the side of the stage every night during Kiss's performance. Paul could feel Jon's eyes on him all the time, watching and learning.

Like Gene, Paul has a signature song in which he too is hoisted up above the stage on wires. Where Gene flies fifty feet straight up on to a platform during 'God of Thunder', in 'Love Gun' Paul is flown over the heads of the audience, guitar in hand, to a podium near the back of the arena. How far he travels, suspended from the wire with one loop to support his feet and another to which he is hanging on for dear life, depends on the size of the venue. The furthest, at a Grand Prix circuit in Mexico in front of 150,000 fans, was 150 yards. Because of the undulating ground, the platform on which he was meant to land was perched on the top of a thirty-foot scaffolding tower, and Paul was so nervous he made me and Doc climb the tower ourselves to wait for him and make sure he landed safely.

But for me the best stunt of all is the fire-breathing trick that Gene performs in 'Firehouse'. A roadie comes on and, taking his guitar, hands Gene a sword, part of which is wrapped in a petrol-soaked bandage. Behind him Gene has two bottles of what looks like water, but one is filled with inflammable liquid and the other – for afterwards – with an antiseptic mouthwash. They are distinguished from one another by different-coloured tape. Gene takes a swig from the red-taped bottle and spits it towards the blade gripped in his hand, and the sword is engulfed in a jet of flame that will flare up as much as five feet high before it dies back down.

With a show this size an army of people is needed to make it happen. Travelling with us from city to city and country to country are nine truck drivers, five bus drivers, seven lighting technicians, five sound technicians, the four pyro technicians, five carpenters, two riggers, an electrician and eight video technicians for all the big screens that the audience look at during the set. Then there are the band's personal technicians, plus the fifty local loaders we employ at every gig. Keeping track of them is a logistical nightmare. Kiss work a system of different coloured tour shirts to identify who is who. Gene's guitar tec, for example, might have five local stagehands to help him, each of whom wears a red T-shirt with 'Kiss local crew' on the back. This way he knows at a glance where his five guys are at any given time. The daily crew get to keep their T-shirts after the show is over, which helps to keep everyone sweet.

With a band like Kiss the wardrobe person plays a vital role. The band have three girls who look after their stage outfits, which is no mean feat with the blood and thunder that each night's show entails. They have two local women at every gig to help them, who spend all day making sure the costumes are clean and ready to wear. There is also a guy who takes care of putting the wigs on, who stands at the side of the stage each night just in case one comes off. Each band member has his own flight case which opens up into a wardrobe, complete with a built-in make-up shelf and mirror. The girls make the dressing rooms into a home from home, with all the band's personal pictures, family, girlfriends and so on; their favourite music, favourite drinks and favourite coloured drapes. It is all in the mind of course, but still it is these small touches that help keep the artists happy, and the bottom line is that that is what we are here for.

To feed the 100-plus workers we have a catering team of four: two chefs and two cooks, who provide the crew with breakfast, lunch and dinner. After the sound check is finished, around 6 p.m., the band and crew will all have dinner together before the show. Usually this is the only time we see the nine truck drivers. Over dinner they will discuss the best route to the next gig with the tour manager, then sleep in their trucks until midnight, when the equipment has all been loaded and it is time for them to go.

The crew travel in tour buses, each of which sleeps twelve. Accommodation is cramped: there are six bunk beds on each side in the centre part of the bus, top, middle and bottom, each of which allows just enough room to turn over. But apart from the fact that there's not much space, the buses are state of the art. There's a kitchen with microwave, a lounge with TV, DVD, CD player, computer games – all the comforts of home. At the back of the bus is the party room, where the crew unwind with drink and drugs and any groupies who are brave enough – believe me, there is never a shortage in any city, and some would stay for weeks. And as long as it keeps the crew smiling it works for everyone.

The crew has one last member – Winston Busdog. Winston is a handsome grey Weimaraner belonging to the production team of Patrick and Diane Whitley. They acquired him as a puppy and he has travelled on the tour ever since. He has his own tour pass which hangs round his neck and his own bunk on the tour bus and his name in the official personnel list alongside his job title: tourdog.

For a band like Kiss, touring on this scale is an expensive business. Merchandising is crucial. Their merchandise is the one thing that belongs to them entirely. Revenue from ticket sales is split with the promoter. Revenue from album sales – royalties apart – goes to the record company. But apart from the merchandisers they employ to sell it, all the revenue from their merchandise goes to the band. When I started out in the seventies merchandising was nothing like so important as it is now. All you got was a T-shirt, and that would only be for a major tour. Back in the sixties when I first saw The Beatles there was no tour merchandise at all. I sometimes wonder what it would be worth today if there had been. Merchandise on the scale that Kiss work on earns the band in the region of $20 per head per show. With an audience averaging 15,000 a night, twenty shows a month for a six-month tour brings in something over $35 million. Not surprisingly, merchandise has become an integral part of the rock industry, and few bands now can afford to tour without it.

★

Both Gene and Paul are anglophiles, and I warm to them instantly. Their favourite bands are The Beatles, The Kinks, Led Zeppelin and The Who. Paul lived in London for a while with former topless model Samantha Fox, and developed a liking for British humour and food – especially liver and bacon with mashed potatoes. Now Paul has a young son, Evan, he has stopped sleeping around on tour. Gene is also a father. He has two children, Nicholas and Sophie, by his longtime partner Shannon Tweed, a former *Playboy* Playmate of the Year. Despite his family status, he does as he pleases while on the road. This means screwing a succession of groupies, fans, models, waitresses; women of all ages and sizes. It is not something he keeps secret: Gene Simmons is rock's most notorious lothario. He and Shannon have an open relationship, which suits him just fine. Gene photographs each of the girls he sleeps with, a collection that numbers more than four thousand.

Gene freely admits that he will fuck anything that moves – provided it is a woman who has reached the age of consent and is not yet drawing a pension. He scoffs at those who are addicted to alcohol and cigarettes, yet his own appetite for sex borders on addiction. The difference is that Gene's habit does not have an adverse effect on his career, nor will it kill him. He is an enthusiastic believer in safe sex, as I discover when he calls me late one night when we are in a hotel in Austria. He has four girls in his room and has run out of condoms. I find a vending machine in the men's room off the lobby and buy ten packets of three.

Gene answers my knock at the door with only a towel wrapped round him, his belly protruding and his thinning hair drawn back in a flimsy ponytail. As I drop the packets into his cupped hands, a girl with breasts bigger than her head peers out from behind him, giggling. An elderly waiter passes us in the hallway, pushing a room service trolley and staring at Gene with a mixture of amusement and disgust.

'What are you looking at?' Gene booms, to the waiter's evident consternation, and then adds for good measure 'Haven't you ever seen a Jew in a towel before?' Warming to his theme, Gene gestures expansively, throwing his arms wide. 'Where's all our gold?' he says. 'What have you done with it? When will we get it back?' It is all good-natured banter, and the waiter, to his credit, gets the joke. Gene winks at me as he closes the door. When you're overweight, balding and fifty years old, and you're getting up on stage every night in a wig, make-up and silly costume to play the God of Thunder, you need a sense of humour.

Gene is a multi-millionaire and has a different girl every night. Time and again, he says what a lucky old man he is. He carries with him a little black book filled with the phone numbers of girls in various cities all over the world. When it is full he adds extra pages that fold concertina-style, so the entries under 'A' for example pull out to three feet long. Other big names in the rock world will call him when they are on tour, asking for names and numbers of the girls he recommends. Gene loves to show off these girls to the rest of the band and get a reaction from other guests in hotels by parading around with a girl on each arm. Yet he also has the air of a gentleman. The girls are never mistreated and always leave happy. Gene can call any of the thousands of girls he has been with and they will always see him again.

One woman that he keeps in touch with on a purely platonic basis is Cher, whom he has known for twenty years. We talk about her at length. He tells me that in the mid-seventies, during a dip in her career, when she needed a place to stay in New York he lent her his loft apartment in Manhattan. They still speak regularly, and it is clear that Gene retains a lot of affection for Cher. The only woman for whom he has greater regard is Shannon. She is charming and elegant, and on the occasions that she joins the Kiss tour, I am amazed at how many people approach her for a picture or an autograph. As the star of several TV shows, not to mention the dozens of movies she has to her name, she is a celebrity in her own right. And as the mother of Gene's two children, she is the most important woman in his life apart from his own mother, who raised him alone in Israel before they moved to America.

Near the end of 1998 Kiss release a new album, *Psycho Circus*, the first in almost twenty years to feature all four original members of the band. The Reunion Tour turns into The Farewell Tour, with dates in Europe, America, Japan and Australia. It is when we revisit Germany in February 1999 that I receive a call from June telling me that my mother Joan is gravely ill. Mum has bone cancer and her condition has been steadily worsening for eighteen months. When I was last home, Dad had made up a bed for her in the living room because she had grown too frail to climb the stairs. At least from there she could look out on to the garden she loved so much. I would sit with her for hours whenever Dad left the house. When he returned, he would always say the same thing to me, a gentle joke to ease the tension: 'Are you still here?'

She has had several operations but the last has been unsuccessful and has left her in terrible pain. Doc gives me his blessing to fly home at once and both Gene and Paul are quick to offer support. Knowing my mother was ill, in Canada Paul had given me a book called *Tuesdays With Morrie*, an inspirational story about a teacher dying of cancer, and how his friend, Mitch Albom, the author, learned wisdom and life lessons from his old mentor until the day he died.

I take a cab from Heathrow straight to the hospital where Dad has been at Mum's bedside for days on end. June and my brother Simon have been making sure that he eats and rests. As soon as I see him, the fear shows in his face. There is fear in my heart too, but I can only imagine what Dad is going through.

I read in *Tuesdays With Morrie* that what a cancer patient dreads most, especially towards the end, is waking up alone. This is the moment they feel most afraid, when dreams give way to reality. Between us, Dad, June, Simon and me, we make sure that one of us stays with Mum for twenty-four hours a day.

For two days she slips in and out of consciousness. She is incredibly brave, as all cancer patients are, but on the second day, as I hold her hand in mine, she asks me to take care of Simon, and a moment later she whispers, 'Let me go.' They are the last words she says to me.

The funeral is held at Saint Dominic's Church in Camden, presided over by Father Malcom McMahon, the Catholic Bishop of Nottingham, who for many years was our family parish priest. He has cut short a visit to Rome to be here, and his willingness to do so clearly means a lot to Dad. After fifty-five years of marriage, Dad appears lost without Mum at his side. She was the heart of our family. Every day at the hospital we knew what we were losing; but the truth is that you're never prepared for the actual moment of loss. Until the person you love has gone you can't begin to measure how big a void they will leave in your life.

Three days after the funeral, Dad tells me I should return to work. He assures me that with Simon, June and my kids to look out for him, he will be okay. He has taken to calling June his guardian angel. I rejoin the Kiss tour in Spain, knowing he is in safe hands.

★

In May 2000 we reach Detroit for two sold-out shows at the 16,000-capacity Palace of Auburn Hills. Detroit is the band's second home. It was here, in 1975, that they recorded the live album which gave them their first million seller and produced their first hit single, 'Rock And Roll All Nite'. The band expressed their gratitude in the 1976 song 'Detroit Rock City', which remains one of their most popular anthems.

In Detroit I arrange a special treat for Paul. It is my chance to repay him for his kindness when Mum died. Paul is a boxing fan, as I discovered during the course of my first Kiss tour. We were in Barcelona and Paul was desperate to see Mike Tyson's world title fight against Evander Holyfield. There were no cable TV facilities at our hotel, but one of the barmen invited us back to his house, where we watched the fight at four in the morning on an ancient black-and-white set. We left at six, still reeling with shock that Tyson had been defeated. Holyfield's trainer for that fight was Emmanuel Steward, and it is Emmanuel that I call after Kiss fly in to Detroit. Emmanuel is an old friend of Dad's and owns Detroit's Kronk Gym, the most famous boxing academy in the world. Here he has trained several of America's greatest champions, including Sugar Ray Leonard and local hero Thomas 'The Hit Man' Hearns, who won world titles at three different weights. British fighters Lennox Lewis and Prince Naseem Hamed have also trained at Kronk. I ask Emmanuel if I can bring Paul Stanley to see the place. He tells me to come by in the afternoon when the gym is busy, so that Paul can get a sense of what really goes into making a pro fighter.

Kronk is situated in the basement of a dilapidated school building in one of Detroit's poorest neighbourhoods: a bleak cityscape of shabby tenement blocks and disused warehouses. This is not the kind of place to bring a limo, so we arrive by taxi. Paul is simply dressed in jeans, T-shirt and leather jacket, but is still unmistakably a rock star. A security guard sits on a folding chair at the entrance to the gym. He waves us inside and points to a flight of concrete steps leading down to the basement. The door to the main gym room is at the far end of a corridor fifty feet long. As we approach the door, we hear the muffled thuds of gloves hitting bags, and a pungent stench fills our nostrils. Nothing else on earth smells like a boxing gym. On the journey from the hotel, I had warned Paul what to expect; a stale odour of sweat and blood, sawdust and saliva, compounded by the training clothes the boxers have been wearing which are draped over the radiators to dry. 'You'll want to heave,' I tell him. 'But you'll soon get used to it.'

Inside, under bright strip-lights, we see twenty boxers at work. Our eyes are immediately drawn to the ring in one corner, where two young middleweights are sparring. Elsewhere, fighters of varying size are at the punching bags or skipping with ropes. The walls are covered in yellowing posters advertising fights dating back decades. On one of the walls is a large one-hour clock, the time marked out in blocks of three minutes, each block followed by a single minute marked in red. At the end of each three-minute block, a buzzer rings out across the room to signal a minute's break from whatever discipline the boxers are working on. Their whole day consists of three-minute segments of perfect concentration and one minute of rest. This is how trainers condition their fighters for the rigours of three-minute competitive rounds. Down in the Kronk basement, ring time is all that matters.

Emmanuel is working with Michael Moorer, a leading heavyweight contender and a giant of a man who must be six foot five and all of 240 pounds. When the buzzer sounds, Emmanuel gestures for us to sit on a bench beneath the big clock. He uses the minute's break to issue instructions to Moorer before resuming their work. Emmanuel wears flat-faced gloves with cushioned palms that he holds up for Moorer to punch at in quick combinations of right and left jabs. When the buzzer rings again, Emmanuel walks over to shake our hands as an

261

announcement is made over the public address system. 'We have two guests here today,' says a gruff voice. 'Please welcome Paul Stanley from Kiss.' The boxers and trainers cheer and applaud and Paul waves to them, a little embarrassed. 'We also have Michael Francis, whose father is George Francis, one of the best trainers ever to come out of England.' More applause: most of the fighters at Kronk are black, and they know what Dad has done for black fighters like John Conteh, Bunny Sterling and Frank Bruno.

We stay, watching sparring, for most of the afternoon. Paul is fascinated and grinning like a kid at a funfair. Before we leave, Emmanuel presents us with Kronk T-shirts and jackets, and Paul invites all of the boxers and trainers to the following night's Kiss show.

Fifteen of them take up the invitation. Twenty minutes before the band comes on, I lead them out on to the stage. I want to give them a band's eye view. They welcomed us into their world, their ring; and in return I want to show them ours. The people in the audience look at these guys as if they are from another planet. The boxers, too, are amazed. They can't believe that the first two rows are filled entirely with beautiful young women. One of the guys who'd been sparring that afternoon turns to me shaking his head. 'I'm in the wrong business!'

On 16 August 2000 I celebrate my fiftieth birthday. Kiss are playing six shows in Texas, Missouri and Lousiana, and for the next nine days we are based at the Four Seasons Los Colinas Hotel in Irving, a suburb of Dallas. But 16 August is a day off for the band, and in the afternoon, two pickup trucks arrive at the hotel to collect Ace Frehley, who has family living nearby. Ace is in an excitable mood because he and his relatives are going out to hunt deer with rifles. As the pickups drive off, each

loaded with men and guns, it looks for all the world like a scene from *Deliverance*.

I spend the day by the pool before heading out into town for a meal with Gene, Paul, Doc and several other members of the band's entourage, among them Tommy Thayer, the tour manager. Tommy has known Gene and Paul for years since he played lead guitar for Los Angeles rock band Black 'N' Blue, whose third album was produced by Gene. Black 'N' Blue never attained the popularity of contemporaries like Mötley Crüe and Ratt, but Tommy is an accomplished guitarist, and therefore a useful man to have around, given Ace's unpredictability. Tommy knows every Kiss song inside out, and on a couple of occasions he has been ready to act as a stand-in for Ace at a gig. At Irvine Meadows in California, the show was delayed by over an hour when Ace missed his flight from New York. Tommy got dressed up in Ace's make-up and costume ready to go on in case, when a call came in to tell us that Ace had landed at LAX. Doc sent a helicopter to fly him direct to the show, and the band went on stage an hour and fifteen minutes late. Only now there were two people made up as Ace – the real one and Tommy, with the audience none the wiser which was which. Maybe we should have put them on stage together: that would have been a new twist to the show . . .

It is one in the morning when we get back to the hotel, but as we walk to the bar we are met by a posse of Ace's relations, all of them trying to talk to us at once. 'Ace has been shot!' they announce.

'Is he dead?' asks Doc, and establishing that he is not, heads once again for the bar. But Ace's relations will not let us go. 'You don't understand,' they insist. 'Ace has been shot!'

It seems that Ace had an accident out hunting. For reasons best known to himself, he refuses to let them take him to a hospital.

His cousins have waited anxiously for Doc to appear in the hope that he can persuade the patient to have himself patched up. Sighing, Doc agrees that he and I should take a look.

We find Ace in his suite, lying stricken on the bed, naked from the waist up and clutching a blood-soaked towel. The heavy silver chains around his neck rattle as he pulls the towel away to show us the wound. A raw red graze ends in a small hole between his ribs from which blood is slowly seeping. One of his cousins explains that Ace's gun misfired and a spent bullet ricocheted into his chest. He does not appear to be in immediate danger – after all, it is several hours since it happened and he is still very much alive. But the injury looks nasty nonetheless, and it is pretty clear that Ace needs to see a doctor.

The problem is that he won't. The suite was trashed by a paintball party yesterday and he doesn't want anyone in it. He doesn't want us in it, let alone a stranger. Nor will he go to hospital, in spite of Doc's protestations. We have no more luck than his cousins did at making him see sense. Doc argues, cajoles and pleads, to no avail. When Ace becomes hysterical it is clear that we aren't helping. What's more it is two in the morning by now and we want to enjoy the remaining hours of my birthday. To be brutally honest we do not feel inclined to be sympathetic, especially since Ace is refusing medical help of any kind. We give up what seems like a thankless task and retire to the bar, where we stay for another hour or so and a bottle or two of champagne.

Twice we are interrupted as the barman hands me the phone. The first call is Ace, but I cannot make out a single word he is saying. The second is Ace's girlfriend calling from Canada. Ace has rung her and told he is dying: I tell her not to worry and that Ace will be all right. Drunk and exhausted, we toss back a final birthday toast and wend our way off to sleep.

I have just stripped down to my boxer shorts when there is a loud banging and shouting at my door. Opening it, I am confronted by a fully armed SWAT team in flak jackets all crouched down in the corridor, firearms raised.

'Are you Michael Francis?' they bark. I affirm that I am. I stand there a moment, blinking, wondering if I am dreaming or what on earth is going on, before I find out they are here because of Ace. Someone has called the manager and told him that one of the hotel guests has been shot. The manager, as the law demands, has called the police. Mistakenly, the police believe that Ace has been shot here on the hotel premises, and by a second party.

As I begin to explain that Ace shot himself out hunting, a green-uniformed paramedic emerges from Ace's suite at the far end of the corridor, followed by two colleagues pushing a wheeled stretcher on which Ace lies supine, straps around his body and a drip applied to his arm. Along the hall I hear an officer asking if he can identify his assailant, but Ace is out of his mind on painkillers and too weak to lift a finger, never mind give a coherent answer to the policeman's question.

A policewoman asks me if anyone else can confirm what I have told them. 'Yes,' I tell her. 'Doc McGhee, the band's manager. That's his room over there.' They bang on his door and Doc, like me, emerges in his underpants. When he learns the cause of the disturbance he is apoplectic. 'Nobody shot the cunt – he shot himself!'

As the senior member of the entourage, Doc is required to accompany Ace to the hospital, where both will give a statement to the police. Doc is fuming. Right now, if he had a gun, the odds are he would happily finish the job.

It is eight in the morning when Doc knocks at my door. He has been at the hospital all night. Ace has had half a bullet removed from his chest. He is weak from loss of blood but there is no lasting damage. The police accept that Ace did indeed shoot himself. The gig tonight will go ahead as scheduled. With some added precautions – a painkilling injection before he goes on and a medic standing by at the side of the stage in case – Ace should be able to play.

Personnel List

KISS

GENE SIMMONS

PAUL STANLEY

ACE FREHLEY

PETER CRISS

ENTOURAGE

DOC MCGHEE .... MANAGER

TOMMY THAYER .... TOUR MANAGER

PACO ZIMMER .... TOUR ACCOUNTANT

MICHAEL FRANCIS .... SECURITY

The Kiss A-Team ... page one of the key personnel list for the US leg of the Farewell Tour.

Doc is shattered and heads off to his room to get some sleep. I am tired too, but as I sit on the edge of the bed it is not fatigue alone that has me questioning why I am here. Maybe it's losing Mum, or maybe it's just that I'm getting too old to enjoy this kind of lark. But I've made up my mind that this tour will be my last.

23

A kiss goodbye

It is barely six weeks afterwards that Ace fucks up again. Kiss
are staying at Chicago's Ritz Carlton Hotel, a luxurious five-
star establishment and a favourite among high-profile
celebrities. The Eagles and Tina Turner are also staying here,
and when I work out in the gymnasium, I see TV icon Oprah
Winfrey and basketball superstar Michael Jordan. On
29 September, following a day off, we are due to fly to
Columbus, Ohio for a show at the 18,000-seater Nationwide
Arena. Almost every day, we follow the same routine. Each
band member receives a wake-up call at noon. Gene and Paul
require just one call and they will be in the lobby fifteen minutes
before our two o'clock departure. I call Peter at twelve, and an
hour later I knock on his door with coffee, milk and cookies to
make quite sure that he's up and ready to leave. I call Ace at
noon, one and one-thirty, but today there is no response. This is

not unusual, but it is getting late. I find Paul in the lobby and we walk around the block for a coffee. If sex is Gene's vice, Paul's is Starbuck's. After a couple of minutes I call Ace on my cell-phone. Again, there is no answer. I tell Paul to bring his coffee with him, as I will have to go to Ace's room. Gene waits in the lobby and rolls his eyes when I say that Ace is not responding to my calls.

I take the elevator to the twelfth floor and bang on Ace's door. After a minute there's still no response so I call again on the cellphone. I can hear the phone ringing inside the room as I press my ear to the door. At every hotel I am issued with a master key-card for use in emergencies. I slide the card into the lock and the door opens a few inches before the security chain snaps tight. Through the narrow opening I can see into the lounge area of Ace's suite. A table is littered with room service trays, on which half-eaten food is piled up beside an empty vodka bottle. At the foot of the table, the light brown carpet is stained red. It might be wine: it might also be blood.

Through the small gap I call Ace's name several times. Silence. Something is very wrong. In my mind I can see tomorrow's headlines: Rock Star Found Dead In Hotel Room. I hope to God that this is not what has happened; I tell myself I have never lost one yet. I call hotel security and inform them that we have to break down the door. And finally, reluctantly, I call the manager. I would prefer him not to see the room in this state, but I have no option. When he arrives he peers through the door and wrinkles his nose at the stale, sour smell.

'We need to call the police.' he says.

'There's no time for that,' I tell him. 'We've got to get in there now.'

He summons the hotel maintenance crew and moments later two more guys appear, dressed in light-blue coveralls like the Super Mario Brothers. One is carrying a pair of steel bolt-cutters four foot long. It is now two o'clock and we should be leaving for the airport. I call Doc on his cell and tell him we have a major problem with Ace. Just then there is a loud metallic snap as the cutters break the chain on the door. I push the door open, expecting some movement from the adjoining bedroom after the noise of the chain busting. The manager voices the fear we have all been thinking: 'Nobody could sleep through that.'

The others wait where they are as the manager and I walk through to the bedroom. I swallow to shift my rising sense of dread. Tentatively, I push the door open and call Ace's name once more. A second set of doors, glass-panelled, leads to the bed. Through opaque curtains I can see two bodies, but I cannot tell if they are alive or dead.

I press open the glass doors and the curtain brushes aside. On the four-poster bed, Ace and his girlfriend lie entwined, naked and still. Both Ace and his girlfriend are painfully thin. There is no flesh on them anywhere – it is like a scene from the Serengeti after the lions and hyenas have had their lunch. Behind us, unable to stop themselves, the security guys and the maintenance men have shuffled closer to see what is going on. I lean in close to Ace's face: he does not appear to be breathing. From the tangle of limbs, I extract an arm. I can only tell it is Ace's because of the twenty silver bracelets he never takes off. Gently, I lift his wrist to check for a pulse.

With a sudden start, the girl sits bolt upright in the bed and screams. Shocked, I let go of Ace's arm, which falls limply to the bed, making everyone jump. Mario drops the cutters, which crash heavily to the floor. The girl struggles to cover herself with a bed sheet. As she squirms and tries to figure out where she is, Ace's arm twitches. I look at his face. One eye opens slowly, then the other. He is alive but he barely knows it.

The girl finds her voice. 'Ace!' she yells. 'Who the fuck are these guys?'

Ace doesn't know. He hasn't got a clue who he is, let alone us. 'Ace!' I shout at him. 'It's Michael!'

As Ace comes to his senses, I usher everyone out, asking the manager to let me take care of it from here. I call Doc to let him know that his guitar player is not dead, then lead Ace into the bathroom to shower. Whatever drugs Ace and his girlfriend have taken – prescription or otherwise – he won't say. But from the state that they are in, I imagine this was a close call.

Ace might be lucky to be alive, but he is in deep trouble nonetheless. His contract stipulates that he must not take drugs or drink to excess while on the tour. Gene and Paul will be furious. We will certainly miss our scheduled take-off slot, which means we will not be able to do a sound check before the show. Doc calls and says that if Ace is not ready in less than thirty minutes, we will leave without him and Tommy will take his place. Somehow, Ace manages to rouse himself. Before we leave the room, he insists on bringing the shoulder bag he carries with him everywhere. Inside the bag are bottles of prescription pills and a reinforced steel box filled with jewellery and cash. The bag is so heavy that Ace is barely able to lift it, but he refuses to let me carry it. When we emerge from the elevator into the lobby, the weight of the bag on his right shoulder causes him to stagger three steps to one side before I pull him by the arm and guide him out to the van where the others are waiting.

As Ace shuffles on to the seat beside Peter, not a word is exchanged between him and the rest of the band. I jump in the back and the van speeds off for the airport, where we board the band's private jet, a GII with twelve seats. The atmosphere is icy cold, and I for one am relieved when Ace falls asleep.

We land in Columbus with scarcely two hours to spare before Kiss are due on stage. The drive to the venue is only twenty minutes, but that leaves no time for anything but make-up – no time to sound check; no time for the competition winners whose prize was a chance to meet and greet the band. Backstage, it feels more like the sad clown's room at the circus. Still nobody is speaking, and no amount of make-up can disguise the mood of each of the four band members.

SATURDAY, MAY 13
POLARIS AMPHITHEATER

COLUMBUS, OH
EASTERN TIME

TRAVEL

BAND	**CREW**
CHARTER TO COLUMBUS	DRIVE FROM CHICAGO 355 MILES/7 HRS ARR. APPROX. 10:00A

HOTEL

BAND
RITZ CARLTON CHICAGO
160 E PEARSON STREET
CHICAGO, IL 60611
☎
FAX:
CONTACT:
RM SERV: 24 HRS
LOUNGE: 11:30A-2A
FACILITIES: H/C, POOL, JACUZZI
TO VENUE: N/A
TO AIRP: 30 MIN

DRIVERS ONLY
WELLSLEY INN
8555 LYRA DRIVE
COLUMBUS, OH 43240
☎
FAX:
CONF:
TO VENUE: 1 MILE

VENUE & PROMOTER

POLARIS AMPHITHEATER
2200 POLARIS PARKWAY
COLUMBUS, OH 43240

MAIN:
FAX:
BLDG. CTC:

PROD 1:
PROD 2:
PROD FAX:
ACCT:
MGMT:

CAPACITY: 20,000
LOAD-IN: 8:00A
DOORS: 5:30P
SHOWTIME: 7:00P
CURFEW: 11:00P

SUNSHINE PROMOTIONS
10089 ALLISONVILLE, SUITE 100
FISHERS, IN 46038

PHONE
FAX:

PROD REP:
PHONE:
FAX:
PAGER:
E-MAIL:

SKID ROW: 7:00-7:30P
NUGENT: 7:50-8:50P
KISS: 9:10-11:00P

AFTER SHOW TRAVEL

BAND	**CREW**
RETURN TO CHICAGO	DRIVE OVERNIGHT TO PEORIA 366 MILES/7.5 HRS

13

A day in the life ... the Columbus show from the Kiss Tour Itinerary.
Note the 7-hour drives at both ends for the crew.

Against the odds, they've made it. The intro music starts and the house lights dim as I walk the guys from the dressing room to the side of the stage. I peek through the big black drapes: 18,000 fans are cheering wildly, many of them with their faces painted like their heroes, some in full costume. Amazingly, the show is running smoothly until Paul gestures to me to meet him at the side of the stage. 'What the fuck is going on?' he yells in my ear over the roars of the crowd. 'My side of the stage is like an ugly farm! Gene's got all the good-looking girls – put some on my side!'

I have a lot of affection for Paul but he is incredibly vain – especially for a guy who has just turned fifty and is wearing an outfit that my Aunt Flo wouldn't be seen dead in. He may no longer play around on tour, but that doesn't mean that he doesn't still bask in female adulation. On my walkie-talkie, I order the security staff to bring twenty good-looking girls from other parts of the arena to front and centre, where Paul can see them. No sooner is Paul smiling again than Gene is calling me over, wanting to know where all the hot girls on Paul's side have come from. In this situation, you can't win. Fortunately Ace is just concentrating on standing upright. The last thing on his mind is pussy. He knows that Gene, Paul and Doc will want a long talk after the show about what happened back at the hotel.

But before then, there is a job to finish, and all is going well until the encore, when Gene trips over one of the sound monitor cabinets at the edge of the stage. For a split second, his 230-pound frame sways precariously as he fights to regain his balance on seven-inch stack heels. Panic flashes across his face – at all costs, he must not lose his wig. But the force of gravity is too strong, and – bang! – the God of Thunder is suddenly flat on his back and wriggling like an upturned turtle.

Paul is in fits of laughter. From the side of the stage, I tell him that Gene reminds me of the boxer Trevor Berbick just before Mike Tyson knocked him out, when Berbick was staggering backwards and forwards like one of those wobbly toys, so much so that Tyson was having trouble landing the final punch. It takes four roadies to lift Gene back to his feet. He stomps around like a miserable adolescent for the remainder of the show, but Paul is still laughing when he bids the audience good-night at the end. 'We love you!' he exclaims. 'Thank you from me, Ace, Peter and Trevor!'

Off stage, however, the darker mood returns. For an hour the band stays locked in the dressing room with Doc. Standing guard at the door, I hear raised voices and angry shouts as Gene and Paul tear strips off Ace. The result is that Ace is given one last chance, for which he meekly offers thanks.

We return to Chicago in better spirits and head to Jojo's Hotdogs, a shabby little diner in a rundown part of town. Jojo's is a legend among bands. It serves the best hot dogs in Chicago, and Kiss always make a point of coming here whenever they are in the city. We devour four hot dogs each before ending the night in a strip club. Exhausted by the events of the past twenty-four hours, I breathe a sigh of relief when Gene says he has seen enough tits and ass for one night, and we can get back to the hotel. It is on days like these that I really earn my money.

Money is the one thing that keeps Kiss going after almost thirty years in a business that is notorious for self-destruction. Two of them – Gene and Paul – love making it and can never get enough; while the other two – Peter and Ace – never have enough, so they have to keep on working. But money is not worth putting your life on the line for, and on one occasion we came uncomfortably close.

The band were booked to play a show in Belgrade, only as the date got nearer the political situation there had become so unstable that nobody wanted to go. There was no doubt it was dangerous. Other bands with tours booked in the Balkans had been pulling out left, right and centre. But of course we had a contract with the promoter, and to cancel at this late date would have cost Kiss a fortune.

After much discussion, the band elects to play. It is too much money to lose. I call the promoter and tell him we need additional security: a guaranteed team of eight who will stay with us from the moment we leave our plane. I also request two rooms at the best hotel adjacent to the airport which the band can use as their dressing rooms for the show. I want them to spend as little time as possible at the venue. This way they can get ready and made up at the hotel and be driven to the stadium just before they are due to go on.

Unless he can meet our conditions, I tell him, the band will not do the show. A few hours later he calls me back and confirms the arrangements are made. A top security team will be waiting to escort us to our hotel; from there to the venue, then back to the airport and safely onto the plane. We are committed. The gig is on.

Our plane lands at 6 p.m. and there on the tarmac, somewhat to my surprise, are the extra security team the promoter had promised. I recognise one – a clean-shaven, handsome guy in his forties who looks like he can take care of himself and is very much in charge. He shakes my hand and says 'Welcome to Belgrade. You are in safe hands.'

I tell him he looks familiar – perhaps we have worked together at some point when I was last in Belgrade, as promoters tend to use the same security teams. As we head for the Belgrade Intercontinental Hotel in a twelve-seater van with an escort of two Land Rovers, one in front and one behind, I begin to feel better about the situation. These guys mean business. We do not even stop at any traffic lights: as we approach each set, the leading Land Rover blocks any oncoming traffic and waves us through. In spite of my unease I am impressed. I have seldom encountered security with that kind of power before.

At the hotel our two rooms are on the twelfth floor, and each of them has an armed guard seated outside. The wardrobe girls and Dave, who takes care of the wigs, have been waiting anxiously for us to arrive. They have been here all day setting up and they are desperate to get out. They say that the guards are as scary as hell: they were really freaked when they saw the guards had guns underneath their seats.

Leaving the band to get ready I go to check the security at the venue, accompanied by our new friend and his men, and I cannot help noticing how much respect he is given by everyone we pass along the way. At the venue itself the atmosphere is tense. The production manager says he has never wanted to get a show over with as much as he does this one. There are guys walking openly round with guns and all sorts of rumours among the crew that the stadium has been used for executions in the past. Outside the gates the fans are already gathering, even though the tickets cost more than the average weekly wage.

Back at the hotel we still have an hour before the band will be ready, so my friend and I go down to the hotel restaurant for a meal. I find myself getting to like him as we talk. He wants to know how I got started and how long I have been in the job – always the first thing a head of security asks you, whatever country you are in. He tells me his wife is a singer, and says that she will be coming to the show.

Then it is show time. The cars are parked right outside the entrance ready to whisk us to the venue; the security team is waiting outside the lifts on the ground floor; and I collect the band. As we emerge from the lift in the hotel lobby, the band in full Kiss costume and make-up – myself first, then Gene the seven-foot demon in his thigh-length stack-heel boots, then the Starchild, the Catman and Ace – the security team falls into step alongside us, four of them each side. Not a word is said as we march across the lobby, but it must look completely bizarre: four men in black and silver jumpsuits, big hair and outlandish make-up being marched in single file by two ranks of grim-faced guards. It feels as though we were heading outside to the firing squad, and if only we'd known who these guys were, that might have been close to the truth.

We have timed it to perfection, arriving at the venue just as our intro tape is starting. It's The Who's 'Won't Get Fooled Again' but I'm thinking it should be The Animals' 'Gotta Get Out Of This Place'. On the inside of the barricade that separates stage from audience, all the security guards are dressed in full paramilitary uniform and appear to be armed to the teeth with both guns and riot batons. I have never seen the band perform so fast: they play a two-hour set in little more than an hour and thirty minutes. The fans are amazing and give the band a rapturous reception, but still we don't wish to prolong our stay and as quick as we can we are back in the van and speeding to the airport. In less than an hour we'll be in the air and I for one will breathe a sigh of relief.

So far so good. But as we approach the airport I realise that it is in darkness, which is strange. The van pulls up by a single-storey building and our new friend ushers all of us inside. In a small room our pilots are seated, which is stranger still, since they should be ready for take-off on the plane. The moment we cross the threshold the friendly atmosphere changes, and suddenly it feels very wrong indeed.

Our friend takes me back outside on to the tarmac, away from the building, out in the darkness where he and I are alone. The airport is closed, he tells me. He needs 5,000 US dollars in order to open up the runway and permit us to take off. It is not for himself, he assures me, but for the greedy bastards who run the place. But in the pitch darkness the big smile has gone from his face, replaced by an almost incredible sense of menace. His eyes are cold, and I am not fooled by the casual manner in which he holds his gun. He has us at his mercy, and he knows it.

This is definitely not a situation I want the band to be in. I look at him and I look at the gun and I do not like it one bit. I do not want to die in the dark on some obscure Balkan airfield for the sake of a concert fee. I think of my wife and kids and at that moment I realise, without pride but with perfect clarity, that if I had to I would leave them there – Doc, the band and all – in order to save myself.

Instead I ask him to give me a minute to speak to Doc.

'Doc,' I say, 'We have a problem. More than a problem in fact. If we don't give them five thousand dollars we're not getting out of here,'

'Fuck that,' agrees Doc without hesitation. 'We'll give them whatever we've got.'

Paco, our tour accountant, hands over $2,000 which is all the cash we have, as we have deliberately chosen not to sell any merchandise at the show. I proffer it to our so-called 'friend', hoping that it is enough. Thankfully it appears to do the business. The crocodile grin comes back to his face and finally I can let the cheeks of my butt relax. Ten minutes later we are safely on our plane and leaving Belgrade behind us, and I have never seen so much drink disappear in the first half hour of a flight.

Some months later we are in New York, watching the TV news in our hotel, when there on the screen, to our surprise, is our smiling extortionist friend. We discover that he is Arkan, leader of the notorious Serbian paramilitary volunteer force known as the Tigers. To half his country he is a national hero; to others he is a war criminal, implicated in massacres of both Bosnians and Croats, for which he was indicted at the Hague. Whatever the truth, he has multiple gangland connections, and has convictions for bank robbery in Germany, Holland and Belgium. And now he is dead, gunned down by assassins in a hail of bullets in the same hotel in which I enjoyed his company over dinner.

This was the man into whose hands we had entrusted our lives. We look at each other and agree it was the best $2,000 we ever spent.

★

On 8 October 2000, Kiss travel home for a lengthy break and I return to London. My younger brother Simon is only thirty-six, but he too has been diagnosed with cancer. A large growth at the base of his spine has left him partially paralysed, and the cancer is so aggressive that doctors are powerless to stop it spreading. In the space of three months leading into February, Simon loses the use of his arms and legs.

I have promised Simon he will not die in hospital, and his doctors have given permission for us to take him home to Dad's. At first they were reluctant to allow it; they said that he was too ill to be moved. So I hire a private ambulance to make sure that we can get him safely home. Before we leave, two nurses help to pack Simon's things and to dress him for the last time. The nurses have grown fond of him, and both of them find it hard to say goodbye. We have made up a bed downstairs for him, just as Dad did for Mum. Like Mum, he wants to be able to look out on to the garden. That afternoon, he has visitors: Sting and his wife, Trudie Styler. My brother Billy has been Sting's tour manager for almost two decades. They live nearby, and over the years have become close family friends. They stay with Simon for an hour, until he falls asleep.

Throughout the night, I take turns with my son Daniel to hold Simon's hand and to be there for him whenever he wakes up. There is little else we can do except make him as comfortable as we can. He asks me to bring him some of his favourite flowers; he asks us to open the curtains to flood the room with light. His last visitor is Charlie George. When Simon was six years old, Charlie scored the goal that won the Cup for Arsenal. Ever since, he has been Simon's hero. Charlie has brought him a special gift – an Arsenal shirt, autographed by every member of the current team. Simon is only just able to speak, but even now, he still has his sense of humour. He points at Charlie and then at the shirt, miming the act of writing. He reckons Charlie signed all those names himself.

Later that day, in the early evening, Simon dies, exactly a year after Mum. Fourteen years younger than I am, he was not much older than my children. For them it is like losing a brother rather than an uncle. For me it is like losing a son. And for Dad, it is somehow more devastating than losing Mum. This, he says, is every parent's nightmare. It should not happen to anyone, to have to lose a child.

★

One month after Simon's death, I travel to Australia with Kiss for the last eight dates of their Farewell Tour. I think about pulling out of the trip, but June tells me I should go. The irony is not lost on us, that I am the one who wants to stay and she is the one who is pushing me to go. But she knows me better than I know myself. She says that I need some perspective, that the change will do me good.

We are in Australia for twenty-four days, but it feels like months. I know that this is the end of the line. I enjoy seeing Gene and Paul and Doc as much as ever, but Ace is soon up to his old tricks. Some people never learn. The final straw is the last night of the tour. Oddly, the date is Friday 13 April. We have less than thirty minutes before the band is due on stage when Ace gets it into his head that the promoter owes him money. He demands 40,000 US dollars in cash before he goes on. Neither Doc nor the promoter has the least idea what this is all about, but Ace is insistent: no money, no show. After several minutes of frantic appeals, Doc hits on a solution. He hands Ace a napkin on which is written an IOU for $40,000, signed by both himself and the promoter. Satisfied, Ace tucks the napkin inside his flight case and calmly resumes his make-up.

After the show is over, the napkin has mysteriously disappeared, and Ace is livid. The promoter has laid on a party – a lavish affair at a nearby hotel – to celebrate the conclusion of the tour, but the night is marred by Ace chasing after the poor beleaguered promoter, heaping him with abuse.

For me, it is one crazy rock star tantrum too many.

It has taken me a long time to sort out my priorities, even though the evidence has been there all my life. It is family that matters: stability, home, love. Life on the road is a chimera, an illusion. It may be exciting, addictive, adrenalin-fuelled; but it isn't real. Performing night after night before crowds of adoring fans, with their every whim indulged by people like me, what this artificial world gives the stars around whom it revolves is a licence not to grow up.

Next morning I bid a fond farewell to Gene and Paul and Doc, and walk away for good from the rock 'n' roll life.

24

The end of the road

It is 8 a.m. and I have arranged to meet Dad at the gym, but he never turned up. I go around to his house, where the lights are on and his car is parked outside, but there's no response. It's unusual; but still, I reflect, it's a beautiful spring morning and he probably went out walking over the Heath.

That evening June cooks dinner at 6 p.m. We are expecting Dad to knock at the door and call through the letter box as he always does: 'It's the lodger again!' It is his little joke, as if he was embarrassed at coming round every night to our house to eat. But we love his company. Since we lost Mum and then Simon, Dad has suffered severe depression; yet over the last few weeks, with the two hours he spends at the gym in the morning and the time he spends with us in the evening, talking to June and joking with the kids, he seems to be sleeping much better, and has even come off the tablets he has been taking.

At the gym he has started teaching some of the younger trainers to box. One of the members is Gareth Rhys Jones, a film director and boxing fan, who is keen to make a documentary about Dad's life in boxing. Dad loves the idea, and all of a sudden he has that broad smile back on his face, and he loves the respect that he's getting from the young guys at the gym. Since he and Frank Bruno had finally hung up their gloves, he has missed his old friends and the hustle and bustle of the boxing world; and now he has got his old training bag out, with the skipping ropes and the boxing gloves that so many world champions have used over the years, and is looking forward to doing what he does best.

7.00 P.M.

The knock on the door and the call through the letter box. Dad has had his hair cut and is wearing his best jacket over a new white shirt. I tell him he looks good. June tells him he is late for dinner, but he says that tonight he has not come for dinner, he just wants a cup of June's tea.

It is a family joke that June makes a better cup of tea than Mum did, so Dad has a cup of tea and a sandwich. It is the first time he has refused a dinner. He tells June several times how much he appreciates what she did for Mum and for Simon not just over the last three years but over the last thirty. I tell him I looked for him at the house this morning after I waited to meet him at the gym. He says he had been to the Garden Centre to get all Mum's favourite spring flowers and has been up the top of the garden planting them out. 'Wait till you see it,' he says to us. 'Mum would have loved it.' Spring was always her favourite time of year.

He tells us how proud he is of our kids. Grant had taken his girlfriend Lucy and their new baby Lia round to see him on Sunday, and they had played in the garden for hours.

Dad gets two keys out of his jacket pocket and gives one to me, telling me it is the key to his safe in case anything should happen. He hands the other to June and says it is for his front door. She reminds him we already have one that he gave us years ago but he tells her to take it anyway, so that we have a spare. He asks for another tea, which is strange as he never has more than one, and while June is in the kitchen he tells me to take care good care of her. At ten o'clock he asks for his coat and gives us both a hug. 'If I don't make it to the gym,' he says, 'come round to the house and see Mum's flowers.' Then he shakes my hand as he says goodnight.

'See you tomorrow.' I say.

WEDNESDAY 5 APRIL

Wednesday morning I get to the gym but again Dad has not come. Gareth has brought the proposal for his television programme, and is disappointed to find Dad is not there. It looks amazing and I can't wait for Dad to see it, so, as he requested, I go round to his house. No answer. I am puzzled but not alarmed. I walk round the corner for a coffee, pausing on the way to talk to Claud. Claud has run the fruit and vegetable shop for thirty years or more, and it is where Simon had his first Saturday job. Dad has to go by Claud's to get to the Heath and would call out 'Good morning, Frenchy!' as he passed. I ask Claud if he heard Dad this morning. He thinks he might have done but he is not sure. I wait an hour and then go back to the house. I know how much it will cheer Dad up to look at Gareth's proposal and I badly want him to see it. Still there is no one in.

June calls at 5 p.m. and again at 6 to see if he is coming up for dinner. We put one by just in case: we still expected the knock at the door and his voice, 'It's the lodger again ...', but he never came.

THURSDAY 6 APRIL

It is just past 4 p.m. and I have had meetings most of the morning so I have not been to the gym today to meet Dad. I am reading a book that one of my children gave me for Christmas, but something is not right. I cannot shake off the feeling that there is someone else in the house, even though I know that I am alone. I walk from the living room into the kitchen and back but the feeling is getting worse until it is almost overwhelming and suddenly I hear voices outside our front door. I hear a scream which I know is June though it seems to come from somewhere deep in the ground. As I turn to the sound it's as if I am in slow motion. Even though I know it is only seconds, it feels like it takes me a lifetime to reach the door.

On our front step a policeman and a young policewoman are bending over to help June to her feet. June is screaming to me that it is the kids, that something has happened to one of our kids; and as I stand there my world shatters. You go through life being in control and thinking that you are protecting your family and in that one fragmented instant it's all gone. I don't want to hear what the policeman is trying to tell me. All I can see are the faces of my three children. Joanne, Daniel and Grant. I understand what Dad had meant about Simon, that losing a child is the worst thing that can happen, and I understand what that must have done to his heart. At the same time I hear the policeman's voice: 'Mr Francis, it isn't your children, it's your father,' and at first all I feel is a curious sense of relief that the kids are safe. Then for the first time I hear what the policeman is saying. 'I'm afraid it's your father, Mr Francis. He's hanged himself.'

Calmly I close the door on them with myself and June inside. Then it is my turn. I look at June and a howl of denial comes rising up inside of me and goes on and on and on.

Dad left me a note dated Tuesday night and timed at 10.30 p.m., half an hour after he left us. He said that he knew I would understand because we were so alike, and asked me to ask the family to forgive him.

George Albert Francis died 4 April 2002 of a broken heart. A very brave man.

★

At the funeral many of Dad's champions come to pay their respects. Frank Bruno is one of the coffin bearers. For him, too, it is like losing a father. When I greet Frank, I remind him of the pride and happiness Dad felt when he won the WBC world heavyweight title in 1995. He made Dad's dream come true.

In the procession Bunny Sterling walks with John Conteh. During the past few years, Dad and John had grown close once more after many years apart. Seeing John at the funeral, older and wiser, reminds me of what Dad said to me after I was fired by Jon Bon Jovi. 'Nothing surprises me, son,' he told me. 'Conteh was like a member of our family, he slept under our roof, and he fired me because people told him he could make more money else-where. But people change.' Maybe one day, Dad said, Jon and I would look back at the good times we had together, as he and John Conteh had done. 'Remember the good stuff,' he said to me, 'not the bad. Life's too short.'

Doc McGhee calls me at home shortly after the funeral. He recalls the time he asked Dad to come to America to look at a promising young boxer. The guy had won twenty amateur fights and Doc wanted to know if he had the makings of a professional. He flew Dad first class to Chicago to work with the boxer for a week, but after just one day Dad called me to say it was hopeless. 'The boy has a great jab,' he told me. Punches hard with both hands. But the trouble is he's got a wooden leg. He's okay going forwards, but he can't go back or sideways. He's never going to be a champion.' As Doc reminds me of this story, he makes me laugh for the first time in many days. It means all the more to me since Doc has recently lost two members of his own family. Somehow it feels as if we are on the same journey.

'Don't think about what you've lost,' Doc echoes Dad's own words. 'You had a lot of good years with him. You're lucky.'

★

Doc's right. I find myself thinking over what he said, and not just because of Dad. I have been unbelievably lucky. I have lived a life I never could have dreamed of, and done things that figure in most people's wildest fantasies. I have travelled all over the world. I have flown in private planes, attended the most lavish parties, stayed in the best hotels, and dined in the finest restaurants. I have even played golf on the hallowed turf of Augusta, where the sport's greatest players contest the US Masters. For a golfing fan, playing this course is the equivalent of being invited for tea at Buckingham Palace. I played in a four-ball with Doc, Richie and Tico during one of Bon Jovi's American tours. Tico wore red and white checked trousers, a red shirt and a white fedora hat, and looked like he was auditioning for a part in *The Great Gatsby*. He could not hit the ball straight; his slice was so heavy that he would play every approach shot facing forty-five degrees to the left of the pin. We couldn't stop laughing each time he prepared to strike the ball, but he still finished with a better score than mine.

I have worked with some of the biggest stars in rock, and been fortunate to call some of them my friends. I can't pretend to have liked them all; it would be nothing short of a miracle if I had. Looking after stars, you don't have to like them as people. That isn't a part of the job. But you do have to respect them. I could not work for a star I did not respect. And yet I can say that in all my years I have only known one or two on whom I would not waste my coffee to put them out if they were on fire.

To some of them I have been close. When you are on the road with the same people 24/7 for months on end you get to see them as they really are. Social barriers get stripped away. You see them warts and all. You see their foibles and their fears. You get to share their good times and their bad. Yet you also learn that friendships forged in such artificial conditions can be fragile, precarious, especially when money and ego are involved. This is something that Doc understands too well. Doc is one of the wisest people I know. He works incredibly hard for his bands, giving them all 110 per cent. He has more vision than anyone else I have

288

met. More than one major band owe him their careers, and he is equally adept at reviving the fortunes of a flagging band as he is at breaking out a new one. But Doc has no illusions about the business that we work in, and how its relationships last. He said to me once: 'In the end the artist is the enemy. One day you will get a fax from their attorney advising you that they do not need your services any more. That's as sure as that one day you will die. It is simply a matter of when.'

So I count myself doubly lucky, since some of the friendships I made on tour have lasted for many years.

I have seen my share of the darker side of rock. It wasn't all high times and parties. Jon Bon Jovi received twenty death threats in the time I worked for him, although no one ever laid a finger on him while I was at his side. But the one thing you can't protect people from is themselves. The rock business is as hard-hearted as it is hedonistic: if you have the least tendency to go off the rails, given half a chance it will give you a shove and merrily wave goodbye. In a world where almost anything is available, a world without restraint, the temptation is always there. The lethal cocktail of pressure combined with accessibility takes tremendous force of character to resist.

I think of the people I know who didn't make it.

John Bonham at thirty-three, the world at his feet. He should have been indestructible – or so he seemed to us.

Paul Gardiner, Gary Numan's talented bass player, with his London wide-boy manner and his taste for dope and pills. Paul was found dead in a children's playground in1984. He had overdosed on heroin. There were few headlines when Paul died, and not many people remember him. But he was full of spirit and personality. He was just a kid who wanted to live the rock 'n' roll dream – until the dream turned sour. And the saddest part of what happened to Paul was that he had a child of his own.

Peter Grant died of a heart attack at the wheel of his car in 1995. Where Paul was a kid who had barely achieved a modicum of fame, Peter was a colossus who had had it all: power, wealth and notoriety. Yet he too was a casualty of the unforgiving business, his body unable to cope with the damage of years of cocaine abuse. The irony was that in the eighties, after increasing problems with his health, Peter had given up drugs entirely. At the time of his death he was clean and had lost the better part of 150lb. I met up with him in the early nineties and was amazed how well and happy he appeared. It was as though, with the cocaine no longer in his system, all that legendary drug-fuelled aggression had simply melted out of him, and what was left was the real Peter, the inner man, whose kindness and good humour I had always known was there.

John Bindon died of pneumonia in 1993, a penniless alcoholic in a tiny Belgravia flat. His capacity for provoking casual violence had made him increasingly unemployable as an actor, and in 1978 he was tried for the murder of gangster Johnny Darke. He was acquitted of all charges but the case effectively ended his career; his final screen appearance being, appropriately enough, in *Quadrophenia*, Franc Roddam's film version of The Who's epic album of the mod culture of the sixties, which was released in 1979. Bindon was one man whose death can hardly be laid at the door of the music industry: he was a deeply damaged person whose life would have spiralled out of control no matter what he did. But after the film world threw him out the rock world took him in and gave him all he needed to finish his self-destruction: booze, drugs and no shortage of people with whom to fight.

I may have seen people destroy themselves but I've also worked with remarkable survivors. Cher is one. She has so much depth and so much inner strength that I truly believe she can survive whatever the business may throw at her. In contrast to the wild reputation that followed him in the seventies, Paul Rodgers has come through better than almost anyone else I know. Looking fit and tough and younger than his years he lives in America now, where he has carved out a solo career in classic blues and rock. Paul is the kind of musician who earns other musicians' respect. In 1999 he received a lifetime achievement award from the Los Angeles Music Awards Association; and shortly after that a music magazine poll voted him the greatest British rock vocalist of all time. The rock cognoscenti have taken to calling Paul 'The Voice' – an epithet he shares with Frank Sinatra, with whom I was also privileged to work.

Bad Company too have stayed the course, although mostly minus Paul. Rising from the ashes of that soul-destroying tour and re-forming in the mid-eighties they went through several successful incarnations with various founder members before Rodgers himself rejoined the fold in February 2001.

Led Zeppelin never reformed despite lucrative offers from tour promoters. Live Aid was the last time that the three surviving ex-members played together in public under the Zeppelin name. Of the three, Robert Plant has enjoyed most success as a solo artist. He and Jimmy Page reunited in 1994 to record two albums and tour the world playing a mixture of new songs and Zeppelin classics. John Paul Jones has recorded several solo albums of experimental music. Now in their late fifties, Page, Plant and Jones are among rock's most dignified elder statesmen. Page left his drug problems behind years ago.

In June 2003, a new Led Zeppelin live album – called *How The West Was Won* and compiled from tapes of two Los Angeles shows from the summer of 1972 – was a chart success on both sides of the Atlantic, going straight to number one in the US. In the same month a DVD of some of their seventies concerts also topped the music video charts. It was an astonishing feat for a band that broke up twenty-three years before, and testimony to their legendary status as the ultimate rock gods.

Gary Numan is yet another whose star is in the ascendant.

Known as one of the godfathers of electronica, his songs have been sampled by all-female pop group Sugababes and dance act Basement Jaxx, and covered by modern rock icons Marilyn Manson and The Foo Fighters. I read in the *Independent* in January 2003 that 'the once and future king of electropop, Gary Numan, is cool again. After 25 years he is a defining influence on a new generation of pop stars.' Gary would probably argue he has never been away. Through his years in the musical wilderness, he has carried on making the music he wants to make for the fans who want to listen. It's a good way to cope with the vagaries of fortune: keeping your integrity, maintaining creativity, waiting until the pendulum swings and your time comes round again.

In 1984 I got to tour with the greatest survivor of all. Sinatra was almost seventy years old when I worked with him and the voice was no longer the legendary instrument that had held a generation spellbound for three decades in the forties, fifties and sixties. Nevertheless to watch him work his audience was like nothing else I have seen. He would walk on stage and light up a cigarette and before he had even sung a note they would be in the palm of his hand. It was mesmerising. I could well believe that twenty years before the advent of John, Paul, George and Ringo, Frank had already made thousands of teenagers scream and swoon and cry.

Even before The Beatles, I grew up with Frank Sinatra. Along with Dean Martin and Nat King Cole, he was always in our house. Every spare minute Dad had he would listen to Frank. As soon as he got up the first thing he did was go over to the old record player built into the sideboard he won as an amateur boxer and put on one of his precious 78s. Dad loved those records. The sleeves looked like they were new, and heaven help anyone who got a mark on them. That little corner of our house was like a shrine, with its photo of Mum and Dad on their wedding day and Dad's boxing trophies lined up alongside the records. When I was a kid it seemed to me that even our budgie respected it. As far as I remember, he never landed on it.

So when the call came from Alf Weaver, Frank's right hand man, to work with Frank in Europe, it seemed somehow fitting that I should be getting paid to hear him sing. Like many of the stars I worked with, Frank loved boxing. His own father had been a boxer when he was young, and once Frank found out that my dad was George Francis he would talk boxing to me whenever he had the chance. On the last night of his tour at the Royal Albert Hall he invited my mum and dad to his dressing room after the show. That was a rare honour: normally only his closest friends or one or two major celebrities were allowed in his inner sanctum, and it was a story that Mum and Dad would tell for years. Of all the big stars I have worked with, Frank was the only one that my parents really wanted to come and see. I was so pleased to be able to give them something back in return for all they had done for me; a gift from my life to theirs.

For myself, I was starstruck. The fact that I had been a part of this rarefied world for almost ten years by then did not mean I was any less thrilled to be working with Frank Sinatra. Working with stars never made me immune to the charisma they project, and Sinatra was the best. Everyone has heroes, and he was one of mine. To stand on the stage with Frank at the Royal Albert Hall on that last date of the tour was one of the highlights of my career, and a night I would not swap for any other.

Sinatra sold tens of millions of records, nine of which won him a Grammy. He also made more than sixty films, two of which earned him Academy Awards. Friend of both presidents and mobsters, he remained a star up until his death at the age of eighty-two in 1998, four years after the release of his last recorded album. Yet Frank's life was no bed of roses. Three of his marriages failed. His early career was almost derailed by a backlash in the forties, sparked by a hostile press and reports of links with the mob. He was labelled a communist sympathiser and dropped both by Columbia Records and by MGM. A series of drink and health problems threatened to ruin his voice. In the fifties he came back stronger than ever, but the mafia rumours continued to dog him throughout the successful sixties, until he retired, disillusioned, in 1971. Even then he was not finished, and his comeback album in 1973 immediately went platinum. A similar cycle of trouble and triumph repeated the pattern again in the eighties and nineties.

What makes a survivor? Resilience, belief in yourself, ability to roll with the punches: any or all of these? Balance is crucial – a valid sense of who you really are. But whatever the ingredient that pulled him through the bad times, Frank must have had it in spades.

If there's one thing I've learned it's that no matter who you are, fame always comes at a cost. You can be the sanest, most level headed person imaginable – it doesn't matter. There will still be a price to pay.

For George Michael, with whom I toured in the early nineties, it meant living a lie in public for the best part of a decade. Within the music industry, it was an open secret that George was gay. He kept his sexuality hidden in order not to alienate the millions of female fans for whom his saturnine good looks and smash hit, near-the-knuckle songs like 'I Want Your Sex' made him an object of fantasy and a worldwide sexual icon. Also George was very protective of his close-knit family and went to extraordinary lengths to maintain a private life – a difficult proposition when you are one of the most famous people on Earth. Whenever he appeared in public he had two or three beautiful girls at his side, but all the time I was with him the paparazzi never stopped sniffing around him for the real story.

On the American leg of the tour, George went out and partied every night, but where Bad Company or Bon Jovi would go to rock clubs and strip bars, George preferred discos or gay clubs. He especially loved the clubs in New York, which were filled with all kinds of outrageous characters, from male models to transsexuals.

George did not do any drugs, nor did I ever witness a fight in any of these clubs in all the time we were on the road. The trouble came from the press, who would set traps for him using attractive young men as bait. My job was to ensure that he could relax and enjoy himself without being hassled or photographed. I made sure that no strangers got near him, which was not easy amongst the crowds at clubs and parties for hours, night after night.

So desperate were the newspapers to get the dirt on George that one reporter even bribed a hotel waiter for the use of his uniform so that he could gain access to George's suite. He arrived with a room service trolley, hoping to surprise George with another man. Instead, he found me, and as soon as I saw him sneaking furtive glances around the suite, I removed the name tag from his jacket and marched him down to the hotel manager's office. After that little incident, whenever George wanted room service, it would be delivered to my room and I would take it to him myself.

Living this double life was tough on George, but he had done it for so long that he had grown accustomed to it. Still, I never stopped wondering how lonely he must have felt.

It must have been so much tougher after he fell in love. It was while he was in Brazil for the Rock In Rio festival in 1991, when we travelled to a small island off the coast for a much-needed break. George, who was both generous and great company, had arranged for ten of his closest friends to fly in from London to join him. The only club on the island was a ramshackle place with two flashing lights over a small dance floor. Behind a bar stocked entirely with beer, the barman had just ten records that he played over and over again on a rudimentary turntable. The only drug was some potent weed supplied by a local hippie for those of us who wanted to partake. It was simple but idyllic, and, most important of all, it was far from the gaze of the world's media. For the first time since I had worked with him, George was able to relax and be himself.

One night in the tiny club a handsome young man got talking to

George. He was Anselmo Feleppa, a Brazilian designer, and when we left for the hotel at three in the morning, he came with us. For the rest of our time on the island, and for many months afterwards, the pair of them were inseparable. When the tour finished, George was so much happier than when I had first met him. The transformation was extraordinary; he had opened up so much, he seemed so much more at ease with himself, and not just with his sexuality. George himself said some years later, once it was out in the open, that knowing Anselmo had changed his life completely. When Anselmo died of a brain tumour in 1993, George was devastated. And yet, throughout this time, their relationship remained a secret, both from the press and from his fans. I think that by then George had tired of the masquerade and would dearly have liked to have had the truth acknowledged. Only, short of standing on top of Nelson's column and shouting to all and sundry, 'I'm gay' – not an option for someone who was still at heart a deeply private person – he couldn't see how to do it. When, after several years' recording silence, he released the critically acclaimed album *Older* in 1996, the album was dedicated to Anselmo, and both the album and its number one single 'Jesus To A Child' were filled with allusions to love and his sense of loss.

George was also making much more overt references to the truth about his sexuality in interviews, only now, where once they had doorstepped him in order to get the answers, everyone seemed to want to ignore the message. It was as if they had all been turning a blind eye for so long that the press and the public had begun to collude despite themselves, and were somehow determined to carry on playing the game. So when George was arrested in 1998 on a charge of 'lewd behaviour' in a Los Angeles toilet, it was something of a blessing in disguise.

At least it enabled him to drop the increasingly burdensome charade. Since he was 'outed' he has spoken both freely and frankly about his sexuality. He is comfortable with it, and happy. Secure in himself, he has nothing to hide, and nothing to regret.

George is well equipped to cope with the pressures of his

celebrity. He has a brilliant sense of humour, which has helped him to get through. He told one journalist: 'I see a lot of famous people get into trouble and they never seem to handle it very well when, in fact, laughing at yourself is the only answer.'

Also George was wise enough – or self-aware enough – to realise what fame was doing to him and to deal with it before it was too late. He summed up the fame trap succinctly to *Hello*: 'Everybody wants to be a star. I certainly did. And I worked hard to get it. But I was miserable, and I don't want to feel that way again.'

It is harder to stay grounded in a band, where several super-charged egos may be pulling in different directions. I have seen it happen time and time again. All bands start out with dreams. Guys – and girls – in bedrooms and garages, wanting their names in lights. Setting out on an adventure, intent on getting famous, and maybe making great music along the way. Most never get there, torn apart by the constant grind of trying to make it big. But even if they succeed their problems are only just beginning. Dreams are no protection when millions are at stake.

Of all the bands I have worked with Bon Jovi seemed the best equipped to handle their success. They were so close back in 1987: a tight-knit unit. They spent years playing in clubs, paying their dues and keeping their dream alive, before they even signed a record deal. Then, with *Slippery When Wet*, all their hard work paid off. They became rich and famous. They could have anything they desired. But as they got bigger and bigger and were making more and more money they forgot what it was that had got them there in the first place. The music signs were overtaken by dollar signs; and somewhere along the line, they lost their brotherhood.

Jon has been smart enough to have kept the band together – albeit without Alec John Such, who left in the early nineties. Since he has taken charge of his own affairs, he has proved himself an astute and sensible businessman who knows how to manage his interests and who makes very sure that no one will rip him off. That is how he survives, by acknowledging rock is a business and making it clear that he is in control. But that special bond between them was left on the road out on the New Jersey tour, and once that is gone, you can never get it back.

Fame, wealth, power and ego can poison the wisest mind and the kindest heart. But when I reflect on the people with whom I have worked it is always their human qualities I remember. When I think of Jon Bon Jovi, I don't think of him as a rock star but as a friend. I remember Cher's wit and her earthy sense of humour: George Michael's sense of fun; the laughs I had with Sheena Easton back in the early days; how brilliant Paul McCartney was with his kids.

Paul is perhaps the one I admire the most, not just because he was part of the biggest band ever but as a human being. He is one of the most famous people on the planet, yet he is one of the nicest people I know. He has never lost that essential part of himself, not even when he has had to make tough decisions; not even though The Beatles' protracted break-up had to have left its mark.

Famous or otherwise, all of us carry scars. It is how we deal with them that counts. Between the ages of fifteen and eighteen, I was a criminal. I have to live with that. It is something I cannot wipe out. But I thank my stars I escaped that life, and I owe that to the people who gave me the means to leave it behind. Paul McCartney and Peter Grant. They gave me the chance and I took it.

Lucky again.

In October 2002 I return to New York City for a few days' break with June, our son Daniel and his new wife Donna. We stay at the Plaza Hotel. It was here that I stayed when Jon Bon Jovi was arrested in Central Park in 1989, and again when he and Dorothea celebrated their marriage a few months later. And later I stayed here with Cher in 1992. She and I spent many hours discussing our favourite movies. Knowing that mine was *The Godfather*, she had arranged a special surprise for me in New York. Half an hour before she went on stage for a charity performance at the Paramount Theater, she led me to a reception room where her friend Francis Ford Coppola was waiting. I was bowled over to meet him. He laughed when I told him that my entire family watched *The Godfather* every Christmas, and that my dad always said, 'That's how a family should be run.' During the show, a guy in a white raincoat jumped on to the stage and tried to get at Cher: I cut him off as he ran for her, overpowered him, and dragged him off the stage, where he was arrested. Afterwards, Coppola told me he had enjoyed seeing me in action. Back at the Plaza Hotel that night I thought to myself how much I loved my job.

I always stayed in the same room at the Plaza, overlooking the park. Partly out of habit and partly out of nostalgia, I have booked this room once more for June and me. On our second day in the city, I wake to find an envelope slipped under the door. Inside is a single sheet of paper: an itinerary for Bon Jovi. By one of those curious ironies fate sometimes throws in your way, the band also happens to be staying here ahead of a show in New Jersey. The itinerary must have been delivered to our room by mistake.

'What is it?' June asks. When I tell her, she groans. 'You're not going . . .'

'Don't worry,' I say. 'I won't.'

I keep my promise. I pass the test. I do not go to the show. But all through the day, my thoughts keep returning to Jon and the band. Memories: none of the bad stuff, as Dad had said, but the good. I think of how much I would like to sit with Jon for a couple of hours, just the two of us, as we used to, with a bottle of good red wine and a CD of *The Last Night Of The Proms*. Jon has three kids of his own now, and I would love to talk about our respective families, and all the times we shared. Memories crowd into my mind and I realise how much they mean to me. I savour them. I treasure them. I would not change a single one. I do not go to the show, and I do not let on to the band that I am here. But I feel comfortable with it. It feels as if a ghost has been laid to rest.

★

I know how lucky I've been. Many times people have said to me what a fortunate bastard I am to have led this crazy life.

There is an old saying in boxing: *let me mark your card*. Dad used it all the time. It comes from the referee's practice of marking a boxer's performance after a fight, telling him how he has done and which of his skills could use some work. It means to give good advice, to pass on the kind of inside knowledge that only comes with time.

I have shaken hands with Elvis and stood on stage with Frank Sinatra. I have lived with Cher and watched from the wings as Bon Jovi played their homecoming gig at the Giants Stadium in front of a crowd of 100,000 people. I have walked to the ring with the Heavyweight Champion of the World, and many more things that plenty of people would give their right arm to have done. If there's one thing I've learned, it's that those things are superficial, fantastic as they were. What is important are family and friends, since they are the foundation of a full and happy life. I have been blessed with a family who were brought up surrounded by love, because most of the time that was all we had. I still have the friends I had at school, all of whom are worth their weight in gold.

So if you will let me, I'd like to mark your card ... You should never be afraid to tell those you love how much they matter and what they mean to you. You never know what the next phone call or the knock on the door will bring.

'Fame is a vapour, popularity an accident; the only earthly certainty is oblivion.' *Mark Twain*

INDEX

INDEX